Raid

Raiders of the Deep

by Lowell Thomas

With an Introduction and Notes
by Gary E. Weir

BLUEJACKET BOOKS

Naval Institute Press
Annapolis, Maryland

Naval Institute Press
291 Wood Road
Annapolis, MD 21402

First Bluejacket Books printing, 2004
ISBN 1-59114-861-8

The Library of Congress has cataloged the hardcover edition as follows:
Thomas, Lowell, 1892–1981.
Raiders of the deep / by Lowell Thomas; with an introduction and notes by
Gary E. Weir.
p. cm. — (Classics of naval literature)
Originally published; Doubleday, Doran & Company, 1928.
   Includes index.
   ISBN 1-55750-722-8 (acid-free paper)
   1. World War, 1914–1918—Naval operations—Submarine. 2. World
War, 1914–1918—Naval operations, German. I. Title. II. Series.
   D591.T5 1994
   940.54'51—dc20
                      94-23138

Printed in the United States of America on acid-free paper ∞
11 10 09 08 07 06 05 04 9 8 7 6 5 4 3 2 1

Introduction

"Look at this! Lowell Thomas! I read this book when I was a boy!" my father-in-law exclaimed upon seeing *Raiders of the Deep* in the study of the small house my family and I occupied on Cape Cod during a summer of research in 1993. For him and a generation of Americans who experienced the Great Depression and twenty years of isolation from the international community after World War I, Lowell Thomas's fifty books, countless newspaper features, and frequent radio broadcasts opened a door that led to an exotic world of adventure and excitement. Thomas's activities as a war correspondent during the world conflict of 1914–18 turned the eccentric scholar and intelligence officer T. E. Lawrence into the popular hero Lawrence of Arabia. Forty-six years on the airwaves made "so long until tomorrow" as familiar and identifiable a phrase as any in the history of radio and television. Unlike many writers of history, who rarely manage to inspire a wide readership with history's allure and adventure, Lowell Thomas made these aspects of the past his forte.

In *Raiders of the Deep* he explored the fascinating, mysterious, and exciting world of German U-boats and those who went to war in them from 1914 through 1918. In telling this story, he had no desire to analyze the war or measure the larger, revolutionary effect of the conflict or the submarine. This was popular adventure journalism at its best, not the probing prose of Siegfried Sassoon or Erich Maria Remarque. Although books like *All Quiet on the Western Front* demonstrated war was indeed hell and described a generation of numbed survivors lost to the trenches, Thomas wove his story around the unusual, the daring, and the heroic in the great struggle.

Accustomed to treating his readers to a combination of thrills and frontline journalism as a war correspondent, the reporter Thomas understood his American audience. The people to whom he appealed found war at once stimulating and forbidding. They did not seek conflict but were intrigued by its realities, by the suspension of peace and normalcy, and by the interesting characters who inevitably gained prominence in this extraordinary environment. If all of this took place high in the air, under the scorching sun of a near eastern desert, or deep under the ocean—so much the better.

Raiders of the Deep represents a naval variation on the classic style of adventure literature that turned many flyers of the Great War into interwar legends. No doubt, Thomas thought the adventures of his submariners every bit as appealing and their achievements equally heroic; he also recognized a good story when he heard it. In the enhanced reality of Thomas's *Raiders of the Deep,* one can find the roots of the enormously successful submarine techno-thrillers of today.

Like many writers of the 1990s, Lowell Thomas found all of the excitement his readers sought in this undersea world. Like the airplane, which also made its military debut in the Great War, the submarine took its crew into a threatening environment in the midst of the most destructive episode in human memory. Instead of soaring through the air, however, the submarine's crew dove blindly into a completely forbidding world. They entered the ocean deep in a fragile vessel armed with only a limited supply of air, a handful of torpedoes, one deck gun, and the essential *asparagus,* the U-boat commanders' pet name for their periscope, whose lenses permitted a submerged, cyclopian view of a world at war.

This was the stuff of mystery and adventure and Thomas made the most of it. In the course of his research for *Raiders* he traveled to Germany in pursuit of the daring U-boat commanders who nearly severed Great Britain's maritime supply lines and cost all of the Allies dearly in men, material, and ships. These officers of the Imperial German Navy defined the strategy, tactics, and art of undersea warfare in its infancy. In *Raiders,* Thomas provided them with a forum for relating their own version of their wartime exploits. Although his journalistic instinct for the exciting led him to enhance and mildly embellish these tales, he essentially presented his readers with oral histories from men who lived through experiences extraordinary by any standards. Although professional historians would immediately warn their audience against the pitfalls involved in uncritically accepting these accounts as genuine, Thomas did not greatly concern himself with the need for critical evaluation. He wanted to inform and entertain, and that these stories had any truth at all seemed enough to amaze masses of readers uninitiated in the new world of undersea warfare.

Even though informing and entertaining always remained Thomas's primary goal, the subject and people he presented in *Raiders of the Deep* forced him to grapple with the human consequences of U-boat warfare: the terrible hazards facing the officers and crew of a submarine submerged or under attack. In a war at sea, the ocean environment inflicted discomforts and posed dangers frequently unanticipated. Every submariner endured terrible living conditions: their boats were small and lacked privacy and creature comforts, their food went stale or rotten with disturbing speed, and the air they breathed usually stank. While submerged, each crewmember occasionally recalled with anxiety the possible consequences of the relentless ocean pressure on the hull of his boat. All of Thomas's *Raiders* acutely felt the vessel's blindness save for the periscope and feared the uncompromising doom that could well follow carelessness, technical malfunction, or successful efforts at antisubmarine warfare (ASW) by determined surface hunters.

But what of the civilians? Thomas naturally used the ever-present specter of discomfort and death to describe the nature of undersea warfare and to enhance the thrill of the U-boat war. He could hardly, however, ignore the object of the hunt, merchant or passenger ships carrying both war cargoes and noncombatants. The deaths of civilians during the war and the general public outrage outside Germany and Austria-Hungary at the loss of innocent life always called into question the legitimacy of U-boat warfare and the activities and moral character of Thomas's raiders. Indeed, this major moral dilemma played a large part in bringing Americans to the battlefields of Europe. After the conflict had ended, thousands of Americans and Europeans still questioned the morality of U-boat warfare and found the use of stealth and surprise in the war at sea thoroughly dishonorable. Although Lowell Thomas the journalist felt obliged to mention the issue of ethics in his discussion of unrestricted submarine warfare, the popular adventure author sought an explanation for his readers that would neither diminish the honor of the men whose story he told nor brand them war criminals. No doubt, Thomas found himself caught up in their amazing adventures. For that reason and to assure his audience that these men deserved a place in Western culture's pantheon of adventure heroes, he covered them in the mantle of warriors obeying orders. Did not all naval officers and enlisted persons in every navy find themselves in this situation? They received instructions and their oaths of allegiance bound them to carry out the plans of their superiors.

In his treatment of the terrible fate of civilian passengers, however, the reader can discern Thomas's discomfort. Part of this feeling doubtless derived from a general recognition of the horror of war. The balance of his uneasiness he shared with every person involved in World War I who questioned the wisdom and necessity of threatening non-combatant populations with submarines and airplanes. Brutal reality thrust these ethical dilemmas into the limelight, and only political opportunists or those who placed a very low value on human life did not find themselves moved to wrestle with the morality of it all.

At the turn of the century, relatively few understood U-boats and their capabilities. Even fewer could actually build these curious and disturbing vessels. In 1906, the Krupp Germania Shipyard in Kiel supplied the Kaiser with the navy's first submarine, *U-1*. This facility boasted Germany's largest shipyard and one of the best submarine designers and engineers in Europe, Hans Techel. Admiral Alfred von Tirpitz, chief of the Imperial Naval Office and architect of Germany's prewar naval expansion, cared little for submarines. He authorized the creation of an alternative to Krupp at the Navy's Imperial Shipyard in Danzig only to satisfy his critics. Tirpitz's progressive liberal Reichstag adversary Eugen Richter and a number of officers including the retired Vice Admiral Karl Galster and Captain Lothar Persius proclaimed very openly that the U-boat showed great potential against the capital ship. Those who publicly criticized Tirpitz complained that the French and Russians had already found a place for the new vessel in both their fleet and strategic thinking. Furthermore, they feared a possible Krupp monopoly of U-boat construction in the event of war. Tirpitz reluctantly addressed their anxiety with the Danzig facility. His strategic views and successful political career rested on an all-big-gun battleship fleet and his personal variation on the strategic writ of Captain Alfred Thayer Mahan, American apostle of the battleship and the decisive battle. This viewpoint provided no place for a commerce-raiding submersible with an ill-defined role that might compete with the battleship for construction funds.

Danzig received the contract for the *U-2* in the same year that Krupp delivered the *U-1*. Designs for Imperial Germany's second submarine emerged from the Imperial Naval Office construction department and called for a small, petrol or gasoline-electric boat capable of a 13-knot maximum speed. On the surface, internal combustion engines burning gasoline as fuel drove the boat at barely over 13 knots. The powerful, air-breathing petrol engines required access to the atmosphere and a place to dispose of exhaust, neither of which existed below the ocean surface. Thus, when submerged, two Siemens-Schuckert electric motors and two electric generators furnished enough power for roughly 9 knots. Tirpitz's Danzig alternative immediately demonstrated its value by building the *U-2* more cheaply and giving it greater speed and range than Germania's *U-1*. Over the next eight years, Danzig delivered twenty-one U-boats to the Imperial German Navy, exactly the same number as Germania. In spite of Danzig's respectable output and the more modest cost, Krupp's size, diversity, and strength would have made it very awkward for the navy to carry on without the firm in peace and still more so in the event of war. The industrial giant's immense resources and wealth as well as its political clout had already presented Tirpitz with an almost unmanageable monopoly in armor production. The Imperial Naval Office was spared a repeat performance only when both Bremer Vulcan and A. G. Weser, major shipyards in the city of Bremen, proposed building U-boats in 1914 to complement the effort already under way in Kiel and Danzig.

In 1914 and 1915, the small German U-boat force, clearly a stepchild in the navy Tirpitz built, seemed an unlikely tool to use against Britain's mighty Royal Navy. The German Admiralty could call upon only twenty-nine boats for operations against the Allies in January 1915. From 1898, when the Reichstag initiated naval development in earnest with the passage of two fleet laws sponsored by Tirpitz, German naval planners did not seriously view the U-boat as the giant killer it quickly became at the outbreak of war in 1914. Indeed, Tirpitz viewed the submarine as an expensive diversion from the true focus of any future naval war, the battleship and battlecruiser. When in 1914 conflict came long before the German High Seas Fleet could hope to engage the British Grand Fleet successfully, the U-boat offered the best alternative to throwing Germany's surface forces into the decisive battle Tirpitz had always viewed as inevitable. For, although Tirpitz felt differently, the Kaiser viewed engaging the Grand Fleet in the early months of the war as a suicidal waste of valuable assets.

The opening months of the war provided relatively easy targets for the U-boats, as the Allies had not yet come to terms with their new submerged adversary. Reading Thomas's account of the exploits of Lieutenant Otto Weddingen in *U-9* reveals not only the role played by chance in his boat's encounter with three desirable targets after a gyrocompass malfunction and a severe storm, but also the complete absence of submarine awareness on the part of the Royal Navy. On 22 September 1914, three British armored cruisers of the *Cressy* class, HMS *Hogue, Cressy,* and *Aboukir,* fell victim to *U-9*. When the first of Weddingen's torpedoes hit, the captain of the *Aboukir* thought he had struck a mine. When the other two vessels came to his aid, *U-9*'s hat-trick was complete. If the experience of fighting from a submerged position presented a novel problem to the Imperial German Navy, addressing the U-boat threat demanded universal recognition of the danger posed by this peculiar type of warfare and the creation of a new system of strategy and tactics.

Meanwhile, Otto Weddingen continued his exploits, as did his fellow U-boat officers. Just a few weeks after *U-9*'s notorious success against the three British cruisers, *U-26* sank the Russian armored cruiser *Pallada* in the Gulf of Finland. On the last day of October 1914, *U-27* destroyed the seaplane carrier HMS *Hermes* off Calais. In January of the following year, the British battleship *Formidable* fell victim to *U-24* off Portland. While accumulating these victories, the U-boat force lost seven of its own vessels. Even if the price seemed a bit high, the significance of undersea warfare obliged both the Allies and the Central Powers to acknowledge the potency of the new submarine weapon and address the possibilities and challenges for the future.

Having chosen to use its U-boats as a primary offensive naval weapon, the Germans found that acting on this choice revealed the complexity of trying to introduce and refine a new style of warfare in the midst of a major conflict. What sort of command and control structure would suit the U-boat fleet and what sort of strategy would exploit the strengths of the new warship? The command organization and strategies employed went hand in hand, reflecting determination, confusion, and adjustment to the submarine.

Germany's U-boat command structure demonstrated the navy's uncertainty about the vessel's role. From 1905 to 1913, the Inspectorate of Torpedo Development exercised authority over all submarine matters until, in the last days of peace, the navy briefly placed the boats under the newly created Inspectorate of Submarine Development. From the outbreak of war through the armistice of 1918, the U-boat force was scattered among many commands to accomplish a variety of missions. Those U-boats attached to the High Seas Fleet, Imperial Germany's primary naval fighting force, fell under the command of the Leader of Submarines (FdU), later changed to Commander of Submarines (BdU), who answered to the chief of the High Seas Fleet. U-boats operating out of wartime bases in Flanders eventually came under the command of the Leader of Submarines–Flanders, and the long-range boats assigned to Kiel in the last two years of the war fell under the Commander of Submarines in Wilhelmshaven, Captain Andreas Michelsen. Further east, the admiral in command of the Baltic Fleet, a position held in 1914 by the Kaiser's brother, Admiral Prince Heinrich, took responsibility for boats in the Baltic Sea for almost the entire duration of the war. The navy did not resolve this muddle of locations, tasks, and assignments until the creation of both the U-boat Office in 1917 to coordinate submarine production and the centralized Naval High Command [Seekriegsleitung or SKL] under Admiral Reinhard Scheer in 1918.

In the Mediterranean and Adriatic Seas the situation was further confused by the alliance with Austria-Hungary. Kaiser Franz Josef insisted that every U-boat, German or Austrian, fly the red-white-red Habsburg naval ensign upon passing through the Strait of Gibraltar. The Imperial and Royal Navy of the Austro-Hungarian dual monarchy carried all of the Mediterranean U-boats on its lists, even if the vessel was German, and Vienna did not take measures to centralize its U-boat command until June 1917, when the Habsburg Kaiser appointed a Leader of Submarines–Mediterranean (FdU–Mittelmeer).

In spite of the fragmented command structure, effective strategies and tactics emerged as the U-boat force gained valuable combat experience. From the war's very beginning to its bitter conclusion, Germany's three successive Admiralty chiefs, Admiral Hugo von Pohl, Vice Admiral Gustav Bachmann, and Admiral Henning von Holtzendorff, relied heavily on the U-boats to sink Allied merchantmen and warships, to provide intelligence through reconnaissance and picket duty in advance of the fleet, and by their successes, both to destroy British commerce and help draw the Grand Fleet out of its bases piecemeal, so the High Seas Fleet could engage and defeat its component parts.

As early as the opening days of the war in 1914, Lieutenant-Commander Hermann Bauer, High Seas Fleet FdU, suggested that an unrestricted U-boat onslaught against British commercial supply routes converging on the United Kingdom might place the British Empire in genuine danger of defeat. His proposal met with the approval of his superiors only in January 1915, after the realization that the U-boat could well offer the only opportunity of persistently bringing the naval war to the British. The government of Chancellor Theobald von Bethmann-Hollweg reluctantly complied with the wishes of the armed forces and proclaimed a war zone around the British Isles on 4 February 1915, suspending German observation of the maritime prize rules and placing both warships and merchant vessels in danger of attack without warning. With this step, the German Imperial Navy embarked on an effort to impose a submarine commercial blockade on Great Britain in response to the stand-off blockade of German ports enforced by the Royal Navy since the war began.

The following months brought an increase in U-boat production and unprecedented sinkings in the sea approaches to the United Kingdom. These months also witnessed a series of international crises as U-boats attacked commercial traffic defying the proclaimed war zone. The *Arabic* incident with the United States in August 1915 confronted Germany's political and military leadership with the possibility of American entry into the war in support of the Allies. The loss of the Cunard liner *Lusitania* to Kapitänleutnant Walter Schwieger and *U-20* on 7 May 1915 brought the possibility much closer and prompted an immediate reaction from Bethmann-Hollweg. He convinced the Kaiser and the Admiralty to curtail the sinking of neutrals and attacks without warning. By 26 April 1916, Germany decided to interrupt the blockade for fear that further U-boat activity might cause America to enter the war, an event which would tip the balance in the conflict. Ten months later, the unfavorable course of the land war and the increasing American sympathies toward Britain caused German Admiralty Chief Henning von Holtzendorff to demand the resumption of unrestricted U-boat warfare. He felt that the navy could strangle British commerce before American intervention could change the situation on the western front.

For Holtzendorff, warships were certainly fair game, but Allied merchant vessels carrying noncombatants and neutral commercial ships presented a dilemma. Although the British often flew neutral flags, disguised their Q-ship submarine hunters as innocent merchantmen, and armed some cargo ships and passenger liners, the international standards of war at sea expected belligerent powers to operate within the maritime prize rules. In spite of the notorious sting of its torpedo, a submarine's primary weapon and only true asset was stealth. Visual or sonic detection could mean death for men like Otto Weddingen and the premier U-boat ace, Arnauld de la Perière. Remaining hidden as they carried out their task of destruction offered the possibility of a welcome return home. When the prize rules called them to the surface for reasons of justice and humanity in a barbarous time, they faced the ultimate dilemma, which Thomas captured well. In addition to challenging and legitimate targets, Thomas's main characters encountered Q-ships, merchantmen turning to ram, and freighters that unexpectedly returned fire.

In the spring of 1917, Admiralty Chief von Holtzendorff won the restoration of the war zone around Britain and unrestricted U-boat warfare. Subsequent successes by the Kaiser's submarines helped lead the United States into the war, forced the British to improve defense measures further, making greater use of mines and depth charges, and prompted the Royal Navy to take the advice of those, including the American Admiral William S. Sims, who advocated instituting escorted merchant convoys. In its first war, the U-boat proved a critical factor in both combat and diplomacy.

All through the conflict, Germany's hopes and plans rested upon vessels that would seem miniature by Cold War standards. When Walter Schwieger sent the *Lusitania* to the bottom with one torpedo assisted by volatile dust in the ship's nearly empty coal bunkers, he commanded a vessel roughly one-tenth the size of an American attack submarine of the 1990s. *U-20* displaced a mere 650 tons running on the surface with its ballast tanks empty. Built at the Danzig Imperial Shipyard, the vessel was 64.7 meters long and displaced 837 tons submerged. For propulsion *U-20* sported a pair of two-stroke diesels manufactured by Maschinenfabrik Augsburg-Nürnberg (MAN) and two electric motors for submerged running supplied by Allgemeine Elektricitäts Gesellschaft (AEG). For the sake of comparison, the more familiar American fleet submarine of World War II, frequently portrayed by Hollywood, displaced 1,500 tons on the average and their German counterparts of that era, the U-boat types VIIC and IXC, barely exceeded 700 and 1,000 tons, respectively. According to specifications, such vessels could reach approximately 20 knots on the surface, with the American fleet submarine holding a slight edge. Submerged, they both managed 7 or 8 knots. When compared with the earlier *U-9,* Schwieger's *U-20,* built with four vessels of her class between 1910 and 1913, could manage a speed only slightly greater than Weddingen's boat, 15.4 knots on the surface and 9.5 submerged. In the final analysis, experience quickly taught commanding officers like Schwieger and Weddingen and their Allied counterparts that these paper specifications did not always translate into improved or acceptable performance under wartime conditions. At the end of the war, however, with the bulk of the German fleet interned at Scapa Flow, Allied designers, engineers, and submariners soon realized that the German U-boat was the most reliable and easiest to maintain of all the submarines sent to war from 1914 through 1918.

In one of the more harrowing tales in *Raiders,* Thomas offers a testimony to durability with the story of *U-93,* one of the remarkably reliable emergency wartime "mobilization-" or Ms-boats in the German submarine fleet. At first under the command of Baron von Spiegel von und zu Peckelsheim, *U-93* nearly fell victim to a British Q-ship in the spring of 1917. Knocked from his position on the upper deck during a battle with the schooner *Prize,* which revealed itself at the last moment as the *Q-21,* Spiegel saw his boat sink beneath him in a hail of 7.5-cm shells and machine-gun fire. Only after spending the rest of the war in an elite British prisoner-of-war camp did Spiegel discover that his remaining crew, under command of one of his junior officers, Lieutenant Wilhelm Ziegner, took the boat—leaking, blinded by shell damage to its periscopes, and losing fuel-oil—around the British Isles and south through the North Sea to enter home port at Wilhelmshaven.

This vessel represented the better wartime submarines manufactured for the U-boat arm of the Imperial Navy. The Krupp Germania Shipyard in Kiel built *U-93* between 1915 and 1917 as part of a contract for three submarines of her class displacing 798 tons on the surface and 1,000 submerged. The boat carried two Germania six-cylinder, two-stroke diesels, a pair of electric motors manufactured by Siemens-Schuckertwerke, and might make 16.8 knots on the surface and 8.6 submerged without the kind of damage inflicted by

Q-21. Early in the war, *U-9* could manage 3,250 sea miles at a constant 9-knot speed. By 1917, *U-93*, which did not represent the state of the art by the time she made her amazing return trip from her encounter with *Q-21*, could travel over 8,000 sea miles at 9 knots. By this time the Imperial Naval Office demanded improved range because U-boats needed to avoid the well-protected English Channel and journey northward around Great Britain to patrol the Atlantic sea lanes converging on the British Isles from the west. The Allied navies had long since begun to address ASW more seriously, as the very hazardous, well-guarded choke points like the mouth of the English Channel and the Strait of Gibraltar demonstrated to some careless U-boat commanders, and the deadly determination of the Q-ship showed Baron Spiegel.

The pressures of war also gave birth to larger boats, durable diesels, more reliable storage batteries, improved electric motors, and quicker production methods. By 1918, with the advent of the Scheer U-boat–production program, the submarine had attained absolute priority in materials, labor, and construction in Imperial Germany and the navy accelerated the building pace with the introduction of new shipyards and machine works. Those directing the Scheer Program planned to build nearly 450 U-boats between the end of 1918 and the beginning of 1919 to force the Royal Navy to cease its standoff blockade and to place British commerce in sufficient peril to force an end to the war on terms favorable to Imperial Germany. This program, conceived and launched in the final year of the war, demonstrated not only determination in the face of labor and material shortages and possible defeat but also the final recognition that the U-boat had taken its place as one of the most effective weapons of twentieth-century naval warfare.

Although the submarine has retained its mystery, by
now it has become a very familiar element of war at
sea. The exploits of German U-boats and the American
submarine fleet in World War II have preoccupied the
popular imagination in historical literature, fiction, radio, and film for nearly fifty years. As the undersea
Cold War between the American and Soviet submarine
navies intensified after 1945, devotees of subsurface
warfare discovered wire-guided torpedoes, submarine-
launched ballistic missiles, and 30-knot submerged
speeds. With the proliferation of naval and military
techno-thrillers, contemporary readers fancy themselves among the initiated and have become somewhat
jaded by their familiarity with World War II taken to
the tenth power in our own time by high technology.
Yet, those raised on the black-and-white images of the
Atlantic and Pacific submarine war between 1939 and
1945 and more recently captured by the amazing exploits of American *Los Angeles*–class attack submarines
and Soviet *Alpha*s would do well to pick up this volume by Lowell Thomas. Between its covers, they will
discover a truly remarkable beginning: a world of petrol engines, primitive diesels, and daring about which
they probably know as little as Thomas's first audience
in 1928.

GARY E. WEIR

CONTENTS

LIST OF ILLUSTRATIONS

Raiders of the Deep

"Torpedo! Fire!" A white wake, a dull roar, and another ship starts on its final voyage.

CHAPTER I

IN QUEST OF AN ULTRA-MODERN SEA TALE

High up on Squaw Mountain near the Tornado Mine in Colorado there was an abandoned tunnel. Prospectors had found an outcropping of gold and for a hundred yards or so had followed the vein into the mountain. Suddenly it had petered out. I stumbled on that old tunnel one day and from then on for years it was my pirate cave. Frequently on Saturday afternoons I came here and sat alone beside a blazing fire of pine cones and old dynamite cases. And here it was that I first read one of the rarest imaginative tales ever written—Jules Verne's *Twenty Thousand Leagues Under the Sea.* And here it was that I met for the first time the mysterious Captain Nemo. From then on I was interested in submarines. For that matter, where is the boy or girl or woman or man who is not?

Then the greatest and most terrible of all wars broke upon the placid world, and a race of real Captain Nemos came into being. Here were tales of Jules Verne come true, tales more hair-raising than Verne's wildest imaginings, tales of adventures on voyages of *many hundreds of thousands of leagues under the sea.*

In 1917, with portholes covered, saloon and deck lights out, and all of us forbidden so much as to light a match, we entered the submarine zone. We were on a special mission, assigned to accompany the various Allied armies and bring back a record of events

1

on all battle fronts from North Sea to Persian Gulf. There was a real thrill in that last night out as we zigzagged across the Bay of Biscay toward the mouth of the Gironde River. Hunted—dodging a foe we couldn't see. If we were thrilled, then what of the sensations and experiences of the raiders of the deep lying in wait for us?

Months later, when we started east to join Allenby's army north of Gaza, to elude these new wolves of the sea we crossed from Taranto to Malta on a slim British ocean greyhound, a 22-knot courier boat. From Malta we planned to push right on across the Mediterranean to Alexandria. But for more than a week no ship, save submarine chasers, dared venture beyond the great steel net at the mouth of the harbour at Valletta. A ring of U-boats was said to have encircled the island.

Were we inconvenienced during those days at Malta? Not in the least! We thoroughly enjoyed the enforced delay. By day we visited picturesque old forts and palaces of the Knights of Malta, with their corridors hung with armour. Or we made excursions inland to the tangerine plantations, or across to the spot where St. Paul was shipwrecked. At night in Admiral Lord Calthorpe's box at the opera we attended gala performances in company with American Consul Wilbur Kiblinger, a charming gentleman from Virginia.

But what of the under-sea pirates in the U-boats off the Malta coast? We often wondered. Surely theirs must be an adventurous and desperate game!

On the way back from Lawrence's headquarters in Arabia I spent a short time chasing U-boats with destroyers and seaplanes near the Mediterranean entrance to the Suez Canal. And as I sat up there in the cockpit looking down on the sunny Mediterranean, with a balmy Egyptian breeze whipping past my ears, I often wondered about the nightmare existence of the men who fought under the sea.

At the end of the war, Webb Waldron and I crawled through the Allied lines to witness Central Europe in the convulsions of revolution. We met U-boat sailors everywhere. It was then that I first started gathering material for what I knew would one day be looked back upon as the most unreal, the most incredible, and at the same time the most harrowing and thrilling tale of the World War.

Since then, on trips to Europe over a period of ten years, I continued my search for the men who came within an ace of bringing the combined forces of twenty nations to their knees with their new form of warfare—warfare under the sea!

What stories they were! The gathering of them was like passing through a gallery of thrills and fantastic dangers.

After writing of the deeds of Lawrence, the picturesque hero of the Allies, I sought adventure in high Asia. Then came the chronicling of man's first circumnavigation of the world by air. Meanwhile, I was seeking for some romantic figure, some counterpart to Lawrence of Arabia. Later, on a flying tour of Europe, I found him in Count Felix von Luckner, the cheery corsair who raided the seas in a three-master windjammer.

Von Luckner's sailing ship as a raider in the war was certainly a novelty. But there were other raiders the poles away from to'ga'ns'l and marlinspike—the submarines. There you had the two ultimate extremes of war on the oceans. The submarine with its snaking torpedo was less anomalous, to be sure, than the three-master and its full spread of canvas. None the less beguiling, though. Less romance, perhaps, but more thrill and terror. The campaign of the U-boats held the world spellbound. One of the latest marvels of modern technology, striking a sweeping, fearful blow that threatened to decide the issue of the conflict of the nations—that surely was a thing to clutch the imagination with an iron grasp. And then there were the weird perils of the men who navigated beneath the surface of the sea, who struck their blows from the recesses of the ocean's bosom. The ever-threatening fate of the submerged coffin stands eerie and supremely terrifying. Ah, what stories waited to be told! Not merely stories of mad adventure, but history, important and of intense interest to all men. Surely no chapter of the history of our time needed telling quite so much as this.

And so after a sailor's yarn of scudding the waves with a fair breeze at your back and all sails set, why then a tale of the tight iron shells that ranged the underwater—spectral, fearsome, and deadly.

Of course, there are the two sides to the story: On the one hand, the adventures of the crews in the Kaiser's U-boats; on the other, the no less beguiling tales from the Allied side of the men who fought them. The U-boats logically come first, the stories of the German submarine commanders—then another tale, *Fighting the Submarines.*

In setting down this account of the submarine war, straight from the lips of the U-boat commanders, I have disregarded all controversial ground, or at any rate have attempted to. The right and wrong of under-sea war is not discussed here. The tales I have to pass on are tales of sheer adventure. Stranger than fiction? Aye! And tales, I believe, such as no other chronicler will have a chance to set down in our time. At any rate, we all hope the world has learned its lesson, and may there be peace among men for generations to come!

What manner of men were these chaps who in war time won the hatred and bitter execration of half the

PERISCOPE AND TORPEDO

The track of the "asparagus" (above); the launch-
ing of the torpedo; and its tell-tale white wake.

*Weddigen, the first great victor of
the war under the sea.*

*Officers' mess aboard the U-9. Weddigen at the right. Spiess,
who tells the tale, at the left.*

world? Pirates, they were called, and hanging was the destiny considered just for them. At the same time, it was perfectly clear that they were true stalwarts of the race of adventurers. There was a magic of light and wide airy space in the upper sky where the aviators ranged, but there was a more terrible beguilement in the close embrace of the underwater where men groped with that eerie eye, the periscope.

And then there was the horrible inevitability in the doom of the foundering submarine. The airman shot down in flames was a picture of fright, but the snug iron coffin of the voyager under the sea was a ghostly picture quite as powerful upon the imagination as the flaming coffin of the sky.

What manner of men were they, and what were they doing now? The trade and the course of life that the hero of war follows when peace has returned is always a curious problem. The more so with the submarine commanders of Germany, because Germany is allowed no sea power worth mentioning and the continuance of a naval career is cut off for most of them. After the weird life of war under sea they were thrown abruptly into the placid ways of civilian life in peace time.

I found them in no wise fire-snorting pirates, nor even characters salty with the sea. Quiet, pleasant chaps they turned out to be, most of them rather young—the flower of the German Navy. They had volunteered for U-boat service because it involved the most hazard. As they are to-day, for the most part they would pass anywhere as nicely mannered fellows, matter-of-fact, and rather mild. That, of course, is what one might have expected. The most daring of warriors is likely to be quite a plain citizen in peace time, at least in this day and age. Many of the former submarine commanders are in business connected with shipping. They go to their offices every day, look over invoices, and dictate letters. Others are in engineering, and still others are successful business executives. The war is past and gone. The perilous life in the U-boats is far behind. They think of it but little. They are busy carving out careers for themselves, and the old days come to mind only when former comrades get together for reminiscences or when at social gatherings stories and experiences are related. Herr U-boat Commandant, whom a few years ago the world looked upon as some kind of sea dragon, is, in this year of 1928, a steady-going citizen such as you could scarcely distinguish from a young and enterprising American business man.

And what ethical slant did they have on their deeds and exploits which the millions of us regarded as the black nadir of immorality and inhuman wrong? I found some interesting things here, particularly in the case of the man who sank the *Lusitania*. These will be told in their proper places. Meanwhile, one point is to be kept in mind, a general principle that stood as the ethical background of the submarine commander, his way of looking at things. It is very simple. As a descendant of Adam he was the same as the rest of us. As a man of war, well, he was a naval officer, and a naval officer's business is to obey orders. That was his training, his tradition, his life. All you have to do is to consider the age-long idea of military discipline as you will find it in the United States Navy, or any other navy, then it all becomes clear. The submarine commander obeyed orders, and that is the highest virtue known to the code of armies and navies. Sometimes he undoubtedly went beyond his orders. A few men in all times and all climes have done that.

But how about all of those atrocities which were so liberally attributed to the U-boats? Here, as with the subject of atrocities in general, it is difficult to find any sound evidence, anything more than rumour. The two particular crimes attributed to the U-boats were the sinking of hospital ships and the firing on lifeboats. In the first instance the Germans cite the fact that ships often struck mines and were thought to be torpedoed. There are two authenticated instances in which hospital ships appear to have been sunk deliberately. In the second instance I ran across cases where lifeboats were said to have been fired on. The Germans reply to this by pointing out at least one instance when a seemingly innocent lifeboat tried to sink a submarine with a sudden throwing of bombs, and when it was scarcely more than human for the U-boat to open fire. In that way a great tale of machine-gunning lifeboats might begin. In general I found almost nothing conclusive about atrocities, although many instances of humanity on the part of the U-boats came to me from British sources.

If you want a verdict on these things just ask the men who were in action against each other in the war of the sea. On the whole they speak in high admiration of each other. Seafaring men are built that way.

The tale begins with a vivid picture: a cruiser with guns like the spokes of a wheel and funnels belching smoke—and over there hidden below the waves a sliding, black, cigar-shaped hull, a fearsome fish for any ocean.

In the conning tower of the U-boat is an officer destined for a career that will make him one of Germany's greatest war heroes. His periscope—the "asparagus," as the Germans nicknamed the eye of a submarine—has been on the alert. He has spied the cruiser a long way off, heading toward him. He lies in wait. The sea is rough. In the tossing water he can scarcely keep his boat at the proper level. But the mountainous waves are more of an aid than a hindrance. Spray and foam hide the jumping peri-

scope. On a glassy sea that six-foot asparagus would
be visible from afar to a lookout in a crow's nest. The
cruiser holds its course, swift, warlike, a brave picture
of the dominant power of iron and steam. The submerged raider steals to a point close to the path of the
oncoming vessel. The tossing sea conceals the periscope. An ideal setting for an ambush—the first of
the war.

A deadly, short-range shot. So rough is the sea
that even the path of the torpedo is obscured. The
cruiser hasn't a chance to side-step. A dull roar. At
the water line, just under the forward funnel, it strikes.
The entire fore part of the ship is blown to bits. Fire
breaks out and flames shoot skyward. The cruiser
heaves. Its stern rises until it stands straight in the
air. For a moment it hesitates. Then, bow first, it
dives.

Three minutes have elapsed since the torpedo sped
to its mark. The noise of the explosion has carried
for miles. Torpedo boats rush to the scene. Both
cruiser and U-boat have vanished.

This was the first ship ever sunk by the attack of a
submarine. It was the 3,200-ton British cruiser
H. M. S. *Pathfinder*. The identity of the ship the
U-boat had sunk was not known in Germany until
days later, when word drifted in through Holland.
Out of a crew of 360 less than half were saved. Only
one lifeboat got away before the *Pathfinder* went
down. The other dazed survivors were found clinging to the wreckage. The commander to make this
first underwater kill was Lieutenant Commander Otto
Hersing. His raider was the *U-21*.

But it was an under-sea boat of far older vintage
that was destined to launch the torpedoes that were
to give the world its really spectacular introduction to
this new phenomenon of warfare.

Again and again as I talked with those Captain

Nemos I heard it: "When Weddigen in the *U-9* won the first big victory"; or "When Weddigen in the *U-9* sank the *Aboukir,* the *Hogue,* and the *Cressy.*"

At the very beginning of the World War the news came that a German submarine had torpedoed and sunk three great British armoured cruisers. That newest of new inventions, the submarine, a mysterious and doubtful quantity in the calculus of warfare, had come to the front with a telling stroke. The place to begin, indeed.

Weddigen lies at the bottom of the North Sea, and the *U-9* has long since been consigned to the junk heap. But very much in the land of the living is a youngish, rather dreamy-looking chap, Lieutenant Johann Spiess, Weddigen's watch officer and second in command, who tells in his own words the tale of the raids of the historic *U-9*:

Editor's Note: Lieutenant Johann Spiess was trained as a torpedo specialist after his entry into the navy in April 1907. On the eve of war he was assigned to the Baltic Naval Station in the Torpedo Inspectorate at Kiel, which was initially in charge of U-boat matters.

CHAPTER II

PERISCOPE AND TORPEDO

The twenty-second of September, 1914. How well I remember it! For me it is one of those days a man looks back upon with endless reminiscence, a dividing point for a lifetime. And it has more than a mere personal significance. It stands a marker in the stream of history, a milestone on the long road of terrestrial events. On that day a new piece of action flared big and bold on the earthly scene. The sliding cataclysmic submarine intruded with crashing torpedo shots into the game of nations. We, the raiders of the deep, struck our first telling blow. Already a British warship had been sunk by our comrades of the *U-21*, but now we scored a success that made history. The world thrilled and marvelled, and it was not long before all mankind trembled with the thought of the hand of death that reached out under the sea. On that twenty-second of September, 1914, we sank the great cruisers, the *Hogue,* the *Aboukir,* and the *Cressy.*

Two years before, in October, 1912, I was assigned to the submarine service—to my disgust. At the time I was serving as second torpedo officer aboard S. M. S. *Pommern.* But my one ambition was to get assigned to a torpedo boat, the goal of every young torpedo expert.

The small, swift craft, with their darting attacks, seemed to offer us the best opportunity for hurling our huge, ship-smashing missiles. The submarines? Bah! True, they, too, were for launching torpedoes. But in those days we looked at under-sea craft, along with aircraft and other technical innovations, with a skeptical eye. Would they ever amount to anything in real warfare? Probably not. Nor was life aboard the U-boats anything to look forward to. Even now the submarine is no pleasure barge. In 1912, between close quarters, foul air, and crazy rolling and pitching, a rowboat was palatial compared to the inside of one of those diving dories. There were frequent accidents, too, especially in foreign navies. And death in a plunging submarine was as evil a fate as the imagination could conjure. Death by slow suffocation. Nevertheless, although I did not like it, a submarine officer I became.

The boat to which I was transferred was the *U-9*, of the old kerosene-burning type. (The Diesel engine had not yet been developed.) At that time the *U-9* was quite an up-to-date craft. But technical progress was such that this boat speedily became obsolete.

Nowadays we can look back with an indulgent smile upon that prehistoric era. Any kind of extended U-boat voyage was undreamed of. Only in rare cases did men sleep on board, which was not only uncomfortable but considered dangerously unhealthful. Going ashore at nightfall was the invariable routine. Diving was done as little as possible, and we seldom ventured to go down more than a few yards, and then we looked anxiously about to see if the seams were tight and no water was leaking in. There was grave doubt whether subsurface craft could weather a lively storm. They had never been tried out in a real gale. An attack under water in any kind of rough weather was considered impossible. The prescribed plan under such conditions was to approach and torpedo an enemy craft with the conning tower above water. The supposition was that, with the waves breaking over the conning tower, it could not be seen. Our kerosene motors

Editor's Note: Lieutenant Spiess was not quite correct when he said—or perhaps Thomas added—that the diesel engine had not yet made its appearance. When *U-9* was built by the Imperial Shipyard at Danzig, submarine designers and engineers had not yet adapted the diesel to U-boat propulsion. Rudolph Diesel invented the engine in 1892 and the first practical model was built by Maschinenfabrik Augsburg-Nürnberg in 1893. *U-19* through *22* received the first submarine diesels at Danzig while they were under construction between 1910 and 1913.

smoked like the very deuce, and, as we used electric power only for running under water, we sailed on the surface with a column of kerosene smoke towering over us. We were almost as visible as a smoke-belching steamer. There were fourteen boats of that antiquated kerosene-burning type, the series *U-5* to *U-18*. All save two were lost and lie to-day on the bottom of the sea.

Our commander was Lieutenant Otto Weddigen, already known as an exceedingly capable submarine man. He was a slender, blondish young officer of quiet, courteous manner. He was the very reverse of the martinet. Never blindly set on his own opinion, he allowed the officers under him the privileges of initiative and freedom of ideas. You did not feel like a subordinate when you served under Weddigen, but rather like a younger comrade.

I had never voyaged on a submarine before. The first dive and the first cruise had for me all of that peculiar thrill and nervous sensation that it always has for the beginner. You stand in the conning tower looking through the small ports, which are covered with thick glass. Then you see the water creep swishing over the upper deck. The air clinging to the surface of the boat flows up to the surface in a stream of silver bubbles. Now the water washes up past the glass through which you are peering. With a clear sea and bright sun you can see underwater as far as the bow of the boat. It is a strange and fascinating spectacle.

On your first trip anxious thoughts flash through your mind as the water closes over the boat. Have all the valves and hatches been closed properly? Will the steel body resist the pressure? Is not water pouring in somewhere? My first voyage on the *U-9* was merely from Kiel to Wilhelmshaven, and yet it was enough to give one a bit of nerves. I was standing over the conning tower hatch. A loud bang and a sudden blast of air. I thought it was a misfire in one of the cylinders of our petroleum motors. Then two men came clambering madly up the conning tower ladder, a machinist and a petty officer. They were gasping. Their hair was singed and their flesh scorched. An oil tank explosion had occurred and the engine room was on fire. A fire aboard a submarine is no fun. I can certify to that. But after a bit of warm work we put out the blaze.

The *U-9* was lying at Wilhelmshaven two months later, under a process of having some new technical devices installed, when there was a great sensation in our submarine fleet. Six boats went out on an endurance test in the North Sea. They remained out for six days, most of the time anchored to buoys in Heligoland Bight. That in the bleak month of December. It was considered an incredible achievement. We could not get over the wonder of it. How we congratulated the heroes aboard those craft when they got back!

During naval manœuvres in the North Sea, May, 1913, the *U-9* put out of action—theoretically—three battleships. Our commander, Lieutenant Weddigen, with a quiet smile of victory, won this mythical but glorious victory with his favourite stroke, the four torpedo salvo—executed by discharging the two forward and two rear torpedoes at short intervals.

We were lengthening our cruises constantly, and doing more and more diving. We went down deeper and deeper, too, although we seldom ventured beyond fifty feet. In December of 1913, the *U-9,* in the course of a North Sea cruise, stayed out at sea in a violent storm, and weathered it famously. We ran awash and submerged and even carried out manœuvres in the teeth of the gale. Decidedly the submarine as an instrument of war was picking up and beginning to give hint of good possibilities.

Kiel Week of 1914 came. During June, the Kaiser led the festivities that marked the opening of the Kiel Canal. A powerful British fleet, England's finest superdreadnaughts and cruisers, attended. There were great naval parades. Our submarines took not the least interesting part. Our British guests could not gaze too long at the low-lying little craft. There was music and dancing and feasting. The days were bright and gladsome and the nights brilliantly alight and full of merriment.

But the festivities at Kiel were rudely interrupted. On June 28th, came the news of the murder of the Austrian Archduke and his consort. Warships drew off for their home ports. Thoughts of strained international relations were in every mind. On July 16th, our flotilla commander came aboard the *U-9* to witness a new and difficult operation that we had learned—the reloading of torpedoes at sea, both above water and under. In an underwater attack at periscope depth we fired the two torpedoes of our forward tubes, reloaded, and discharged a double salvo again. All four missiles found their mark, the old hulk S. M. S. *Hamburg*. Weddigen accepted congratulations with a slightly jaunty set of the head. That manœuvre of under-sea firing, reloading, and firing again was something to be proud of.

"The practice and manœuvres of the U-boats now increased to a feverish intensity. The dark shadow of war was drawing ever closer, ready to engulf us, and we could not tell how soon those mimic battle operations of diving and torpedoing might become the real thing. Then came the end of July and declarations of war against Russia and France. England had not declared against us. Nevertheless, a surprise attack by the British fleet was feared.

Editor's Note: Dreadnoughts were an extremely significant ship type for the time. At the turn of the century, the major naval powers, led by Great Britain, decided to construct battleships that no longer depended in any way on intermediate guns. In 1904, Admiral Sir John Fisher, then Britain's First Sea Lord, decided that the first-line battleships of the Royal Navy should possess more speed and much more firepower. The Royal Navy's *Dreadnought* carried ten 12-inch guns in her five turrets, which made her far more powerful than any other ship afloat. She could also make 21 knots on

At three hours past midnight, August 1st, the German submarine fleet slid out of harbour at Heligoland to do patrol duty in the North Sea. Silently and secretly, in the darkest hour of the night, as befitted the nature of our weapon, we sailed into the World War. At sundown on August 2d, while we steered from patrol back to our base, Weddigen and I stood beside the conning tower. A scarlet sun was setting amid fiery clouds. A big gray liner with four stacks foamed past us, headed north, a liner sallying forth on duty as an auxiliary cruiser. For a long minute the splendid ship was silhouetted against the crimson sunset. Weddigen was lost in contemplation of the sight. He seemed very young and dreamily boyish. A shadow of dark thoughts was in his face.

"Spiess," he said in a low voice, "you see how red the light is. The whole world seems bathed in blood. Mark my words, England has declared war on us."

It was a presentiment inspired by the ominous sight of the auxiliary cruiser hurrying past the ruddy splendour of the setting sun. And, indeed, before the *U-9* drew up alongside the dock, I deciphered the radio message: "Be prepared for military offensive measures by England, starting to-day. Signed: Flotilla Commander." England had taken the jump.

Were we prepared? By land our German military arm stood alert and ready. On the sea, although outnumbered by Britain's might, our battleships, cruisers, and destroyers were swift and strong. But what of our submarine fleet? It was as good as any in the world—but not very good.

Ah, what if, in 1914, the technical science of underwater craft had reached the height of three years later? Ah, what if at the beginning of the war we had had the kind of submarine fleet we had at the end? The course of history would have been changed. As it was, we entered the world struggle with a handful

---

steam turbines, a significantly better speed than her predecessors. The appearance of this ship obliged all other navies to follow suit. Although other countries, such as the United States and Germany, had similar plans, Fisher's decision placed the Royal Navy in the lead and bound all others caught up in the naval arms competition to follow. Superdreadnoughts advanced this concept by increasing speed and the power of the main armament. Later British battleships approached 26 knots' speed and mounted 13.5-inch guns.

of U-boats that in the light of a couple of years later were primitive and pitiful—antediluvian.

Twelve strong, the German submarine fleet was sent out to seek the might of the British Navy. We were ordered to hunt over the North Sea for hostile warships and attack them with torpedoes. We left harbour on August 6th, and for a week made a round of the North Sea. For the *U-9* the cruise was uneventful. The North Sea was deserted and we caught sight of no enemy smokestack. So far as we could see the British fleet was in harbour. Nor did the other boats that returned sight any mark for their missiles. Two of them did not return. We received British reports that one, the *U-15,* had been rammed by the small British cruiser *Birmingham.* We gathered that she had been sunk while attempting an attack on a squadron. The other of the missing boats, the *U-13,* disappeared without sound or sight. She may have struck a mine or encountered some accident while diving. At any rate there was no more word of her—the common fate of the submarine.

Our first submarine advance resulted in no damage to the enemy, and we lost two boats out of twelve. Not encouraging. All we could do was to grit our teeth and await a better chance. "Remember the *Birmingham"* was the word. Exact vengeance for the *U-15.* Soon afterward the *U-21* sank the H. M. S. *Pathfinder.* That was a good beginning.

The German march through Belgium was on, and it was thought that England might try to land troops on the Belgian coast. The *U-9* was ordered to take a position along the route that transports might follow and wait an opportunity to attack war vessels or troop ships. That was our duty for long, tedious days to come. In France we were losing the Battle of the Marne, and the fighting was settling down to the long siege of trench warfare.

On September 20th, the boat shoved her nose out into open sea. Our gyroscopic compass went awry, and we found ourselves in sight of the coast of Holland, fifty miles off our course. We turned, and steered during the day with the coast as our guide and at night by the North Star. The next day the weather was stormy and the sea rough, and at dusk the gale was so stiff and the waves so high that we sought refuge beneath the storm-beaten surface. That night we slept quietly fifty feet below the sweep of the lashing combers.

When we rose to the surface in the morning, the dawning of the memorable twenty-second of September, we were agreeably surprised. The light streamed up from the eastern horizon and spread over a cloudless sky. The storm had vanished. Not a cloud was to be seen, the wind was a whisper, and the sea was calm, save for a long swell. Visibility was excellent. The horizon was a clear, sharp line, where sea met sky. A fine day to sink a ship. We threw our motors in, to recharge our batteries and replace the energy we had used up while submerged all that night. The recharging of the batteries was soon interrupted.

I had the watch, and stood scanning the horizon with my glass. Near me Weddigen and the chief engineer paced the short turn around the deck, getting fresh air and exercise. The blazing ball of the sun stood above the horizon and flooded the sea with its beams, as if bent on revealing and illuminating every speck on the ocean. Damn that petroleum smoke! A submarine is supposed to be a secretive kind of craft, but we went sailing like the children of Israel, attended by a pillar of smoke. A few Dutch fishing boats lay shadowed against the sunrise, as if in some vividly coloured print.

"Ship ahoy!" Through my long glass I was able to pick out the tiny tip of a mast showing over the horizon. A cloud of smoke appeared beside it. All doubt vanished. It was not the tip of some wind-jamming sailing ship. I felt like shouting at this, the first sight of an enemy warship. I immediately ordered the kerosene motors to be disconnected, so that that infernal pillar of smoke could not signal afar—"submarine bearing down on you with torpedo ready." Weddigen had gone down to breakfast. I called him, and for a long minute he stood, slender, motionless, intent, with his glass fixed on the speck and smudge on the horizon.

"Make ready for diving." His command snapped out with a crisp, nervous intensity. We leaped below. The hatches banged shut. The sea closed over the *U-9*. Our batteries had not been fully recharged, but never mind. We held the boat at periscope depth and steered in the direction of the mast tip and smoke cloud. The *U-9* moved up and down with the heavy swell of the sea. I took my position in the conning tower behind Weddigen, running the periscope out and bringing it down from time to time, so that, appearing for only a short space at a stretch above the surface of the sea, it might not too easily be detected. Weddigen made the observations. I waited, burning with eagerness for some sign from him that the distant ship had appeared above the horizon. For a long time he said nothing, but merely stood and, when I ran the periscope out, peered intently, his small sharp features drawn and tense. With my nerves tightened as they were, I jumped when he said in a quiet, matter-of-fact voice:

"There are three light cruisers with four stacks."

"Torpedoes!" I cried in response, and asked permission to get the torpedoes ready for firing.

A nod of his head, and I leaped forward to the torpedo room. Three light cruisers? Small ships? Aye! But together they would make a good total.

I ordered reserve torpedoes made ready for the manœuvre of submerged firing, reloading, and firing again, which we had only a few weeks before accomplished successfully for the first time in practice. When I returned to the conning tower, Weddigen was transformed.

"Spiess," and he slapped me violently on the shoulder, "they are three light cruisers of the Birmingham class!"

We stood looking at each other.

"Revenge for the *U-15!*" I shouted.

And now it was hard work. We were drawing close to the enemy, and I had to keep the periscope going up and down. We could show it only a few seconds above surface at a time, else its white feathered wake would have betrayed it. Weddigen steered to attack the middle cruiser of the three, aiming for a short, sure shot from about five hundred yards.

"Make the tubes ready," his order came with a sharp abruptness.

"All tubes clear," was my report. "Which will fire first?"

"First tube, bow shot," was the short, quick reply.

I unscrewed the cover of the first tube firing button and held the thumb of my right hand directly over it, ready for the order to press it down and make the electrical contact. With my left hand I continued to operate the lever of the elevating device, by which the periscope was raised and lowered.

Weddigen gave an order to the central station:

"Immediately after the shot dive to fifteen metres— and do not break surface. We are close to the target." Those old-time boats had a trick of bounding to the surface after a torpedo was discharged. If we were to pop out of the water within such easy range of the guns of the cruisers, it would be "Good-bye *U-9.*"

Then, at 7:20 o'clock came the barked command: "Out periscope. Stand by first tube."

We counted the seconds while he peered into the glass, making sure of the aim.

"First tube—fire! *In* periscope!"

At that instant I pressed the firing key with my right-hand thumb, called simultaneously through the speaking tube to the forward torpedo room: "First tube fired," and with my left hand ran in the periscope.

Now followed those always tense moments after the discharge of a torpedo. I glanced fearfully at the depth indicator to see whether we should break water. No, we were diving. I had the periscope lever clutched with both hands, to make sure that it stayed down. You can see that I was only a blooming beginner at actual warfare. The seconds dragged, and nothing happened. A miss? It always takes an incredibly long time before the sound of a torpedo explosion comes back to you, the time for the torpedo to get to its mark and for the sound to travel back. At our range of 500 yards, thirty-one seconds was the period required. But there are times when thirty-one seconds seem like half an hour.

A dull thud followed instantly by a shrill-toned crash. A cheer broke out from the sailors below. We in the conning tower joined in impulsively. We could see nothing, of course, for we had dived to fifteen meters and were below periscope depth. After our first exultation we looked about anxiously. It was common opinion at the time that the shock of a torpedo explosion, particularly at short range, might seriously damage the boat that had discharged the missile. We half expected to have sprung leaks or that our steering gear had been put out of commission. A short inspection, however, revealed that we had suffered no damage.

"Bring the boat to periscope depth," Weddigen

The old U-9, *most historic of submarines. In one day her crew bagged three British cruisers.*

The men who sank the Hogue, *the* Cressy, *and the* Aboukir. *Weddigen, middle, Spiess on his right.*

The raiding fleet in its lair at the outbreak of the war. It was with this handful of old-fashioned boats that Germany attempted to smash British sea power.

commanded, suppressing his eagerness to catch a glimpse of what was happening on the surface.

I leaned on the periscope lever. Weddigen peered quickly, and then with a triumphant expression turned the glass over to me. It was my first glimpse of a sinking ship, a sight soon to become familiar. The stricken cruiser lay stern-deep in water. Her bow was high and the *ram* bow stuck above the surface of the sea. Her four stacks were blowing off white steam. Lifeboats crowded with men were being lowered. It was indeed revenge for the *U-15* and our lost comrades. England's light cruiser *Birmingham* had struck hard and sure at her submersible enemy, but we had struck just as hard and just as sure at this shattered warship of the Birmingham class.

The other two cruisers, companions of the sinking ship, were standing by to take survivors aboard. What a fatal mistake! British warships never did anything like that again during the length of the war. Weddigen made ready for another attack. I hurried to the forward torpedo room.

I imagined I was passing through a madhouse. Men were running furiously back and forth, a big group of them. First they rushed forward and then astern. The chief engineer at the depth rudder was helping to keep the boat on an even keel by a process of ballast shifting. The running men were the moving ballast, hurrying hither and thither to points where the weight was needed.

"All forward" and "all astern" the commands would ring out, and they would go racing like a crowd of runners beginning a marathon. You can bet the crew was worn out by the time the encounter with the cruisers was over.

"Reload first tube." I gave the command to the men in the torpedo room. And now we started out at our recently learned trick of reloading a tube while submerged. The operation went off as smoothly as when we practiced it under the eye of our flotilla commander at Kiel.

"First tube has been reloaded." Back in the conning tower I gave my report.

"We have a good target," Weddigen observed with a slightly pitying expression, and motioned me to look through the periscope.

The cruiser was lowering her cutter, while signals were being sent from the bridge. At the gaff the battle flag of Britain was waving in the breeze. The guns were trained out like spokes of a fan, and I could see the gun crews in white uniforms at their stations.

More revenge for the *U-15*—but no. I stepped back from the periscope and turned to Weddigen.

"Captain," I said positively, "these ships are not of the Birmingham class. They are not light cruisers. They are armoured cruisers. This ship has double casements, which I can distinctly recognize."

Vision through a periscope was never any too clear, and it was particularly difficult to distinguish in the matter of distance and size. I was sure that the ships we had attacked were bigger than we had thought. We were not avenging the *U-15* by sinking Birminghams. Better—our victims were of the more formidable class of armoured cruisers.

Weddigen studied the picture in the periscope but thought I was wrong. However, he decided to launch two torpedoes. If the ships were really armoured cruisers one explosion might not be enough to insure sinking. At exactly thirty-five minutes after the first hit I pressed the firing key for both bow torpedoes. The range was only 300 yards.

"Periscope *in!*" And again we dived to fifteen metres.

Simultaneously Weddigen gave the order to back with one propeller.

"Why?" I asked.

"Otherwise we may ram him," was the reply.

Indeed, it was possible that a current might drift us against what would probably be a sinking enemy.

Two explosions came with a hollow ring. It was lucky that we did back away. With one propeller running in reverse we were just able to clear the sinking warship. Our periscope almost scraped its side.

The voice of the chief quartermaster came through the speaking tube:

"Captain, how much longer is this going to last?"

With that came the chief engineer's report.

"The batteries are almost discharged."

Because of the sight of the enemy having interrupted the work of charging our batteries, we had made the attack with the batteries only partly stored with current, and now we were running short of electric power. If we did not turn promptly and make away, we might find ourselves compelled to come to the surface to recharge the batteries—and that in these dangerous waters, which were sure to swarm presently with enemy craft. A destroyer station was in the Thames, and called by distress signals from the cruisers, those deadly hornets would soon come charging.

There was iron in Weddigen beneath quiet, mild seeming. Harsh lines were in his face, the expression of a relentless will.

"We will continue the attack," he said serenely.

We had two torpedoes in the stern tubes and a single spare one for one of the forward tubes. This I loaded.

Back to periscope depth, and the glass revealed a terrible picture. Two great ships lay sinking by the stern. One, the first that we had hit, sagged a great deal lower than the other. The third cruiser was standing by. The water was littered with wreckage, crowded lifeboats, capsized lifeboats, and drowning men. The third cruiser was taking survivors aboard as fast as she could. And now we were going to sink her, too.

Why did she stay there, after her two companions had been hit? It is true that British warships had not yet received the standing order to clear away as fast as they could from the vicinity of a torpedoed ship, but that craft had seen her two sisters go and must surmise that it would be her turn next. She was a brave ship, indeed.

Weddigen and I did not say anything to each other as we watched. Our feelings of horror and pity we tried to suppress. We sought to dispel our inward trouble by cursing the British, which we all did in those days.

One hour after the first shot of the encounter our two stern torpedoes left the tubes. This time we were so bold that we did not dive below periscope depth after the shot, but watched. The range was a thousand yards. The ship saw the trail of our torpedoes and tried to elude them at the last moment by steaming suddenly ahead. We waited for the sound of the explosion so long that we thought we had missed. Then a dull crash came. We waited for the second, but it never came. The second torpedo had missed.

The periscope showed the cruiser still standing there with no apparent change. She had not been hit badly enough to cause her to list.

"We'll make sure," said Weddigen, again expression in his ordinarily mild face.

Our last torpedo left the tube. It struck the mark accurately. A cloud of smoke shot up from the side of the doomed vessel and an immense white fountain. And now the periscope revealed a fearful picture. The giant with the four stacks turned slowly over to port.

Men climbed like ants over her side and then, as she turned turtle completely, they ran about on her broad, flat keel until in a few minutes she disappeared beneath the waves.

Weddigen and I watched alternately, fascinated with a sense of tragic horror. Again we unburdened our overcharged feelings by cursing the English. But even that did not suffice. For long minutes we were lost as if in some kind of trance. He called those of the crew he could, and allowed them to look into the periscope. On the horizon were Dutch fishing vessels making away from the accursed spot with a full spread of sail.

"I believe they are armoured cruisers," Weddigen said to me, "although they seem very small."

They did seem small, and as we discussed it, we decided they must be armoured cruisers of the small, swift Kent class (9,900 tons).

Our electrical power was almost exhausted, and we could remain submerged not much longer. I had the watch, and steered north to get clear of the wreckage, and then blew out the tanks and came to the surface. The gray North Sea had closed over the last of the three cruisers. Lifeboats were still picking up men swimming and men clinging to wreckage. The weather was radiantly beautiful, and even the swell of the ocean had subsided. There was no sign of destroyers yet, but it could not be much longer before they would come rushing. In order to conceal our course from the survivors, we steered to the north. In sight of the Dutch coast, we turned inshore. We ran along in shelter of land.

It was not until noon that we caught sight of the pursuing destroyers. One appeared, but was not able to detect us against the shadow of the coast. It presented an extraordinary appearance. We could see only bow and bridge. These craft steam at such high speed that the after part is covered by the stern wave and only the fore part is visible. Thank heaven they are so fast—they disappear over the horizon all the sooner.

At 6:30 P. M. the chief quartermaster relieved me of my watch. I pointed out a storm cloud. Visibility was poor in that direction, and it was the direction from which our friends the destroyers might be expected to come. I was in my bunk trying to sleep when the cry of "Quick dive!" rang through the boat. At that time we had no alarm gongs. The men were so nervous after the events of the day and the order was so suddenly given that the diving manœuvre was clumsily and slowly obeyed. The helmsman, who was the last down through the conning tower, sang out:

"Destroyer close aboard."

The pestilent craft had indeed come out of the storm cloud, and was so near us that we were nearly done for. Weddigen had the regulating tanks filled so full that the boat plunged down and struck bottom sharply with its stern. We all nearly died of fright, but no damage was done. Luckily, this was in the day before depth bombs had been invented. We arose to periscope depth and found the destroyer cruising back and forth. Too bad we had not another torpedo. However, our batteries were now giving about their last kick and we could run submerged no longer. We sank to the bottom to lie there and wait. We heard our enemy's propeller for a long time. Well, we were all exhausted, and might as well spend a quiet night. With the *U-9* lying peaceably on the ocean floor, we turned in.

In the early dawn of the following day the *U-9* once more stuck her periscope above the surface of the North Sea. Nothing was in sight save a clear, lovely morning. We blew out our tanks and in a few minutes were on the surface recharging our batteries. We put up our radio masts and got into communication with S. M. S. *Arkona,* the German cruiser guarding the entrance to the Ems. Our wireless set was not strong enough to reach the main stations. We reported that we had sunk three small armoured cruisers, probably of the Kent class.

A few hours later, as we approached the Ems, a German steamer passed close beside us. Her crew gathered on deck and raised wild cheers. They called out eagerly news of which we had no suspicion. Through Holland the word had come to Germany that we had sunk the big armoured cruisers, *Aboukir, Hogue,* and *Cressy* of a total displacement of *36,000 tons.* The minimizing effect of the single-lens periscope had caused us greatly to underestimate the size of our prey. It was a far cry from small vessels of the Birmingham class to the giant ships we had sunk.

In port we received an enormous ovation. The Kaiser awarded Lieutenant Weddigen the Iron Cross of first and second class and the Iron Cross of second class to every member of the crew. Later Weddigen was the first German naval officer in the World War to be cited for the rarely awarded Pour le Mèrite, the famous order founded by Frederick the Great, and Germany's greatest war decoration. In the four years of the war less than thirty U-boat officers were awarded this decoration.

A little later detailed British accounts of our victory filtered into Germany. We hit the *Aboukir* first, then the *Hogue,* and then the *Cressy.* After the torpedoing of the *Hogue,* the *Cressy* spied our periscope and opened fire and tried to ram us. A gunner reported that he had hit the periscope, that our conning tower had then appeared, and that he had hit it. An officer standing near the gunner believed the shell had hit a piece of floating wreckage. He, of course, was right. The crew on deck, though, were certain that the submarine had been sunk and raised a cheer. Then our torpedo hit them. The British believed that two submarines had engaged in the attack on the three cruisers.

CHAPTER III

NEW HORIZONS FOR THE U-BOATS.
WEDDIGEN SCORES AGAIN.

Lieutenant Spiess continued his story:

Off on a long cruise. It was the autumn of 1914, those months of blood when the British and Germans were fighting the first of their savage series of battles in Flanders. Our orders read: "Search the area between Orkney and Shetland Islands and Norway for enemy men-of-war." It was in those northern waters that the British blockade line was drawn tight—a likely place to hunt for game. A flotilla of U-boats went out. They were to operate singly. And so in the middle of October the *U-9* steered north. After a run of several days, with half a dozen alarms, attempted attacks, quick dives, and escapes underwater, we found ourselves with boat submerged and breakfast on the table in northern latitudes—and cursing the British. As a result of the amount of underwater running we had had to do, the boat needed ventilation badly. The air was foul. It was enough to give you a headache that you would never get over. I was having my cup of coffee—and coffee was still good and not yet *Ersatz* in Germany—when the chief quartermaster on watch at the periscope sang out:
"Three British cruisers ahoy!"
We ran to the conning tower, and Weddigen stared into the periscope.
"They must want a torpedo," he commented with

the habitual whimsical smile of his mouth turning slightly wry.

I gazed at the little picture of the upper ocean. The distant three cruisers were some wide space apart, but were converging, were steering for a point and that point apparently in the vicinity where we lay. No wonder our commander thought they must want a torpedo.

We imagined they were bent on joining forces and steaming together, but it presently became apparent that they intended to exchange signals, drop a cutter in the water, and deliver mail or orders, and then go their respective ways. We steered at full speed for the point toward which they were heading, our periscope showing for only a few moments at a time.

The cruisers, big armoured fellows, came zigzagging. We picked one, which afterward turned out to be H. M. S. *Hawke,* and manœuvred for a shot. It was tricky work. She nearly ran us down. We had to dive deeper and let her pass over us, else we should have been rammed. Now we were in position for a stern shot at an angle, but she turned. It was a fatal turning, for it gave us an opportunity to swing around for a clear bow shot at 400 metres.

"Second bow tube—fire!" Weddigen snapped out the order, and soon there sounded the telltale detonation.

We dived beyond periscope depth, ran underwater for a short distance, and then came up for a look through our tall, mast-like eye. The *Hawke* had already disappeared. She sank in eight minutes. Only one boat was in the water. It was the mail dory that had been lowered before the torpedo explosion. At the rudder the boat officer hoisted a distress signal on the boat's staff. That little dory with half a dozen men aboard was all that was left of the proud warship.

Seldom has a ship sunk so quickly and carried so many men to the bottom of an icy sea.

The two other cruisers were vanishing on the horizon. At the moment the torpedo explosion crashed out they turned tail and ran as fast as they could. It may have been inhuman for our adversaries thus to abandon the survivors of the *Hawke,* scores of men struggling in the icy water, but by this time the British had learned not to repeat the mistake of September 22d.

Not many major naval units were sunk by submarine attack during the World War, but of the few our old and already obsolete *U-9* accounted for four of them. No wonder they began to call her the *Lucky U-9.*

After the sinking of the *Hawke* we continued our cruise, and presently ran into one of those moments that stamp your memory with a seal of flame. Successes and triumphs leave their vivid impressions, but nothing bites so deeply into your very fibre as when disaster and frightful death is upon you and it seems as if you cannot escape.

"Destroyer ahoy!" and we submerged and steered an underwater course, seeking to steal up on our prey.

The swift little warship zigzagged along. She seemed to be one of the H class and apparently a flotilla leader, as a beautiful diagonal cross was displayed on the pennant flying from her main peak. We could not get in a shot at her. And now another destroyer, also apparently of the H class, appeared. No success with her either. We seemed to have slid into a nest of those hornets. It was a deucedly uncomfortable neighbourhood. We steered to the east so that we might come to the surface and get a better look around. It was about noon. The sea was a dead calm and the day was a bright one.

"Destroyer ahoy!" Again the call sent us below

the glassy surface of the sea. There were four oil-burning craft also of the H type. They came steering directly for us.

"They're giving us the shot of our lives," cried Weddigen, and his sharp, eager features were alight with the exultation of a hunter who sees the game spreading out in perfect array for his gun.

The four destroyers were steaming abreast, one about a thousand yards from the next. The *U-9* was in position to get in between the two on the left wing. Weddigen's orders came quickly and with a deadly precision. He manœuvred the boat so that, as the two destroyers passed one on each side of us, our bow would point toward one and our stern toward the other. Bow torpedo for one and stern torpedo for the other—a splendid double shot. Weddigen often had a placid, stolid look. Not so at this moment. His eyes were shining.

A periscope and the white wake behind it is a thing for a blind man to see on the smooth, crystalline sea. We dared show our long, flagpole eye for only the briefest seconds. We were in position for the double killing. I ran the periscope out for the captain to make his shot.

"Damn it!" he growled. "One of those fellows is out of position. We can fire only the bow tube."

A few quick orders to the helm and engines and then the command:

"First bow tube—fire!"

I pressed the button. Weddigen turned the periscope for a glance at the destroyer that had not kept its place in line. He looked, and jerked around with fright written in his face. His voice rang out with a loud volume and an accent of despair.

"Trim down the boat—quick—quick! Periscope in! All men forward! He is ramming us!"

There was mad activity down below. At that fearful cry the helmsman leaned on the depth rudder and the men rushed forward frantically to force the bow of the boat down.

Weddigen and I stood side by side like paralyzed creatures and gaped with distended eyes at the depth indicator. Would we never dive? The indicator crept up a little, but so slowly, along the mark of the metres, nine metres, ten metres. Could we possibly escape? Thirteen metres . . . at that instant a tremendous roar struck our ears, like some overwhelming thunder. The boat rocked as if she would turn over. Through the unscreened port in the rear of the conning tower I could see a black shadow that loomed and disappeared. The destroyer had charged straight over the top of our conning tower. We had gone clear by an inch. A second more and we would have got the murderous impact of the ram bow. The roar of the enemy propellers had been so deafening that when I turned to the captain, wiping the sweat off my forehead, I attempted a feeble joke.

"He must have dropped his anchor on our deck."

As for the other destroyer, our torpedo had missed. Perhaps it had been seen and the boat had manœuvred to avoid it, or perhaps it had not been set for a sufficiently shallow run to hit the light draft vessel. When we had discharged it the usual big air bubble that accompanies a launched torpedo had broken on the glassy surface. It had been seen by the destroyer that was out of position. Perhaps it had already seen our periscope. Anyway, the craft turned with hard rudder and full speed to ram us.

"Everything in order below decks," came the welcome report. In the conning tower we could scarcely believe it.

We submerged to twenty metres and stole away. The destroyers scoured the sea for a long time. We could hear the grinding roar of their propellers.

When we returned to our base we learned that one of our companions, the *U-17*, was close by when we sank the *Hawke*. She had sighted the three cruisers at about the same time that we had. We had beaten her to the attack. Imagine the surprise of the officer at the periscope of the *U-17* when he saw the *Hawke* suddenly torpedoed in front of his eyes. The *U-17* then turned its attention to the other two cruisers and manœuvred for a shot as they fled. They steamed too fast, though, for a torpedo to find its mark.

A little later, on the same cruise, the *U-17* won a small victory that attracted no attention over the great world but that was of epoch-making importance so far as the World War was concerned. She sighted the British merchant steamer *Glitra*, carrying a cargo of sewing machines and whiskey. Steering alongside on the surface, she ordered the crew to their boats. A boarding crew from the U-boat sank the *Glitra* by opening her sea cocks.

This was the first time in history that a submarine had sunk a merchant ship.

It was entirely unexpected. Attacks on commercial steamers had not been foreseen. The possibilities of that kind of warfare had not been anticipated. The U-boats were not equipped with guns, prize lists, contraband rules, or any of the paraphernalia necessary for a campaign against oceanic trade.

In fact, Lieutenant Feldkirchner, the commander of the *U-17*, had exceeded his instructions, and put into port a badly worried man. How could he tell but that he might get a court-martial for his unauthorized sinking of the *Glitra?* The commander-in-chief, however, O.K.'d the procedure.

The matter went further. The U-boat fleet in general was authorized to make mercantile captures. A little later, our under-sea craft were provided with machine guns, grenades, and formal instructions for prize crews, pertaining to contraband and such. Lloyd's Register, which contains a complete list of the ships of the world, could not be obtained in Germany in sufficient quantities at that time, and for the while we had to dispense with these.

So, that sinking of the *Glitra,* more than the torpedoing of a big British cruiser, was the major result of that October cruise of our U-boat flotilla. Briefly, the idea of the submarine blockade was born—and a fateful idea it was.

Shortly after our return, Weddigen, who had wrenched his leg, relinquished command of the *U-9.* Later he was given the *U-29,* one of the newest and best-equipped under-sea raiders to slip down the ways. At Heligoland he took leave of his *U-9* pals and of the old lucky boat in which he had sunk the *Hogue,* the *Cressy,* and the *Aboukir.* Little did we realize that we should never see him again. After a brief career of brilliant successes in the restricted war on merchant shipping, on March 26, 1915, he tackled a whole squadron of British battleships, singlehanded. But one of Jellicoe's giants rammed him just as that destroyer had tried to ram the *U-9* on our historic October cruise. The *U-29* was not so lucky, and thus perished the first great victor of the submarine war. Out there somewhere on the floor of the North Sea, where he had sent so many of his victims, lies the first of our great raiders of the deep, with his battered submarine for a coffin. Not a man was saved.

This was all that Commander Spiess had to tell about his former commander, and it was to the British that I went for the story of Weddigen's last fight and of his voyage to the last haven of many a German Captain Nemo. A gallant English naval officer related the tale:

"The Grand Fleet had been divided into two parts

for a sham battle. The sea was calm, with a slight swell, and our squadron of eight battleships was making sixteen knots on a straight westward course through the North Sea toward Fair Island Strait to the north of the Orkneys. From the foretop of H. M. S. *Vanguard,* where extra submarine lookouts had been posted, came the report that a conning tower had been sighted on the horizon twelve miles away.

"Several of us were standing with me on the bridge of H. M. S. *Colossus* at the time and one of my companions was a marine officer who fitted to perfection the type of Englishman you so often see caricatured on the New York stage. The silly-ass type, you know. 'Bah Jove,' he drawled, 'do you observe that deucedly curious streak on the water? The track of a bally destroyer, eh what? One might almost mistake it for the track of a blooming torpedo, don't you know? Damn it all, old bean, *it is a torpedo!* What?'

"And it was. The track was clearly visible off the port side. We saw it curve to the right. The gyroscope apparatus on it had failed and the torpedo was not running true. It passed under the stern of the H. M. S. *Superb,* the fourth in our line. However, I think it could have been avoided even had it run straight, because of the distinct white wake it was leaving.

"Every ship altered course toward the supposed position of the submarine. Warning signals were flashed to the other squadron, coming up from the east. One of the ships in that group was H. M. S. *Dreadnought.* Her officer of the watch saw the ship in front of him suddenly alter her course to port and hoisted the signal, 'Submarine in sight.' Almost at the same instant the *Dreadnought* lookout sighted two or three feet of periscope sticking out of the water twenty degrees off the port bow and proceeding at high speed.

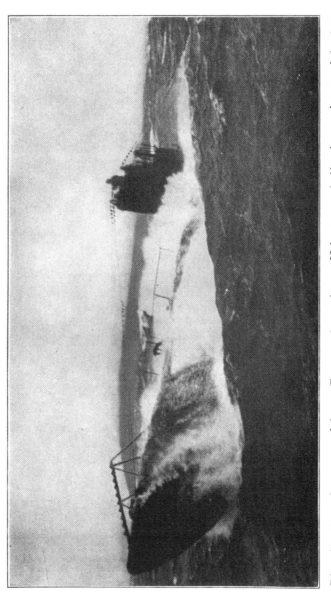

Plunging through spray and foam. Even on the surface a U-boat runs half submerged most of the time.

Ramming home a torpedo. Rather informal handling of a temperamental baby.

Mail from home. The torpedo room of a U-boat from whence the missiles of death were launched.

"It is quite probable that Weddigen miscalculated his attack, due to having to keep his periscope out of sight so much of the time in the calm sea. Immediately the officer of the watch of the *Dreadnought* altered course for the periscope. 'Full speed ahead,' he shouted into the engine-room speaking tube. A few minutes later came the shock of a terrific collision. The *Dreadnought* had been making nineteen knots, and the U-boat must have been sliced squarely in two. She fell away to starboard and her bow popped out of the water, spun around, then seemed to stand vertical for a few seconds as the *Dreadnought* sped past. On it, in plain sight, were the numbers *U-29.* Then it shot beneath the waves. Our destroyers steamed about the spot looking for survivors. There were none—nothing to be seen except a few pieces of débris floating about. The man who had destroyed the *Hogue,* the *Aboukir,* and the *Cressy* had joined his victims on the floor of the North Sea."

CHAPTER IV

RAIDING RUSSIAN PORTS

Commander Spiess, who had told us the dramatic and well-nigh incredible tale of how a little cigar-shaped craft, the *U-9*, had won the first great naval victory of the World War, went on with the story of his adventures:

On February 4th, six weeks before Von Weddigen took the long dive to the bottom of the North Sea, the Emperor arrived at Wilhelmshaven. He inspected the naval forces and we all were presented to him. At the conclusion of the ceremony we were informed that the All Highest had signed a proclamation "declaring the waters around Great Britain and Ireland a war zone." That meant the opening of the so-called "unrestricted submarine commerce warfare," which was to be waged against all enemy merchant ships encountered in the waters that had been declared a war zone. The U-boat was proving itself to be a far more effective weapon than any of us had dreamed. With its success came the idea of a submarine blockade. Meanwhile the war in France had settled down to the stalemate of the trenches, and it looked as if we were in for a much longer struggle than we had expected.

I took command of the *U-9*, and off we went on our first cruise, the purpose of which was to play havoc with Allied merchant shipping. One of our tasks was to drive the great British fishing fleet away from its regular haunt. We captured and sank scores of smacks off Dogger Bank. This was far less glorious than gunning for armoured men-of-war, and less exciting. But it supplied many unexpected thrills, at that. I remember one breath-taking moment. We had sighted a fishing steamer, the *Merry Islington.* A shot across her bow, and her crew nearly jumped out of their so'westers in clambering into their boats and pulling for shore. Why, they were on the beach even before we had time to draw alongside their deserted craft. Our chief engineer and his detail were about to shin up her side, pile below, and open her sea valves, when our quartermaster sang out:

"Destroyer ahoy!"

Ach! What a start that gave us!

A heavy fog hung over the sea, and the destroyer had stolen up on us through the mist. She was heading straight toward us. On she came, charging at full speed. Our old U-boat was not one of the quick kind, and there was no time to dive.

"Starboard engine full speed astern—port engine half speed ahead!" I barked. Mere instinct caused me to do it.

A moment later, and we had slid around behind the hull of the fishing boat. There was a chance in a thousand we had not already been observed. If we could only keep out of view of the onrushing destroyer! The swift enemy swept churning along. As she passed quite near us our boat was completely concealed behind the fishing smack. What luck! She hadn't seen us at all. On she sped and quickly disappeared in the fog. Then we proceeded to sink our prize.

It was now July, and of the fourteen older boats that we had at the beginning of the war, the class of which the *U-9* was one, seven had been lost. The *U-9,* which had been put into commission before some of the boats with the earlier numbers, was now the oldest under-sea craft in the Imperial Navy. We overhauled her and then came orders for us to head for the Baltic on a cruise. Russia was very much in the war news then. The Muscovites had hit Austria hard, and we were in the position of having to do something to help our Allies. Besides, most of our U-boat activities had been discontinued in the North Sea.

On that voyage adventures against the Russians came thick and fast. Ach! I'll say they did! If you want the *n*th degree in thrills, try running right into an enemy harbour in a submarine.

The penetration of an enemy harbour is one of the rarest and most daring exploits asked of a submarine captain. But August 25, 1915, found our faithful old *U-9* dodging mines and stealing stealthily into the Russian fortified harbour of Uto. This Russian naval stronghold had been bombarded by a squadron of our armoured cruisers only a short while back. Our big man-of-war, the *Von der Tann,* had exchanged shots with the Russian cruiser *Makaroff* as she lay in the shelter of the fortifications. And now, we of the *U-9* were on our way right into Uto Harbour in the hope of slipping near enough the *Makaroff* to treat her to a torpedo. We got through the mines and cautiously ran up our cyclopean eye. Lo and behold, the *Makaroff* was gone!

We scouted around the harbour, submerged of course, and were taking a periscope look at what was to be seen when suddenly, as I studied the picture of bay and shore, I spied a Russian submarine. It was hardly distinguishable against the rocky background, but there it was, lying on the water in a small inlet. Alongside was a small steam launch, such as we had often seen on Russian warships visiting Kiel. The situation seemed clear. The Russian submarine officers were leaving their boat to spend the night on shore or aboard the submarine tender that lay a little distance away. The submarine would stay where she was for the night—unless she took an unexpected dive! Ha!

"Here's a fish like ourselves for our day's bag," I said to my watch officer, who stood behind me in the conning tower.

All we had to do now was to enter the channel on the side across from our Russian cousin, then turn in a quarter circle, and, with a torpedo tube pointing at him, let her rip. I steered for the entrance of the channel and ordered the bow torpedoes made ready for the shallow run.

The steam launch left the Russian submarine and started out for the tender.

"Ach! Just as I thought," I mumbled to myself. "We'll send that turtle kicking in a jiffy."

We were entering the channel, sliding along near one rocky bank. I took a leisurely look around with the periscope to make sure that there would be no interference, no destroyers steaming suddenly into the harbour or similar unpleasantness. No sign of any danger. The water was aglow with the setting sun and the encircling shore dusky with the shadows of evening.

When I turned the "eye" to the enemy again, whew! My hair nearly pushed my cap through the steel hull. That submarine was coming toward us! My scheme had gone wrong. What a fool I'd been! Here they were, headed right for us, or at any rate bound for the open sea. Our one chance for a shot now was a lightning quick turn and a pot shot at her on the wing—or on the fin. Our old *U-9* always turned like a fat old lady. Doing a ballet turn was not in her line.

"Hard aport," I called through the speaking tube. "Port engine full speed astern. Starboard engine full ahead. Leave periscope out."

We came around with our most powerful turning movement, while I watched the Russian as he slowly approached us. Then came a shock, a lurch, and a horrible grinding noise. In swinging around, we had hit the rocky projections on the side of the narrow channel.

I stopped both engines, not knowing what was going to happen. I could hear shots popping. The Russian was firing at our periscope.

"In periscope," I called mechanically and, I fear, rather hopelessly.

The chief engineer on his own initiative trimmed the boat down to eight meters in an effort to clear the rocks. It seemed impossible to me that the collision of our stern with the ledge had not damaged our propellers and depth rudders and put us out of commission. The voice of the helmsman in the conning tower sang out:

"She obeys the rudder!"

That one cheering announcement seemed to jerk me out of my fit of hopelessness. I ran the periscope out and cautiously started the port engine. She steered. Hurrah! We were getting clear of the rocks.

Now came the worst. I had to look through the periscope to see that we were steering away from the craggy bank. The Russian, who was watching, saw the stick, of course. It gave him his mark. I saw a track of bubbles coming at us and my blood ran cold. It seemed to lengthen out ever so slowly. I had never thought a torpedo could dillydally along like that. But, of course, it was only my fear that made it seem so slow. I swung the boat as best I could to avoid it. Thank heaven, she missed! But would it bang into the rocks behind us? For a moment I did not realize that the Russian was lying up channel from us. But, even so, the torpedo might hit a projecting rock near us. I waited with a panicky feeling for the explosion. None came. The torpedo had slid on out into the bay.

Our periscope was down now. The whole thing must have seemed eerie and mysterious to the Russian —too mysterious, perhaps, for we saw no more of him. As for ourselves, we were glad enough to get out of the harbour before night fell. Next day, in the half light before darkness came, to make up for that scare, we bagged a fine head of game, a large Russian naval auxiliary steamer. Then we started for home.

The *U-9* was on her last cruise. We steered for the mouth of the Gulf of Finland, and lay off the port of Reval. It was very late in the season—December, that December of 1915 when Henry Ford was sending the Peace Ship over "to get the boys out of the trenches by Christmas." We lay submerged. There was a light frost and the weather was brilliantly clear. Through the periscope I saw a heavy fog bank drift toward us and engulf us. We came to the surface to recharge batteries. As I jumped out on deck I slipped and slid and sat down ignominiously and slid some more. I was just able to keep myself from going overboard. With the fog bank had come intense cold. The thermometer showed 20° below zero. As the boat had emerged, the sea water clinging to her had instantly frozen, and she was a sheet of ice.

When we were ready to trim down we found we couldn't lower the radio masts. The supporting wires were coated with ice and would not rove through the blocks. We knocked away the ice with hammers. The conning tower hatch wouldn't even close. Finally we melted the ice with a blow torch. When we did contrive to get below surface I stared at the instrument board in amazement. We went down by the stern and stuck fast at seven metres. Then I understood. The instruments were all frozen. When we ran the periscope out *it* froze. A thick layer of ice covered the objective lens. Our one eye was put out and we could not see while below surface. In short, when the temperature gets down to twenty below a submarine is a submarine no longer—we had to run on the surface. Luckily for us, winter already had sent the Russians to the snug relief of their ports.

On our return trip we saw a remarkable sight. Near the Island of Odensholm lay the wreck of the German cruiser *Magdeburg,* which had been sunk. The U-boat, sliding along, passed close to the foundered warship. Masts, spars, and smokestacks stuck out of the water. The waves dashed over them at times and they were covered with cataracts of ice, forests of icicles, thick layers of glistening ice, and tens of thousands of glittering streamers that hung from the spars like some weird kind of lace. The light played fancifully and gleamed in the crystalline shapes. The ill-fated *Magdeburg* had been transformed into a fantastic sea palace of the ice king.

That April the *Lucky U-9* closed her venturesome career. Mechanical progress had passed her utterly. Despite her great record and her victories over John Bull's proud cruisers, she was pitifully obsolete, a leftover from a primitive time. What a difference one lone year can make! She was taken out of active warfare and turned over to the submarine training service. From then on she played a passive rôle as a school ship for cadets.

CHAPTER V

THE DESTROYER OF BATTLESHIPS
LEAVES HIS POTATO PATCH
AND TELLS HIS TALE.

"I read the orders. Then I sat and thought. They were of a kind to make a man swell with elation and, at the same time, think soberly of a heavy task ahead. The *U-21* had been selected to do the biggest submarine job that the mind of man had been able to invent up to then. The voyage was one worthy of the wily Odysseus—yes, even of that grim Jules Verne hero of fiction, Captain Nemo. Destination: Constantinople! Then upon arrival to play a hand in one of the most tremendous and spectacular games of war ever enacted on the human stage—the fight for the Dardanelles."

The speaker of these words was one of the German Kaiser's most spectacular under-sea raiders during the first years of the war. But the setting was anything but warlike. In fact, it was as peaceful as that hill outside Bethlehem where the shepherds were watching their flocks the night the Prince of Peace was born.

The tiny village of Rastede lies on the flat North German plain, thirty miles from the North Sea. The cottages are quaint and old-fashioned, surrounded by gardens and fruit trees. The church spire, covered with ivy, dates back to the Fourteenth Century. Near by is the great estate of the Grand Duke of Oldenberg—a splendid castle—and around it some seven thousand acres laid out as an English park and stocked with deer, game birds, and other quarry for the hunter. The gamekeepers wear green jaegers' uniforms that vaguely remind one of Robin Hood and his merry men. They dropped in very frequently, it seemed—for beer at the little inn where I was the only foreign guest, and, in their hunting green, provided the final touch of Old World atmosphere.

Hard by the Grand Duke's estate, across from the castle, is another and smaller park and mansion. The Grand Duke's daughter lives there, a lady whose contemporary romance has made much noise in this busy world. She was the wife of Prince Eitel Friedrich, son of the Kaiser. After the war the family traditions of the Hohenzollerns seemed to break with their political fortunes. There were unseemly divorces and unseemly marriages. The Grand Duke's daughter divorced the Kaiser's son and married an army officer who was in no wise of royal rank. She took him to live on the smaller estate across from the vast Grand Ducal Park.

Within sight of both princely establishments is a comfortable house on a small plot of land. There you will find, living the life of a country squire, Germany's most acclaimed under-sea raider, Otto Hersing. Indeed, the question might be asked: Who was the epoch-maker in under-sea warfare—Weddigen or Hersing?

It was Hersing who was the first to sink a ship by submarine attack when he torpedoed the small English cruiser *Pathfinder* in early September of 1914. But the event did not startle the world because the *Pathfinder* wasn't an important enough victim. Then, two weeks later, Weddigen won his victory. Three big cruisers fell victim to the wizardry of his attack, and in such a fearful, spectacular fashion that the whole world gaped with the realization that a new dimension had been added to warfare at sea. Hersing, however,

Editor's Note: Lieutenant Otto Hersing entered the Imperial Navy in March 1909, became a torpedo specialist, and was assigned to the Torpedo Inspectorate at the Baltic Naval Station in Kiel at the coming of war.

went from one spectacular attack to another. He was a trail-blazer of the seas in those first days of submarine warfare. He was the first to embark on extended U-boat voyages, and now followed a series of little-dreamed-of long cruises into distant waters.

Hersing was the first submarine commander to ply the Irish sea and to harry British commerce there. No sooner was that over than he embarked upon a memorable Odyssey from the North Sea to Contantinople. This was a prodigious feat of submarine navigation, and it climaxed in a feat of grim warfare no less prodigious. Off the shore of that flaming furnace of war, Gallipoli, Hersing torpedoed and sank two giant British battleships, H. M. S. *Triumph* and H. M. S. *Majestic,* one of the greatest naval victories of modern times. For this, every member of his crew was given the Iron Cross, while he himself became the first under-sea raider to really wear the Pour le Mèrite. The same decoration was given to Weddigen, but was conferred after his death dive.

Weddigen was lost early in the war, lost in the depths of the sea. But Hersing remained, a bodily form to acclaim, and he flashed from one exploit to another until the end of the war. Nor did he retire from naval service until 1924. And even after the fighting was done he struck a blow that gained honour for him among his people. He was ordered to turn his boat, the *U-21,* over to the British. He did. But the *U-21* never reached England! It was in tow of a British ship when in some unexplainable way (Hersing tells this with a sardonic smile) it sprang a leak and sank.

Among former submarine men he is talked of as the habitual doer of the extraordinary. Every man in the under-sea service toyed with death daily. Every commander made decisions by the hour that took him skating along the brink of doom. But Hersing seems

to have specialized in doing the impossible. To his
seemingly reckless daring, they say, he owed his life.
Many a time, if he had not taken the audacious course,
he would have been caught in the toils from which
escape appeared impossible.

In those days, when Germany staked its all on the
under-water campaign, the millions in the beleaguered
country gaped breathless over the doings of the
U-boats. Inevitably, the most spectacular of the submarine commanders became a national idol. Hersing
was fêted and lionized. Hundreds of articles were
written about him. No illustrated magazine or pic-
torial was complete without a picture of him. Postal
cards with his photograph on them were sold over
every stationery counter, and posters were put up with
his likeness and one word—Hersing. Poems were
written about him, and songs. The gallant Admiral
von Scheer and other high naval officials vied with
each other in praising him. Every possible decoration
was conferred on him. Cities from the Rhine to the
Russian frontier hastened to make him an honorary
citizen and showered him with elaborate documents
all dressed up in parchment and tooled leather.

Nor were his enemies any less negligent about com-
plimenting him. The British put a price on his head;
and even after the war, the French authorities in the
occupied German provinces along the Rhine were so
eager to snare him that they offered 20,000 marks to
anyone who would lure him into territory they con-
trolled. In 1924 a woman in Wilhelmshaven, where
Hersing was stationed, thought she might as well reap
this little reward. She asked him to give a talk about
his war experiences before a society in Hamburg, and
told him an automobile would be sent to take him there.
Hersing agreed to the seemingly innocent proposal,
when, at the last moment, he was tipped off that the
plan was to get him into the automobile, hold him,

and carry him speeding over into territory under French jurisdiction.

British naval historians, who have been writing since the war, have given high praise to the under-sea prowess of Hersing. That distinguished English officer and author, Lieutenant Commander E. Keble Chatterton, R. N. V. R., who has written many books on naval warfare, says: "A very large portion of this successful, enterprising spirit which was actuating the German U-boat service was owing to Hersing. His cruises were certainly extraordinarily daring, and showed considerable endurance. In other words, they afforded invaluable data from which to deduce the theory that much more could be expected of submarines, provided they were multiplied in numbers and built of improved designs."

The German naval authorities during the war used the greatest precautions to keep the real number of Hersing's boat a secret. They made a practice of giving out confusing reports about the commanders and the numbers of the U-boats. Often a boat took a higher number than its real one, this to make the enemy think that Germany had more under-sea craft than was actually the case. Hersing's boat throughout the war was the *U-21*. It was always referred to as the *U-51*. Thus, in their hunt for Hersing, the British were on the lookout for the wrong boat. I had read a good deal about him in English books on war-time subjects, and had known his boat as the *U-51*. When I got to Germany and heard of the *U-21* I was confused. It was not till I was told of the substitution of numbers and the reasons for it that the puzzle was solved.

The British told me that when Hersing arrived in Constantinople with the number *U-21* on his boat the morale of the Turks went up about fifty per cent. But when Hersing went out on his first raid he returned with the number *U-51* on the boat. "Fine!" exulted the Turks, "fine! Another U-boat sent to us by our good friend the Kaiser. Allah is indeed on our side." Whereupon their morale went up a few more notches.

I found the celebrated under-sea raider to be a tall, dark, slender man, with all the dignified and hospitable courtesy of a German rural proprietor. The pictures I had seen of him—war-time pictures—showed a lean, striking-looking young chap with a keen, hawk-like face—a devil of a fellow to all seeming. He looked much older nearly ten years after the Armistice. The best description I can give is that he is strikingly like Fred Stone. He told his callers that he was troubled by rheumatism, a malady that submarine men commonly contracted from the continual dampness of the boats. When we asked him what he was doing, he replied:

"I grow fine potatoes."

And that resigned philosophy seems to set the mood of the retired monarch of the deep. While most of the submarine commanders have turned to active business and have passed from that fantastic war-time life of periscope and torpedo, and the constant presence of frightful death, and have gone on into other absorbing activities, Hersing has buried himself in the quietude of country and of growing crops—and remembers the more poignantly because of this. He was the only one I met who gave any aching expression of grief and bitterness over Germany's present lot. The others seemed to take it as a matter of course, the natural attitude of active men who accept hard facts without useless repining.

The day we passed in Rastede was a rare one. Commander Hersing and his gracious wife plied us with cordial hospitality, with food and excellent beer, and with the stories of warfare under the sea for which I had come. In the evening they took us back to the inn where we were stopping, and we sat and talked U-boat shop till late. The green-uniformed gamekeepers from the Grand Ducal game preserves sat around with steins of beer, and hearty village people drifted in and out. In another room a meeting of some local war veterans' association was being held. When it broke up the members surrounded the U-boat commander with friendly greetings. I could sense the affection and respect with which they regarded him. When they were introduced to the stranger who was writing about the adventures of the warriors who voyaged under the sea in ships they became more cordial still, and stayed and talked and sang old songs. Altogether, it was simple and festive and jolly—but the pictures of conning towers and of sinking ships were in the background: the tale of men inside a cigar-like shell a hundred feet below the sea and depth bombs bursting around. After it was told an old German melody was sung by lusty voices.

Hersing's story was like a piece of music in which an impressive introduction leads with swift, staccato stroke to the big theme. He told briefly of a succession of earlier events, and then the great adventure:

In the *U-21* he won the first victory of the undersea warfare, the sinking of the British cruiser *Pathfinder,* and then promptly added another "first" to his record. Another boat, the *U-17,* captured and sank the merchant ship *Glitra.* This was the first mercantile craft to be accounted for by a submarine. With the idea thus suggested, the German Admiralty authorized the U-boats generally to take merchant ship prizes—and the "restricted" warfare against Allied shipping was on. Hersing steered forth in the *U-21*.

A thick November mist, a rough sea, and a U-boat running awash off the French coast. A steamer appeared through the fog—the French ship *Malachite.*

A shot across her bow and she hove to. Hersing steered the *U-21* alongside. The sea was running so high and there was so much probability of warships appearing suddenly that he did not venture to send a boarding crew on to the deck of the captured vessel. The *U-21* must remain ready to dive at any moment.

"Bring me your papers," Hersing shouted to the French captain.

The Frenchman lowered a boat. A few hearty strokes with the oars, and the papers were handed to the German. They showed the *Malachite* to be carrying contrabrand from Liverpool to Havre. A lawful prize of war.

"Abandon ship!" Hersing issued the sharp command to the crestfallen skipper.

Now lifeboats are pulling lustily for the near-by shore, and the *U-21's* stern gun is cracking. Under the impact of a couple of shells the *Malachite* lists and sinks. It stands on record as the first ship sunk under the orders that launched the U-boat campaign against merchantmen. Three days later, in these same French waters, the British steamship *Primo,* carrying coal from England to Rouen, joined the *Malachite* in Davy Jones's locker. When he sank the *Primo* Hersing made the second score of the "restricted" campaign.

Then, in January, came the first of the *U-21's* record-breaking cruises. The submarine war, although just begun, had already set nautical nerves tingling with fright. The U-boats were sinking merchant ships with a monotonous regularity. Something of that fear that later swept the oceans like a chilly wind now made eyes scan the waves for that ill-omened, moving stick, the periscope—but only in the near-by waters of the war-swept North Sea. To the west, between England and Ireland, all was yet serene. Ships sailed the Irish Sea to and from Liverpool as trustfully as if war had never been heard of. A U-boat in the Irish Sea!

A list and a plunge and down she goes to Davy Jones.

Hersing, the destroyer of battleships.

Two of his victims at the Dardanelles: H. M. S. Majestic,
left, and H. M. S. Triumph.

Who had ever heard of a submarine voyaging so far from its base? But now the *U-21* was on its way to the Irish Sea.

The route might have been through the English Channel or around the north of Scotland. The Channel was full of mines and nets, but around the north of Scotland was too long a jaunt to think of in those days. The *U-21* stole under water through the perilous Channel. War craft swarmed. Transports, with their fleets of ranging, protecting destroyers, ferried over England's hundreds of thousands to the battlefields of France. Small chance had a U-boat of launching a torpedo with those cordons of hornets looking for its periscope. The *U-21* lay as low as possible, dodged the nets, with their telltale buoys, and trod its way among the mine fields. It was simpler than Hersing had expected. The narrow waterway was full of mines, but in their first mine-laying the English had made a small miscalculation. They had set the deadly iron bulbs too near the surface. It was low tide as the *U-21* stole through and the mines lay on the surface in plain sight.

Up through Saint George's Channel and into the Irish Sea toward Liverpool. Not far from the great seaport Hersing ventured a rare piece of impudence. Near the docks at Barrow was a flying field with a fine row of hangars. Airplanes lay on the fields and circled the sky above. The *U-21* stole close to shore and opened fire with its small gun on docks and hangars.

The astonishment on shore must have been tremendous. It was quickly succeeded by pertinent activity. Coast defense batteries opened fire on the insolent U-boat. A fountain or two leaped out of the water around the *U-21*. That was no kind of a fight for a submarine. Under-sea craft are not designed to exchange bombardment with forts. Where the Arabs would have folded their tents, Hersing closed his hatches, and stole away under water.

Six miles outside of the harbour of Liverpool the captain of the 6,000-ton steamer *Ben Cruachan* gaped with wide eyes. A shot across his bows—a submarine had popped out of the water. A few minutes later Hersing was scanning ship's papers. Pleasant reading it was. The *Ben Cruachan* was loaded with coal bound for the British Grand Fleet at Scapa Flow. A neat trick for a tiny craft 250 feet long, and with a crew of thirty-eight, to rob Admiral Jellicoe's mighty squadron of a shipload of coal. A few bombs placed on board, and Admiral Jellicoe's coal settled to the bottom of the Irish Sea. Three hours later, the steamer *Linda Blanche* took the downward tack and, later in the afternoon the *Kilcuan.*

Things began to grow hot. The word of a U-boat sinking ships off Liverpool was certainly startling enough. Destroyers and patrol craft of all descriptions swarmed to the scene and went scurrying far and wide in search of a periscope. The water became too hot to hold any reasonably prudent submarine. Homeward bound, said Hersing—and the *U-21* nosed her way back through the Channel and to Wilhemshaven.

And now comes the memorable voyage to Constantinople and the sinking of the two great battleships off Gallipoli. Commander Hersing told of it in a rapid, eventful narrative as we sat there in the inn at Rastede, while the gamekeepers of the Grand Duke of Oldenburg, in the green Robin Hood uniforms, lounged at tables in an adjoining room and laughed and sang:

CHAPTER VI

BY SUBMARINE FROM NORTH SEA TO
THE INFERNO OF GALLIPOLI

We German naval men naturally took the greatest interest in the Dardanelles affair. The Allies had just begun their famous attack on Turkey. England and France were attempting to force a passage through to the Golden Horn. They had gathered ships and a powerful fleet and had set out to rush the ancient straits of Hellespont, that narrow lane of water that runs between cliffs from the broad expanse of the Mediterranean to the pre-war capital of the Turks. Ships against forts—an old familiar theme in the art of naval warfare.

The prodigious guns of the Allied squadron had opened fire with a rain of 16-inch shells upon the Turkish fortifications along the straits. The bombardment had begun with a violence that was the talk of the world, and now was progressing and thundering with an increasing intensity. The Turks had asked the Kaiser for U-boats to aid in repelling the attack. Our naval authorities had decided to accede to what was a most difficult request to fulfill. They had ordered me to do the deed. A trip from Wilhemshaven to Constantinople was an unprecedented task for a submarine. But the attempt must be made. A lone boat must try it first. The *U-21* was selected. We of the *U-21* felt like shouting the extraordinary news to everybody.

It was all very well to feel like shouting, but secrecy

was the word of the day. The preparations for a pioneering voyage like that were necessarily extensive. Of course, they had to be kept secret. The prime idea was to take the enemy ships before the Dardanelles by surprise. They would never dream of a German submarine popping up in the Mediterranean. And there were certain private arrangements to be made. On the long jaunt to Constantinople there was no friendly harbour where we could put in for provisions and for fuel, until we reached the Austrian port of Cattaro on the Adriatic Sea. And that was four thousand miles away. No U-boat then extant could be expected to carry enough food and oil for so long a cruise. We should have to reprovision and refuel somewhere between Wilhemshaven and Cattaro. The Admiralty arranged for one of our Hamburg-American steamers, the *Marzala,* to meet us off the coast of Spain and transfer to the *U-21* a store of provisions and fuel. Naturally, that plan needed the greatest secrecy.

By the time the *U-21* was fitted out, the main naval attack on the Dardanelles had run its course. The land forts had beaten off the attacking fleet with a heavy loss of ships. It was clear that it was impossible to fight ships against forts and force the Dardanelles. The Allies gave up the attempt. But this merely meant that the struggle at the Dardanelles flared up with an enlarged and bloodier violence. The idea now was to force the straits by a land attack, to throw troops ashore and advance along the sides of the long slip of water. We had word of a great concentration of troops for the task, and on the very day the *U-21* stood out to sea for Constantinople, the Australian and New Zealand regiments landed on the dread, fiery beaches of Gallipoli, and the fearful tragedy of Gallipoli was under way. Very well, ships would have to take a large part in the land attack on

the Straits. They would be swarming around. A
U-boat might be able to play a neat part in the flaming drama. We wondered what the future held for
us, and if we should ever get to Constantinople.

On April 25, 1915, we nosed out of the harbour of
Wilhelmshaven and set a course north. The English
Channel by now, with its entanglements of nets and
mines, was exceedingly dangerous for U-boat navigation, and we were not to take any more chances than
we had to until we reached the scene of action. So we
took the long route around Scotland, the northern tip
of the Orkney Islands. We went along minding our
own business. Any ships that hove in sight might be
good game for some other U-boat, but they meant
nothing to us.

North of the Orkneys the fog lay heavy on the
sea. We kept along above water, when rather suddenly the mist cleared.

"*Donnerwetter!*" my watch officer exclaimed in a
ludicrous tone of surprise. I was standing on deck
beside him. We were among patrol boats. There
were a number of them, scattered on all sides of us.

"Heave to," the nearest one signalled before we
were able to make ready for a dive.

At the first glance through the still-lingering mist,
our patrol-boat friend thought we might be a British
sub. With that comfortable assurance, we took our
time about diving, and finally did not have to dive at
all. A fog bank drifted over the sea. The mist closed
around us again, and we slid full speed ahead. The
patrol boats groped around blindly for us and in vain.
Thus, covered by the fog, we had an easy passage
through the net of the British blockade.

A week after leaving Wilhelmshaven we were off
the northwesternmost coast of Spain and nearing Cape
Finisterre. A warm sun and a quiet sea, and my
watch officer and I stood on deck scanning the horizon

as eagerly as if we were looking for a British super-dreadnaught to torpedo. We saw a smudge of smoke on the line where the sky met the sea. It grew more distinct. The outline of a ship became clear. Yes, that was it—the *Marzala,* our supply ship. Presently we were close enough to the friendly craft for an exchange of signals. The *Marzala* headed toward the coast. The *U-21* imitated her obediently. We followed her into the Rio Corcubion, where at night we lay alongside and took aboard large supplies of food and more than twelve tons of fuel oil and two tons of lubricating oil. A brief fraternization in that secret nocturnal meeting, hearty handshakes all around, and forth we sailed again, rejoicing in a well-stocked larder and heavily laden oil tanks.

Confidence soon darkened into gloom. The oil we had got from the *Marzala* refused to burn in our Diesel engines. We worked and experimented and struggled with it, but no use. We tried mixing it with our own oil, but it was a case of a bad egg spoiling a good one. The mixture was as bad as the *Marzala's* oil, itself. So, here we were almost two thousand miles from home and more than that distance from Cattaro. We had started out with fifty-six tons of fuel oil, and had twenty-five tons left.

I was called upon to make a decision that, although I did not suspect it, had perhaps some influence on the course of the World War. Should I turn back toward Wilhelmshaven or go on to Cattaro? Neither alternative was pleasant. We had used up thirty-one tons of oil getting this far and had twenty-five tons left for that long trip back home around the north of Scotland. It was likely to be not enough. It was less likely to be enough for the longer trip to Cattaro. I had no notion of the important part the *U-21* was presently to play in events around the Dardanelles, or I should have had less hesitation. However, I have always liked the bolder course. And then we were more likely to have to use up oil bucking bad weather on the northern route than on the southern.

"We go to Cattaro," I said to my crew. "If we are lucky we shall be able to make it."

They raised a cheer. Our success now depended on the amount of diving we had to do. The business of submerging uses up oil at a great rate. If we did not encounter hostile vessels, which would compel us to sneak under water, I thought that by keeping on at our lowest speed we could just about make it. On the other hand, if we were bothered over much, our oil would run out and we should have to seek refuge in some neutral harbour and be interned. That left us in the peculiar position where enemy craft by attacking us could put us out of commission even if we succeeded in eluding their attacks.

Of all the lazy voyages I have ever seen, that one was the laziest. We merely crept along on the surface, and kept as far as we could from the shipping lanes. Whenever we saw a smoke cloud, we gave it the widest berth possible. The run from Cape Finisterre to Gibraltar took four days. Days of sunshine and placid sea they were. We idled away the hours, sleeping or playing cards on deck, and did not have to submerge once.

At Gibraltar nobody thought of U-boats except in dreams. There were no patrol boats scouting around. We were so careful about wasting our fuel on needless diving that we brazenly put our nose into the Straits, running above water. It was May 6th. We hugged the African coast, keeping as far away from the British ships and guns across the narrow strip of water as possible. We got through peaceably, but in the afternoon two little British torpedo boats hove in sight. Would they spy us? They were headed in our general direction. Yes, they had sighted us.

Too bad, but there was no doubt about it. They turned with a sudden starboard helm and made straight for us at top speed.

"Clear for diving," I gave the reluctant order.

We easily got away from them, but that was no complete relief. I was hoarding my oil with the mean avarice of a miser hoarding his money. And then the news of a U-boat in the Mediterranean was out. That would alarm the ships clustered around Gallipoli and, what was more immediate, send British destroyers out searching for us. That would mean more diving and more oil used up.

We stole along on our way more slyly than ever, keeping to the most out-of-the-way route. "Ship ahoy!" and a big British steamer was coming our way. Undoubtedly she was armed. There was nothing else to do. We took a dive. I gazed anxiously at the fuel gauges. The oil was getting low. And then—destroyers ho! Two French boats saw and charged us. Another dive. I'll tell you it was getting nerve-racking.

The *U-21* entered the Adriatic a week after leaving Gibraltar and eighteen days after leaving Wilhelmshaven, and on May 13th was taken in tow by an Austrian destroyer. We had 1.8 tons of oil in our tanks. I may forget other numbers, my birthday, my age; but that figure is indelibly fixed in my mind.

At Cattaro, we got detailed news of the state of things around the Dardanelles. The British and the Turks on the peninsula of Gallipoli were locked in one of the most savage of death struggles. The Anzac regiments were attacking the Turkish trenches day after day with a relentless fury and courage, and the Turks were resisting with that dogged endurance for which the Ottoman soldier has long been renowned. The British attack was supported fully by ships. His Majesty's Navy was lending the heavy weight of its fire to the attacks of the battalions on land. The great

Editor's Note: Cattaro was the principal Austro-Hungarian naval base in the Adriatic Sea just inside the Strait of Otranto.

ANZAC was the acronym of the Australia and New Zealand Army Corps fighting under British command at Gallipoli.

warships of England were standing off the coast and pouring the devastation of their 16-inch guns into the trenches of the Turks, a bombardment with tons of high explosive, to which the Turks had no possible chance to reply. In my mind's eye I could see a U-boat stealing up on those flame-belching giants that stood near the shore. It wasn't often that a submarine commander was lucky enough to find British battleships outside of the shelter of protected ports, at least not stationed in a given place as if ready-placed targets.

The *U-21* lay for a week in Cattaro, making repairs and taking aboard supplies, and then stood out to sea. We slipped down the coast and around the Grecian archipelago and across the Ægean to the blood-drenched peninsula of Gallipoli. The British had sown these waters with mines, and, to keep away from these fields of ugly underwater turnips, we had to creep along in the shadow of the coast. We edged along on the surface all the night of May 24th, heading southward toward the tip of the fateful tongue of land—that battle-scarred, desolate tip where the battle was raging its fiercest. Under cover of darkness we got through the line of patrol boats unobserved.

CHAPTER VII

THE SINKING OF THE BATTLESHIP
TRIUMPH

Day broke. Ahead of us was the shore, with its beaches and cliffs and hills a bare, burnt yellow. There was no sound of guns. The day's battle down the coast had not yet begun. The sea was a dead calm— anything but ideal for our kind of work. A periscope had better not show itself too plainly in these embattled waters. We plunged and nosed our way on to the hive of war farther down.

Ships appeared in the eyepiece. No chance for leisurely inspection. Periscope up for a hasty glance into the lens, a pious hope that the asparagus would not be spied during its few seconds above the glassy surface, and then periscope down. We sighted British battleships off Cape Hellas. I could distinguish three big fellows. A glance into my fleet book, and I could tell from photographs and descriptions there that they were giants of the Majestic class. They were firing salvos with their heavy guns, battering the Turkish positions among the hills with tons of high explosive projectiles.

A hospital ship stood near by. Around were dozens of patrol boats, torpedo boats, and destroyers that wove and circled, nervously on the lookout for intruders. Had reports of our presence in the Mediterranean inspired all this elaborate lookout? Whether yes or no, it was clear that the British were using all possible precautions to shield their battleships from submarine attack, while the fire-spitting monsters hurled their shells upon the shore-lining trenches of the Turks.

"Rare game for a U-boat," I cried exultantly to my watch officer, and steered the *U-21* cautiously toward the three fire-belching leviathans.

"Periscope in!" I shouted quickly. A destroyer was headed toward us. I don't know whether it had seen the periscope or not: but I did not want a submarine warning to go out until I had had a chance to strike a blow.

We ran blindly under water for a while without daring to show our periscope. I did not like the idea of showing any asparagus again in that neighbourhood for the present. Our course lay north from the tip of the peninsula, toward Gaba-Tepe. There the periscope showed another battleship in front of the northern beaches. My reference showed the vessel to be of the Triumph class. Again the inevitable swarm of patrol boats and destroyers circling around to protect it from submarine attack, like pigmies guarding a giant.

"In periscope!" And we dived to seventy feet and headed toward the monster, passing far below the lines of patrol craft. Their propellers, as they ran above us, sounded a steady hum. For four and a half hours after I caught sight of the ship, which was in fact H. M. S. *Triumph* itself, I manœuvred the *U-21* for a torpedo shot, moving here and there and showing the asparagus on the smooth surface of the sea for only the briefest moments.

In the conning tower my watch officer and I stood with bated breath. We were groping toward a deadly position—deadly for the magnificent giant of war on the surface above.

"Out periscope!" H. M. S. *Triumph* stood in thundering majesty, broadside to us, and only three hundred yards away.   Never had an under-sea craft such a target.

"Torpedo—fire!"   My heart gave a great leap as I called the command.

And now one of those fearfully still, eventless moments.   Suspense and eagerness held me in an iron grip.   Heedless of all else, I left the periscope out. There!   And I saw the telltale streak of white foam darting through the water.   It headed swiftly away from the point where we lay, and headed straight— yes, straight and true.   It streaked its way swiftly to the bow of our mammoth adversary.   A huge cloud of smoke leaped out of the sea.   In the conning tower we heard first a dry, metallic concussion and then a terrible, reverberating explosion.

It was a fascinating and appalling sight to see, and I yearned with every fibre to keep on watching the fearful picture; but I had already seen just about enough to cost us our lives.   The moment that dread white wake of the torpedo was seen on the surface of the water, the destroyers were after me.   They came rushing from every direction.

"In periscope!"   And down we went.   I could hear nothing but the sound of propellers above me, on the right and on the left.   Why hadn't I dived the moment after the torpedo left?   The two seconds I had lost were like years now.   With that swarm converging right over our heads, it surely seemed as if we were doomed.   Then a flash crossed my brain.

"Full speed ahead," I called, and ahead we went right along the course the torpedo had taken, straight toward the huge craft we had hit.

It was foolhardy, I'll admit, but I had to risk it. Diving as deeply as we dared, we shot right under the sinking battleship.   It might have come roaring down on our heads—the torpedo had hit so fair that I rather expected it would.   And then the U-boat and its huge prey would have gone down together in an embrace of death. That crazy manœuvre saved us. I could hear the propellers of destroyers whirring above us, but they were hurrying to the place where we had been. Our manœuvre of ducking under the sinking battleship was so unexpected that no hint of it ever occurred to the enemy. We were left in tranquil safety. Keeping as deep as possible and showing no tip of periscope, we stole blindly but securely away. When I ventured to take a look through the asparagus, we were far from the place where the *Triumph* had met her disaster.

Commander Hersing heard the rest of the story after he had put into port many days later. The battleship he had torpedoed was indeed the *Triumph* herself, with a burden of 12,000 tons and an armament of thirty-two guns. It had come to the Dardanelles from Chinese waters, where it had taken part in the attack on Tsingtau. For days now it had been lying offshore, shelling the Turkish trenches, galling and racking them with heavy gun fire to which they had no possible means of replying. All around the *Triumph* heavy torpedo nets had been let down. These, it was believed, would afford her sure protection from U-boats. But the British felt doubly secure because they little dreamed there were any under-sea raiders in those parts.

The men in the trenches, Anzacs and Ottomans, lay facing each other that morning, with the usual bloody routine of sniping and trying to keep out of the way of shells and hand grenades, when they heard an explosion offshore. They saw the *Triumph* leap like a stricken giant. Then she was hidden from sight by the giant geyser of water, smoke, and débris thrown into the air by the explosion. A few minutes after the geyser subsided, she turned turtle, with her great keel sticking into the air. In thirty minutes she disappeared. Meanwhile, scores of patrol boats and destroyers were scurrying about, taking survivors from the doomed ship and hunting for the U-boat that had stolen in and struck so unexpectedly.

On prosaic desk duty in the British Admiralty in London is the commander of one of the destroyers that caused Hersing to take his reckless dive under the sinking battleship. "That German torpedo," he said, "went through the torpedo net like a clown jumping through a paper hoop. Then came the explosion, and when it had cleared away the *Triumph* was listing ten degrees. Every patrol boat and destroyer anywhere about was either looking for the U-boat or hurrying up to take off our survivors. The *Triumph* herself opened fire after she had been hit, aiming at the place where the periscope had been seen for a moment. In the confusion, she hit another British ship.

"I saw what was happening. The *Triumph* was starting to keel over. Men were scrambling over her sides like flies and leaping into the water. I remember seeing one Chinese stoker clinging for grim life to one of the torpedo booms. Then came the terrific lurch as the battleship capsized. That terrified Celestial was for once shaken out of his racial stolidity. The overturning ship sent him hurtling fifty yards through the air into the water. Fitzmaurice, the captain of the *Triumph,* was another man who was hurled through the air as though he had been shot from a gun. One of the destroyers picked him up a few minutes later—according to rumour, with his monocle still firmly fixed in his eye!

"I can remember the comic episodes now. That doesn't mean I've forgotten the other side. That sinking battleship was a terrible sight. The water was filled with struggling men, and boats trying desperately to pick them up. In the midst of them was the overturned battleship, still floating bottom up. It looked for all the world like a giant whale. Nothing struck me so much as the ignominy of it. What an end for a man of war! It remained like that for a half hour. Again there was a sudden lurch. The stern shot up into the air, and then the big fellow, very slowly, sank under the water."

The *Triumph* had taken her place at the bottom of the blue Ægean with the thousands of other craft that lie on the bottom of that historic sea—ships from the day when the Achæan Armada sailed forth against Troy.

In Hamburg I talked with Admiral Wilhelm Tägert, who had been Chief of Staff of the German forces with Turkey.

"The sinking of the *Triumph*," he told me, "was so tremendous a sight that for the moment warfare was forgotten on shore. The soldiers in both lines of trenches on the Gallipoli hills stood up in plain sight of each other, forgetting everything in their intense excitement. They watched, fascinated, until the *Triumph* had taken her last plunge, then jumped back into the trenches and began shooting at each other again."

CHAPTER VIII

HERSING BAGS ANOTHER BRITISH GIANT. AN ADVENTURE WITH A FLOATING MINE.

Hersing continued his story:

The northeastern corner of the ancient Ægean was a warm place the afternoon that followed that eventful morning. With the alarm spread far and wide, every possible Allied craft was pressed into the hunt. Hundreds of craft were searching for us. Every time we peeped through the periscope we could see boats chasing here and there. With that kind of hunt going on, we did not dare show the tip of our conning tower above water. We ran submerged until our batteries ran out. We had been under water since dawn and did not emerge until night—twenty-eight hours under the surface. Inside our iron shell the air grew so foul that we could scarcely breathe. It was an almost impossible effort to move about. We grew drowsy and heavy. When we came up into a clear, fresh night, we drank the pure, cool air as men who are half dead from thirst drink sweet water. We recharged our batteries and lay on the surface for the rest of the night.

On the following morning the *U-21* started out on a wide circle. I thought I might find the Russian cruiser *Askold,* which we had sighted on our way across the Ægean to Gallipoli. I covered the route we had taken on the previous day, hoping that the Russian

might be cruising somewhere in the neighbourhood.
No use, not a glimpse of the *Askold* or any other
warship. When night came I steered south again.
Under the cover of darkness the *U-21* stole back to
the scene where the *Triumph* had gone down.

Day broke with a rough sea running. Yes, there
was the shore and there the trench-lined hills; but no
ship was in sight. We cruised around. Sundry craft
appeared, but no battleships. It was clear that there
would be no more sea giants cruising slowly back and
forth all day, hurling their tons of high explosive on
the Turkish trenches—no more such easy marks for
a submarine. Well, the Turks would be relieved that
much. I steered south toward Cape Hellas at the tip
of the peninsula.

"Something doing down this way," I observed to
my watch officer. The periscope showed large activity
on the beach and the near-by waters. Soon it became
clear that troops were being landed. Several large
transports lay near the beach, and they were not alone.
Five hundred yards from the shore a huge battleship
of the Majestic class, a third again as large as the
Triumph, lay at anchor. She was covering the landing.
It is singular that, as in the case of the *Triumph,* this
vessel gave her name to her class. She was the *Majestic* herself.

The submarine scare of the past few days had,
indeed, had its effect. The *Majestic* was surrounded
by an almost impenetrable patrol of boats of all kinds.
Not only was there the difficulty of getting near her,
but also the possibility of one of the small boats cutting
across the path of a torpedo and getting it herself.
The manœuvring I had to do for a shot was as
intricate as a fine combination. Fortunately, we did
not have to work with the disadvantage of a smooth
sea. A brisk wind was up and the Ægean ran with
choppy waves that helped to hide the asparagus.

My watch officer behind me ran out the periscope.

"Six hundred yards," I said to him, "but I think it is the best we can do."

I had a good bead on the battleship, but those pestilent little boats kept cutting across the track the torpedo would take. They were so annoying that even if one had appropriated a torpedo for itself and blown up properly it would have relieved my irritation. It took a lot of patience, but finally the road was clear. A little craft was bearing down, but it would have to travel fast if it were anxious to make the acquaintance of a torpedo.

"Torpedo—fire!" I gave the often-repeated command. "Periscope in!"

We dived at once and ran under water. I was sure the asparagus had not been seen, and that the path of the torpedo was not clear enough in the turbulent sea to give away clearly the position from which we had fired the shot. I waited for the report of the exploding torpedo, ready to shoot the periscope up for a quick look.

A distant ringing crash—we had hit our target!

"Periscope out!" A quick glance and I saw the *Majestic* listing heavily.

No time for any more rubbernecking. The destroyers were coming. Their shells cut the water above us as we plunged down to sixty feet. We had a good start and easily ducked away, sliding along under water until we were a comfortable distance away from the dangerous scene. After an hour, I sneaked back for a look. Like the *Triumph*, the *Majestic* had turned completely over, with her keel sticking above the surface of the sea. Half a mile away was a flotilla of destroyers and patrol boats. They were systematically searching the water and working along in my direction. That was too uncomfortable even to watch.

The *U-21* went away from those parts as fast as she could.

I was later told how the Turkish regiments on shore, who were directing a fierce fire on the landing Anzacs, suddenly saw a great column of water, smoke, and débris shoot up beside the big ship. In four minutes the *Majestic* had capsized. She had been torpedoed in only nine fathoms of water, and even when she sank a few minutes later, her keel remained above the surface. She didn't completely drop out of sight for years.

Hundreds of men had been caught in her torpedo nets, through which our missile had torn its way. They were carried down with the foundering vessel. Most of the *Majestic's* crew, though, were saved by a French torpedo boat that had turned swiftly to the rescue when the ship was hit.

For two days the *U-21* cruised around looking for more battleships. None were to be seen, though. The British had withdrawn their large ships into the harbour that they had established at the Island of Mudros. Our one small craft had driven away England's battleships during a critical period of the fighting at the Dardanelles. The Anzacs, who were conducting the bloody futile attacks on the shore, were deprived of the aid of the monsters that had stood offshore and shattered the Turkish trenches with the fire of their 16-inch guns.

Who knows but that our 250-foot craft may have had an important bearing on the issue of the Dardanelles campaign, and that the decision I had to make when we got our store of unburnable oil off the coast of Spain may have affected the course of the World War? At any rate, the great British ships of the line and their 16-inch guns were seen no more belching their flame and high explosive at Gallipoli—especially when it presently became known that another U-boat had come from Germany to aid the Turks. The enemy turned to the use of smaller ships to support his land forces. Boats of light burden, such as monitors, stood offshore and threw their shells. From the conning tower of the *U-21* we saw many of these, but they did not lie deep enough in the water to make good marks for torpedoes.

The Turks had established stations for the U-boats at several points on the coast. We put into one of these for a day, and then returned to the war-torn beaches of Gallipoli, vainly hoping that the battleships might have returned. We ran along and through the periscope studied those fateful ten miles of beach, where one of the world's most savage battles was then being waged. On June 1st, the *U-21* turned its nose into the Dardanelles, for the winning of which all that agony was being endured and all that blood spilled.

At the entrance of the Straits we got into a terrific whirlpool. The boat pitched and whirled—and was sucked down. On we went, down and down, and no power the boat had was able to force it up. We were in the clutch of some relentless force, some dread power of nature, and I thought surely we were lost—that we should be dragged down to a depth where the pressure of the water would crush the shell of our boat. Inch by inch, struggle as we might, we were hauled down, until we were below a hundred feet. Then we were able to hold our own, and presently the grasp that held us was released. We slid ahead, and when we came up we were in front of Turkish mines and nets. An opening had been left in them. The *U-21* slipped through, kept on through the Sea of Marmora, and on June 5th, forty days after we left Wilhelmshaven, we caught sight of the minarets and domes of Constantinople—with only a half ton of oil left in our tanks. A slim margin, indeed.

We were received with intense enthusiasm. Enver Pasha, one of the ruling Turkish Triumvirate, assured us that we had arrived just in the nick of time. News came that the English had put a price of £100,000 on my head. Then followed a month in Constantinople, overseeing the usual repair work on my boat by day, and idling in the cafés of bizarre Stamboul by night.

We stood out to sea again on July 4th. With the Sea of Marmora and the Dardanelles safely passed once more, the periscope revealed a possible victim. We were off Gallipoli, and the ship in sight was the 5,600-ton French transport *Carthage*. She had just landed a load of munitions and was ready to take on her return cargo.

First a bit of careful manœuvring. Then:

"Torpedo—fire!" A square hit. Through the periscope I could see a column of water spouting as high as the masts, then dropping in a cascade on the decks. The stern dipped out of sight and the bow rose vertically out of the water. Clouds of black smoke belched from the funnels. The *Carthage* was 500 feet long. The water was shallow and almost at once her stern touched bottom, although her bow still stood high out of the water. Then another heavy explosion and the blowing off of steam. She sank a few moments later—another ship as spoil for the Ægean, to join the company of Athenian galleys and Levantine corsairs.

A stop at one of the Turkish submarine stations, and the U-21 headed back. I was perpetually drawn to that strip of shore where the war of trenches was blazing and off which the *Triumph* and *Majestic* had gone down. I could not get over an instinctive expectation of seeing another British battleship.

No battleships, only a couple of puny little fishing

steamers. I studied them through the periscope with contempt. One of them turned and steamed full speed toward us. He had seen the asparagus.

"Dive to twenty metres! Speed there! He is ramming us!"

To twenty metres we went. And then the fun began. Not that there was any danger of our being rammed. It was a case of something worse than that—a mine. There was a frightful detonation behind us, and our lights went out. The sudden darkness seemed like the pall of death. Something, I don't know what, had set off a mine near us, and it had nearly blown the boat out of the water. I waited with a sinking heart, expecting the sounds that would tell that the boat was filling with water. Everything was deathly still.

"Report on all compartments," I shouted.

The examination of the compartments was made with the aid of flashlights. She was still tight, but her diving apparatus had gone awry. It seemed for a while as if the diving mechanism were so badly out of gear that we might sink. We worked and sweated with it—and were not able to get it to work right. All we could do was to hold the boat at periscope depth and limp our way back into the Dardanelles as fast as possible—hoping against hope that no patrol boat would come along and pick us up. Old Father Neptune was good to us. We got back to Constantinople safely, but it was almost a case of our having once too often revisited the place where those two battleships had sunk.

The *U-21* remained in the Mediterranean for nearly two years. There was no further work at Gallipoli, and we carried on war against Allied merchant shipping. It was exciting enough, but even exciting work, when done over and over again, becomes routine. One adventure, though, was exceptional.

It was in the spring of 1916, off Sicily, not far from Messina, that I sighted a small steamer flying the British ensign. A shot across her bow, but she didn't seem to understand our language. She kept straight on her course. I repeated my request with another shot. This time she replied with a language of her own—a shell from a little gun mounted on her bow. It fell so short that it meant nothing more than an irritating expression of defiance.

"She wants a fight," I remarked to my watch officer, "and we'll oblige her."

We were standing on the deck beside the conning tower. I ordered full speed—and to the gun crew working our bow gun: "Give it to her as fast as you can."

We drew up, prepared to fight it out at close range. That puny little gun at her bow was something to inspire contempt.

She turned on us. The bulkheads on her deck dropped and revealed the muzzles of two big guns. If she put up her war ensign, I did not see it; but it was clear that she was a decoy ship—one of England's famous Q-boats. It was my first experience with that kind of nasty customer.

Those two big guns crashed out with rapid fire. Fifteen centimeter shells exploded in the water all around us. One of them hit and exploded in the water just in front of me. A burning pain in my arm—in my leg—in my face. I scarcely noticed them in the excitement; but three pieces of shell had hit me and I was streaming with blood.

My first idea was a quick dive. But if we did that she would know where to look for us, and do her searching with depth bombs. We had another way of hiding—a smoke screen. Behind it we could run with our good surface speed, and submerge when we had got a safe distance away. The shells were cracking on all sides when I gave the order for the smoke screen. I stood half blinded, half fainting, with the blood streaming down my face. The smoke puffed up in a dense cloud. The shells did not drop so near now. We ran for dear life, and then in a few minutes submerged.

In March, 1917, I made the cruise back to Germany, where every boat was needed for the climactic campaign against England's commerce.

Hersing cared little about sinking merchant ships. Tramps, windjammers, or even big freighters made little appeal to the imagination of this bold marauder of the depths. Another U-boat commander told me that Hersing frequently would pass up a half dozen humble merchantmen if he even suspected that a man-of-war was anywhere within his hunting range.

Another of his important victories took place on February 8, 1916. On that date Hersing encountered the French armoured cruiser, *Amiral Charner,* just off the Syrian coast, and sent her to join the two British men-of-war that he had bagged at the Dardanelles.

Pick up almost any British history dealing with the naval side of the World War, and you will find it filled with tributes to the wizard Hersing. Here, for example, is a typical one that I ran across while going through the archives of the Imperial War Museum Library at South Kensington. The reference mainly concerns the sinking of the *Triumph* and *Majestic.* It is copied word for word from the *British Official Naval History,* edited by the great English naval historian, Corbett:

For the brilliant way in which the enemy submarine had been handled, both services (the British Army and Navy) had nothing but admiration. It was, indeed, no more than was to be expected from the man in command. For later on he was known to be none other than Lieutenant Commander Hersing, the determined officer who in April, in spite of every difficulty, had brought the *U-21* into the Mediterranean by way of Gibraltar, and thus demonstrated the possibility—till then not credited—of navigating a submarine to the Adriatic without a halfway base of supply. Reaching Cattaro on May 13th with only one-half ton of oil in his tanks, he had remained a week and then continued his voyage to the Dardanelles. The grave moral effects of his remarkable feat could not be disguised. Hundreds of thousands of Turkish troops, depressed by loss and failure, and demoralized by the heavy shell fire from the sea, had seen the stampede of the ships they most dreaded; thousands of our own men had seen the loss of the ships as well, and they knew there was nothing now but the cruisers and destroyers to support them in their daily struggle in the trenches.

So, is it any wonder that Commander Otto Hersing became a national hero in his own country? A hundred years from now, when the Muse of History takes up her pen to chronicle the events of our time, there is little doubt but what the name of a squire of Rastede, who now grows potatoes, will stand out as one of the most remarkable naval figures of our era. Why, the total tonnage of the great Spanish Armada was less than the tonnage of the mighty men-of-war and armed merchantmen that fell victim to the torpedoes and guns of this one audacious U-boat raider. But there were others. Many others, in fact, who bagged more game than Hersing.

CHAPTER IX

THE BEGINNING OF THE REIGN OF FRIGHTFULNESS

Although the U-boats struck spectacular and startling blows against British sea power during the first months of the war, it was soon evident that thrusts from under the sea were not destined to cripple or even seriously damage the King's Navy. Twice as many warships were sunk by submarine attacks during the first year of the war as during the other three years combined. In fact, after the early field day for the sub-surface boats, during which Weddigen and Hersing won their fame, it was indeed a rare event when a U-boat made a successful attack on a major naval unit, a cruiser or battleship.

Against warships, stationary or steaming along in an ordinary, old-fashioned way, the U-boats were deadly. But the Allied naval authorities learned quickly. They found an easy and sure way to parry the submarine blow against their combat fleets. They simply kept their capital ships in harbours, the British usually in the snug, safe inlets of Scotland, where they were protected by screens of mine fields and nets and by patrols of destroyers. The U-boats had small chance of penetrating these harbours, and the only Allied craft that were ordinarily to be seen at sea were light cruisers, whose speed and swift zigzagging foiled U-boat attack, and destroyers, the natural and most formidable enemies of submarines. Many a U-boat skipper did not catch sight of a single major enemy warship throughout the war. When the larger ships did go out on cruises they kept a zigzag course and were heavily protected by destroyers—two measures for baffling submarine attack that seemed to best the cleverest of the U-boat commanders.

The U-boats, checked in their successes against warships, turned the more energetically to the campaign against merchant shipping. The "restricted" campaign was the first stage, and while it was in progress the U-boats acted in pretty much the fashion that surface raiding craft had always done. Their orders were to make such prizes as were allowed by international law. Vessels were to be warned, and passengers and crews were to have an opportunity to get away in lifeboats. Indeed, this was an ancient, unwritten law of the seas. That meant the familiar shot across the bow, an order to the merchantman skipper to abandon ship, and the sinking of the captured vessel—or, sometimes, a prize crew was put aboard and the craft was taken to port as a spoil of war. It was not so spectacular as torpedoing battleships, but it was risky business just the same.

The "restricted" campaigns against merchant shipping inevitably developed and expanded—passed out of the limits of international law. The system whereby a U-boat on the surface stopped a ship and sank it after passengers and crews had taken to the boats was countered on the part of the Allied powers by arming merchantmen, especially the large ones, with guns of a calibre that overmatched the armament of the submarines. In February, 1915, while the Allies on the Western Front were preparing for their first great "Spring Drive," the first "unrestricted" campaign was declared. The German Government announced that it would treat the waters surrounding the British Isles as a war zone, in which any ship might be sunk without warning. This meant the torpedoing of merchant ships. With the announcement the sinkings without warning began, and a few months later the world was horrified by the tragedy of the *Lusitania*.

Still, under the "unrestricted" campaign, the U-boat commanders all affirm that they gave ships warning whenever they could. They were, their own people insist, ordinary men carrying out orders, and did so as humanely as was normal for ordinary men who were living the abnormal lives of under-sea raiders. Also, it was economic wisdom to torpedo ships only when they could be sunk in no other way. A U-boat could carry only a limited supply of torpedoes, and these big missiles were mighty expensive. So there was this economic incentive for stopping vessels and sinking them by gunfire, in which case there was an opportunity to give warning and permit passengers and crews to take to the boats. For the most part, throughout the war, the submarines gave warning in the usual way—a shot across the bow and the command: "Abandon ship."

But there were the terrible exceptions, where big ships were torpedoed, sometimes with fearful loss of life. The *Lusitania* was the most startling example, and there were others.

CHAPTER X

THE CAPTAIN AND THE CREW THAT SANK THE LUSITANIA

The gayest of all the raiders of the deep was the boat that sank the *Lusitania*—one of those jolly crafts, loud with laughter and rollicking fellowship, with more of the spirit of an old three-master, full of hearty shipmates, than of an ultra-modern shell crammed with mechanism of intricate and deadly precision and designed to grope beneath the surface of the sea. Often, in listening to the stories of the submarines, I caught the note of cold, eerie adventure that took me back to Captain Nemo and the *Nautilus,* but there was no such note in the account of the *U-20.* Some of the yarns about her reminded me a bit of my jovial friend Count Luckner, the Sea Devil, and his raiding sailing ship, the *Seeadler,* and some of his joyous adventures—take, for example, his prodigious capture of the steamer loaded with 20,000 cases of champagne. And yet it was this mirthful boat, the *U-20,* that sank the *Lusitania,* that wrought the deed that set the world aflame with the fiercest anger and horror of our time.

Her commander, Walther Schwieger, the officer who gave the order that loosed the fateful torpedo, was lost in the war. I sought out men who had served under him aboard the *U-20* and came upon Lieutenant Rudolph Zentner in the ancient city of Lübeck. Most of the submarine commanders look young, but he looked even younger—a slender, pleasantly smil-

Editor's Note: Rudolph Zentner, who served with Walter Schwieger on *U-20,* was an ensign and weapons specialist still in training with barely a year in service when the war consumed Europe.

ing chap with fiery red hair. His mother was born in New York, and he spoke excellent English. Since the end of the war he has been in the wine importing business. I sat and talked with him in his office, and the place had a fragrance that reminded one of the old-time establishments on the corner before the days of prohibition. Zentner told me that he was an officer on a battleship when the war broke out, but that he, together with twenty-four other junior officers of his acquaintance, decided between themselves that they would probably see more action in the submarine service. They did. Out of the twenty-five, four survived the war.

Zentner ran one hand through his fiery hair, tucked a monocle under one bushy brow, and leaned back in his swivel chair.

"You want to know what kind of boat the *U-20* was? Well, I'll tell you some of the things that happened aboard—not the big things but the small ones."

"Righto," I responded, giving him a light for his cigarette while I lighted my pipe.

"It was my first cruise. The *U-20* stood out to sea on the day before Christmas, the first Christmas of the war. Instead of rigging up a tree with candles in a comfortable house sitting down to mid-night supper with many a toast, it was a case of standing on watch on deck or in the conning tower, of keeping an eye on more dials and gauges than one might ordinarily see in a lifetime, and of living and sleeping in the most cramped quarters imaginable, while the *U-20* stole its way along. That is not the best way to spend Christmas Eve, but war is all that your General—*Ja,* Sherman, *Ja, Ja*—said it was. Our task was to patrol the North Sea off the mouth of the Ems and to shoot a torpedo at any enemy warship that came within range.

"Christmas day broke with a bright sky, frosty air,

and a calm sea. Apparently the enemy was at home spending Christmas as a Christian should, because never a sign of British craft did we see. We had the ocean to ourselves. Nevertheless, duty is duty, and we kept a vigilant patrol all day. Night was something else again. No use watching in the dark, and the only thing to worry about was the possibility of being run down by some pagan craft that happened to be prowling around. No use of risking that. We might as well celebrate Christmas serenely and with nothing on our minds.

" 'Close the hatches for diving,' Commander Schwieger commanded.

"The *U-20* took a comfortable dive and settled on the bottom.

" 'And now,' cried Commander Schwieger, 'we can celebrate Christmas.'

"The boat found a snug resting place on the muddy floor of the North Sea, and we were comfortably settled for the night sixty feet below the surface of the water.

"The tiny messroom was decorated in style. A green wreath hung at one end as a Christmas tree. We didn't have any lighted candles on it. They would have been too risky in the oil-reeking interior of a submarine. The tables were loaded with food. It all came out of cans, but we didn't mind that. That one night officers and men had their mess together. It was rather close quarters. We had a crew of four officers and thirty-two men. We were all in our leather submarine suits. It was no dress affair. No stiff bosoms, no tail coats. No 'fish and soup' as you call them.

"In short, there were many drawbacks, but good spirits were not one of them. In the tight, overcrowded little mess room we ate and talked. The dinner was washed down with tea mixed with rum, and

I lost count of the number of toasts that were drunk. No dinner is quite complete without an after-dinner speech. Commander Schwieger arose and delivered one, and a jolly oration it was. After dinner came a concert. Yes, we had an orchestra. It consisted of three pieces, a violin, a mandolin, and the inevitable nautical accordion. The Berlin Philharmonic does better, but our concert was good.

"Even if it hadn't sounded well, it would have been worth watching. Those sailors played with soul, especially the artist who handled the accordion. A rare fellow he was. He was not much taller than a ship's bulwarks and as broad in the beam as a ferry boat. He had tiny, twinkling blue eyes, and such whiskers you have never seen. His red beard spread all over his chest. When you looked at him you could understand the origin of those bearded gnomes you find in old German legends. He was a fisherman from East Prussia and could neither read nor write—the only German sailor I have ever seen who had to sign his name with three crosses. He was always laughing, but I rarely heard him speak a word.

"You would not take this worthy for a likely knight on the rose-strewn fields of Venus; and yet he seemed to be constantly engaged in complications of sentimental romance. Before we set out on the cruise he had asked for leave to go home to get married on Christmas. It was refused as he was needed on the cruise. When we got back there was a letter to the Commander himself from the lady in question. She reproached him mournfully for not having allowed the fisherman to go home for the ceremony. The little one, she added by way of postcript, had already arrived, and it was now too late. Several months later Commander Schwieger got another letter from a lady about our fisherman. She urgently requested that he be given leave to come and marry her. And this was a different lady!

"But, whatever this fellow's morals may have been, his talents were excellent—for the accordion played on Christmas night. If you had no soul for music, you could look at him and laugh. His little eyes were half closed with ecstasy and his bearded mouth was curved with a grin that was like the crescent of the moon, as he pumped the 'squealer' in and out. Perhaps there was the spirit of a Mozart behind the grotesque semblance."

"Feasting like that wasn't the rule, was it?" I asked laughing.

"It might have been," Zentner replied with a shaking of his head and a lugubrious grimace, "if it hadn't been for the food.

"We captured dozens of merchant ships, ordered their crews off, and sank the vessels. With another kind of raiding craft we could have plundered most of our prizes of fresh provisions, but a U-boat cannot always venture to send a boarding crew on a prize and snatch a bit of fresh meat and vegetables. We had to content ourselves with canned stuff, dried stuff, and hard tack, and on long cruises the fare sometimes became intolerable.

"I remember one occasion when we became positively desperate for a decent bite to eat. We managed to capture a fine hogshead of butter. For a couple of days we piled butter on our hard tack and thought it delicious. Everybody said that the butter would do well for cooking, only we didn't have anything decent to cook with it. The sailors positively sang a chorus: 'If only we had something to fry in the butter.'

"Off the French coast the periscope showed a fleet of fishing boats busy at the nets. It was dangerous for a U-boat to show its conning tower in those waters—but we were desperate men. The fishermen saw a submarine pop suddenly into their midst. From the stories that were told of the U-boats, they expected to be massacred at once. They laughed and cheered and got very busy when they discovered that all the U-boat wanted was some fresh fish. We crammed our boat with fish, fine big fellows—bonitos— with a pinkish meat. By way of a joke we gave the fisherman an order on the French Government as payment.

"And now there was fresh fish, fried in butter, grilled in butter, sautéed in butter, all that we could eat. We took a comfortable station, submerged, so that we might not be disturbed, and you can bet that jaws worked until they were tired. Afterward, the orchestra played loudly and merrily, the fisherman with the fancy whiskers doing his mightiest."

This tale of the butter and fish reminded me of an incident related by Commander Spiess, the same who was Weddigen's watch officer aboard the *U-9* when the *Aboukir, Hogue,* and *Cressy* were sunk. He was in command of the *U-19* on a long hard cruise in northern waters. All on board were "fed up" with canned stuff and hard tack. They steered for one of the Orkney Islands, inhabited only by goats. A party went ashore with rifles. The hunt for wild goats was a thing to delight a sportsman's heart. They accumulated a good buck and returned to the boat. That day there was a magnificent feast of roast goat aboard a U-boat in the sub-Arctic.

Zentner was staring at the ceiling.

"Of course," he remarked, "there were times when joy was not exactly unconfined— . . . when it looked as if our goose was cooked."

"For instance," I prompted him.

"It was early in the war," he went on, "when we were rather green. Commander Schwieger sent for the engineering officer to come up to the conning tower, and I took the latter's place in the central station. We were running submerged. Through the speaking tube came a shout from the commander:

"Two buoys sighted. Keep exact depth," he ordered.

"Later on I should have known exactly what they meant, but then they seemed a bit peculiar but nothing more.

"Suddenly there was a peculiar racket. It sounded as if huge chains were banging against the boat and were being dragged over it. The men at the diving rudders shouted to me that the apparatus was out of control. A glance at the gauges showed me that our speed had slowed down and that we were sinking. The boat turned this way and that, lurching and staggering drunkenly. She continued to sink and presently hit bottom with a bump. We were in a hundred feet of water.

"I leaped up the ladder and looked out through the window of the conning tower. All I could see was a maze of meshes and chains and links. Now we knew the meaning of those buoys. They were supporting a net. We had run into the net and now were entangled in it. Later on such a net would have been hung with bombs, like tomatoes on a vine. Thank heaven, they had hung none on the net we rammed! But meanwhile we were caught. It was a new situation and seemingly a hopeless one. We were sure we were caught fast and could never get out of those deadly meshes. You can bet there was no laughing and singing on board now. Each man thought of his home in Germany and how he would never see it again. I did not see our bewhiskered fisherman, but I am sure the smile under his red beard was straightened out.

" 'Reverse engines,' Kapitänleutnant Schwieger

commanded. The only thing we could think of was to try to back out.

"There was a great straining and cracking and clanking, and then we heard a familiar whirr—the propellers of destroyers. They no doubt had been lurking in the distance in such a way that they could observe a disturbance of the net—telling of a big fish. Now they were coming to see if they could make matters worse for us. Luckily, they did not have depth bombs in those days, or we should have been done for. The gauges were the whole world to us now. I had never gazed at anything so eagerly before. Yes, we were backing. With a ripping and rending we were tearing our way out of the net.

"We were clear, and away we went. All that remained to worry us was the sound of propellers. It followed us. The destroyers were keeping right above us. We dodged to right and to left, and still that accursed sound. You can easily tell a destroyer from another ship by the sound of the propeller, which in a destroyer has a much higher note—a shrill, angry buzz. Our periscope was down, but still something was giving us away on the surface, for those destroyers kept after us, no matter how we went. They were waiting for us to emerge, to shoot at us or ram us. We couldn't guess what the trouble was, but merely kept on going, trying in vain to lose those persistent hounds that were on our trail.

"This kept up hour after hour. We ran blindly under water, keeping as deep as we could. We didn't know much about where we were going. Any attempt to rise to periscope depth and take a look through the asparagus, and we should probably have been rammed. Night came on and we plucked up courage. Perhaps darkness was hiding that something on the surface, whatever it was, that was marking our trail.

"About the time that complete darkness settled on

the sea above, we set a wild, weird course, going as fast as we could. Sure enough, the sound of the pro-pellers grew faint, and we lost it altogether. After continuing for a safe distance, we came to the surface. It did not take long to solve the mystery. One of the cables of the net out of which we had torn away had remained fouled, held fast by our upper works. We had been dragging it along behind us. The other end was attached to one of the buoys which had been floating on the surface. We had been carrying with us a floating marker, which the destroyers had finally lost in the darkness."

Through the window as we talked we could see the snow falling in the streets of old Lübeck. People hurried along, wrapping themselves more snugly against the cold wind. Underneath the window two wandering minstrels played German folk-songs on their wailing violins.

"We shall have two feet of snow," said the man with red hair. Then, drumming on the desk with a pencil, he returned to his story. His long, strong face warped with a smile of droll memory. His brown eyes narrowed as he hunted around in memory for incidents and details.

"I had a strange bedfellow aboard the *U-20*," he said. "We were short of room, and when the boat was fully loaded there was one torpedo more than there was place for. I accommodated it in my bunk. I slept beside it. I had it lashed in place at the out-side of the narrow bunk, and it kept me from rolling out of bed when the boat did some of its fancy rolling. At first I was kept awake a bit by the thought of having so much TNT in bed with me. Then I got used to it, and it really made quite a comfortable 'Dutch wife.'

"Then, after a while, I acquired another bedfellow.

"Two hundred miles or so off the coast of Ireland

we met a sailing ship one day. It was Portuguese, I think—the *Maria de Molenos*. Its crew were all negroes. We told them to abandon ship, and they obeyed with a will. A bit of sea was running, but not enough to make a lather, and the lifeboats were sure to be picked up. A bit of gunnery practice, and the *Maria de Molenos* settled down for her bit of vertical navigation. As the gentle swell of the sea closed over her sinking deck all the usual débris that follows the foundering of a ship remained floating on the water. We even spied a cow swimming about. No, it wasn't a cow that was destined to become my bedfellow, although we regretted that we hadn't a stable aboard to accommodate her.

"I was standing on the submarine's deck. Near by was the musical fisherman with the incredible spread of beard. He was a pervasive cuss. One always seemed to notice him around.

"'*Ach Himmel, der kleine Hund!* [Heavens, the little dog!]' He was usually silent, but now he spoke in a loud, pathetic, and even blubbering voice, and pointed out into the water.

"A small wooden box was bobbing up and down in the rough sea. A little head was thrust above it. A black dachshund was in the water, supporting itself on the box with its front paws. The iron soul of the crew melted. We steered over to the box and pulled the dog on deck. Then and there it was adopted into our affectionate family. We christened it after the lost ship—*Maria de Molenos*.

"We already had one dog, and Maria made two. Later it was six. A canine romance had developed, and Maria had a litter of four fine puppies. Our radiantly bewhiskered fisherman made himself the skipper of the canine part of the *U-20's* population and spent most of his time thereafter taking care of the dogs. When we got back to port we decided that six dogs were too many for one submarine. We gave three of the pups to other boats and kept the fourth. That left us with three dogs, which was about right. We were hard put to find decent quarters for them, so they slept in the bunks. I took the puppy into my bed. So every night I slept with a torpedo and a puppy."

"A merry boat, indeed," I agreed with him.

Zentner had a thoughtful expression as he replied:

"She was a jolly boat, the *U-20,* and a kindly boat—and she sank the *Lusitania.*"

I was interested in Commander Walther Schwieger, who had struck the fateful blow, and who had won the execration of millions of men around the globe. I asked Zentner about him.

"If you want a good and pleasant boat," he replied, "you must have a good and pleasant skipper. Kapitänleutnant Schwieger was one of the few U-boat officers who was in the submarine service when the war began. He was one of the ablest officers we had and a recognized expert on submarine matters—one of the few commanders who were consulted by Grand Admiral von Tirpitz and on whose advice Von Tirpitz relied. The records credit him with having sunk 190,000 tons of Allied shipping.

"He was about thirty-two years old when the war started, and was unmarried. Of an old Berlin family, he was well educated and had in the highest degree the gifts of poise and urbane courtesy. He was tall, broad-shouldered, and of a distinguished bearing, with well-cut features, blue eyes, and blond hair—a particularly fine-looking fellow. He was the soul of kindness toward the officers and men under him. His temperament was joyous and his talk full of gaiety and pointed wit. He had the gifts to command both respect and liking and was a general favourite in the German Navy."

What Zentner told me about Commander Schwieger only bore out what I had heard elsewhere about the man. Everyone who had known him spoke of him with regard, affection, and perhaps a trifle of pity. I gathered that the case of the man who sank the *Lusitania* represents one of the curious, poignant tragedies of the war.

CHAPTER XI

VON SCHWIEGER'S ACCOUNT OF HOW HE SANK THE *LUSITANIA*

Thirteen years have rolled by since that tragic day in May, 1915, when 1,152 non-combatants, nearly half of them women and children, many of them neutral Americans, went down on the big Cunarder. No single deed in our time ever came so near to transforming a civilized state into an outlaw among the nations.

I had often wondered just what the truth was about the sinking of the *Lusitania*. The accounts had been rather conflicting. At the time of the disaster, and even years later, when the United States Federal Court conducted its final inquiry, we had only one side of the story, fragments pieced together from the accounts of dazed survivors. The tale they had to relate was of the usual war-time Atlantic crossing interrupted by a sudden explosion; of the listing of the ship; of vain attempts to get away in lifeboats; of the rapid sinking of the liner; of nightmare hours in the water; and then of bodies piled in the morgues at Queenstown. Only 764 of the 1,916 who had sailed on the *Lusitania* lived to tell that tale; 1,152 innocent travellers had been sent to their death by the hand of man—and that man a German.

From the day when the tragedy of the *Lusitania* cast its shadow over the world, and in the opinion of most of us made Germany the common enemy of mankind, many have wondered what the German version of the affair could be. No tale of the U-boat war

Editor's Note: Many historians and speculators have offered explanations for the swift sinking of the *Lusitania*. Each writer has come to terms in some way with the testimony of survivors that there was a second explosion, which they assumed was another torpedo. In his 1972 book, *Lusitania,* journalist Colin Simpson suggested that contraband explosives on board ignited when the torpedo hit or perhaps when volatile chemicals came in contact with seawater. More recent research by Dr. Robert Ballard of the Woods Hole Oceanographic Institution, supported by the informed opinion of marine engineers and steamship veterans, recently suggested a very credi-

could be complete without it. So, from time to time during these thirteen years, I had picked up bits of information concerning the sinking of the *Lusitania*. Pieced together, they provide us with a fairly complete story. Not that it is likely to change our opinions regarding the savageness of the deed; but there is a certain amount of satisfaction in clearing up points that have long been so great a mystery.

Zentner was not on board the *U-20* when she sank the *Lusitania*. During that cruise he remained behind on leave, taking a course in wireless telegraphy. But he was able to tell me about the disastrous event, and I gathered accounts of it from other men to whom Commander Schwieger had told the story. The sum of it all makes a swift, calamitous tale.

The *U-20* stood out to sea on April 30, 1915. Her orders were to patrol the waters to the southwest of Ireland and to enforce the submarine blockade that Germany had declared against England. She was to torpedo any boat she encountered in the zone of the blockade. Apparently it is untrue—in spite of what has often been said, and what most of us thought—that she was sent out with special orders to sink the *Lusitania*. On May 5th the U-boat sank an English sailing ship, and on the next morning sank an English steamer. At noon of the same day she sighted a passenger steamer of the White Star Line, but the ship was too far away to be torpedoed. Later in the afternoon she torpedoed and sank an English steamer. For two days more the *U-20* continued its patrolling cruise off the southwest coast of Ireland. The fog was so dense as to make operations almost useless. No ships were sunk. The oil supply was running low, and only two torpedoes were left. On the morning of the 7th the fog was as dense as ever. The *U-20* turned its nose homeward for Wilhelmshaven and kept its course

---

ble alternative explanation based upon close examination of the wreck in 1993 by the remotely operated vehicles of Woods Hole's Deep Submergence Laboratory. The hold that contained explosives and ammunition shipped by the British showed no sign of explosion. The bunkers just aft of these holds, which would contain very little fuel and a great deal of explosive coal dust at the end of the ship's voyage, exhibited considerable damage. Thus, there is an excellent chance that the explosion following the detonation of *U-20*'s torpedo was the coal dust in the ship's near-empty bunkers.

until two twenty in the afternoon. The fog by now had lifted a bit.

The following is translated from Commander Schwieger's official log kept aboard the *U-20*. It was given to me by Commander ———, a former companion-in-arms of Schwieger:

2.20 P. M.   Directly in front of us I sighted four funnels and masts of steamer at right angles to our course, coming from south-southwest and going toward Galley Head. It is recognized as a passenger steamer.

2.25   Have advanced eleven meters toward steamer, in hope it will change its course along the Irish coast.

2.35   Steamer turns, takes direction to Queenstown, and thereby makes it possible for us to approach it for shot. We proceed at high speed in order to reach correct position.

3.10.   Torpedo shot at distance of 700 metres, going 3 meters below the surface. Hits steering centre behind bridge. Unusually great detonation with large cloud of smoke and debris shot above the funnels. In addition to torpedo, a second explosion must have taken place. (Boiler, coal, or powder?) Bridge and part of the ship where the torpedo hit are torn apart, and fire follows.

The ship stops and very quickly leans over to starboard, at the same time sinking at the bow. It looks as though it would capsize in a short time. There is great confusion on board. Boats are cleared and many of them lowered into the water. Many boats, fully loaded, drop down into the water bow- or stern-first and capsize. The boats on the port side cannot be made clear because of the slanting position. At the front of the ship the name *Lusitania* in gold letters can be seen. The chimneys are painted black. The stern flag is not hoisted. The ship was going about twenty miles an hour.

The log, as far as it pertains to the event, closes with an entry that states that the steamer seemed badly hit and sure to sink—which seems to refer to a possible supposition that two torpedoes might be needed to sink so large a ship—and then goes on: "I could not have sent a second torpedo into the crowd of those passengers who were trying to save themselves."

From Commander Max Valentiner, one of Germany's most widely acclaimed U-boat commanders, I have the story as Commander Schwieger told it to his brother officers. I shall give it in a transcript of Valentiner's own way of telling it:

"One day, shortly after the *U-20* returned from the cruise during which it sank the *Lusitania,* I met Captain Schwieger, who was a very good friend of mine. We fell to talking, and he gave me a full account of the sinking, which was the talk of the day.

" 'We had started back for Wilhelmshaven,' he said, 'and were drawing near the Channel. There was a heavy sea and a thick fog, with small chance of sinking anything. At the same time, a destroyer steaming through the fog might stumble over us before we knew anything about it. So I submerged to twenty metres, below periscope depth. About an hour and a half later I heard the sound of powerful screws—not the propellers of a destroyer. I went up to ten meters and took a look through the periscope. I saw a big armoured cruiser. It had passed right over us and was now disappearing at full speed.'

"Schwieger went on to say how exasperated he was to miss this fine chance. After the early days of the war you rarely had a chance to loose a torpedo at any warship as big as a cruiser, and many a U-boat never caught sight of one during the entire war. The British kept their big naval vessels securely tucked away in port most of the time and did not send them roaming around to act as good targets for U-boats.

" 'After I was through swearing,' Schwieger said, 'I noticed that the fog was lifting. Presently I could see blue sky. I brought the boat to the surface, and we continued our course above water. A few minutes after we emerged I sighted on the horizon a forest of masts and stacks. At first I thought they must belong to several ships. Then I saw it was a great steamer coming over the horizon. It was coming our way. I dived at once, hoping to get a shot at it.

" 'When the steamer was two miles away it changed its course. I had no hope now, even if we hurried at our best speed, of getting near enough to attack her. I called my pilot, an old-time captain of the merchant marine, to take a look at her through the periscope. At that instant, while he was coming in answer to my call, I saw the steamer change her course again. She was coming directly at us. She could not have steered a more perfect course if she had deliberately tried to give us a dead shot. A short fast run, and we waited.

" 'I had already shot away my best torpedoes and had left only two bronze ones—not so good. The steamer was four hundred yards away when I gave an order to fire. The torpedo hit, and there was rather a small detonation and instantly afterward a much heavier one. The pilot was beside me. I told him to have a look at close range. He put his eye to the periscope and after a brief scrutiny yelled:

" ' "My God, it's the *Lusitania!*"

" 'I took my position at the periscope again. The ship was sinking with unbelievable rapidity. There was a terrible panic on her deck. Overcrowded lifeboats, fairly torn from their positions, dropped into the water. Desperate people ran helplessly up and down the decks. Men and women jumped into the water and tried to swim to empty, overturned lifeboats. It was the most terrible sight I have ever seen. It was impossible for me to give any help. I could have saved only a handful. And then the cruiser that had passed us was not very far away and must have picked up the distress signals. She would shortly appear, I thought. The scene was too horrible to watch, and I gave orders to dive to twenty metres, and away.' "

That was the account Schwieger gave shortly after the event. He told it as a man who had a vivid impression, with full and clear details.

To Commander Valentiner's account I can add the statement that it agrees substantially with other stories of the sinking of the *Lusitania*—stories heard from Commander Schwieger and his officers. There is little discrepancy in the various narrations.

Several suppositions seem to be disproved. One is that it was Max Valentiner who destroyed the great liner. He was often charged with the sinking by the British. Another is that the U-boat commander mistook the *Lusitania* for an auxiliary cruiser. Apparently Schwieger did not realize the identity of the ship when he loosed the torpedo, but discovered it immediately after. Still another assumption is that he fired two torpedoes. He fired only one. A fourth belief is that the *U-20* was sent out with particular orders to sink the *Lusitania*. The boat apparently went out on a routine mission of enforcing the submarine blockade that Germany had announced.

Nothing is cleared up about the supposition that the *Lusitania* sank as quickly as she did largely because of the detonation of war explosives she carried aboard. The supposition is well nigh universally held in Germany, where people point to an alleged statement of Dudley Field Malone, then Collector of the Port of New York, that the *Lusitania* had aboard 4,200 cases of Springfield cartridges, 11 tons of gunpowder, and 5,500 barrels of ammunition. But even so, any such explosion does not seem, in the minds of German naval men, to explain sufficiently the rapidity with which the ship sank. It is a theory among some of them that the high speed at which the *Lusitania* was traveling broke down the vessel's water-tight compartments after she was hit. The pressure of the water, they think, would have been sufficient to have broken down

Editor's Note: Thomas refers here to Lieutenant Commander Max Valentiner, who commanded *U-3, 38,* and *157,* and destroyed 141 merchant ships totaling 299,326 tons, as well as one warship of 627 tons. He was the third-ranking U-boat ace of the Great War. Accepted into the Navy on 1 April 1902, he held the rank of senior lieutenant from the end of March 1908 and was qualified for U-boat command before the Great War began. In 1914 he had over eight years in the service and was stationed at the Baltic Naval Station's Torpedo Inspectorate. Valentiner had great longevity in the Gerone partition after another, until the whole was flooded.

But regarding the question as to whether or not the *Lusitania* was an armed auxiliary cruiser carrying war explosives, that was thoroughly investigated by the United States Federal authorities. As a result, in August, 1918, Judge Julius M. Mayer handed down his decision, in which he said: "The proof is absolute that she was not and never had been armed, nor did she carry any explosives."

Upon his return to Wilhelmshaven, Commander Schwieger was congratulated on all sides for his sinking of the giant liner. He supposed, and his comrades agreed with him, that while there had been some loss of life it had not been large, that the ship remained afloat long enough for rescue ships, which did not have to come from any great distance, to save most of the passengers and crew. Schwieger had seen that the vessel was sinking fast, but did not dream that she would plunge the way she did.

Only after reading foreign newspapers did he understand the immensity and horror of the disaster he had wrought. He was appalled to discover the anger of outraged humanity that his act had aroused and horrified at the thought that he was held up all over the world as an object of odium and loathing. Then he got a reprimand from the Kaiser, a condemnation for having sunk the liner. The other submarine officers resented it bitterly.

"Schwieger had merely carried out orders. He had been ordered to sink any ship he could in the blockaded waters. He had seen a big steamer and torpedoed it. Any other U-boat officer would have done the same, would have been compelled to do the same." So they all said. Hence, they believed that if there was any blame, it should be attached to the authorities who gave the orders under which Schwieger acted.

---

man U-boat service, returning to serve in the Kriegsmarine of World War II as a senior captain working as a leading inspector of U-boats under construction. He witnessed the creation of the Federal Republic of Germany and died in 1949.

But more careful scrutiny of the question shows clearly that the U-boat commanders are wrong in their conclusion. The customs and usages of civilized nations had long since established a universally recognized unwritten law. That law decreed that in time of war belligerents had a right to capture enemy merchantmen. It went farther, and conceded to them the right to sink their prizes—*but only after challenging each ship and then allowing all on board to get away in lifeboats.* Apparently, the Germans had been adhering to this unwritten law of the sea up to the time of the *Lusitania* tragedy. Hence, what possible justification could there be for such a deed?

Some months later the German Government again went on record by officially recognizing the existence of this ancient law of civilized nations. In one of its notes to the United States appeared these words:

In accordance with the general principles of visit and search and destruction of merchant vessels recognized by international law, such vessels, both within and without the area declared as naval war zone, shall not be sunk without warning and without saving human lives, unless these ships attempt to escape or offer resistance.

From his own log it is clear that Schwieger neither gave warning nor took the trouble to find out what ship it was that was passing. He found it out, or rather, his subordinate found it out for him, when it was too late, after he had fired his torpedo. He simply sank the great liner, watched her start to keel over, then gave the order to dive, and headed for Germany.

CHAPTER XII

A SURVIVOR TELLS HIS TALE

Although we are all familiar with some of the history of the *Lusitania,* in order to round out this narrative I decided to interview one of the survivors.

NOTICE!

TRAVELLERS intending to embark on the Atlantic voyage are reminded that a state of war exists between Germany and her allies and Great Britain and her allies; that the zone of war includes the waters adjacent to the British Isles; that, in accordance with formal notice given by the Imperial German Government, vessels flying the flag of Great Britain, or of any of her allies, are liable to destruction in those waters and that travellers sailing in the war zone on ships of Great Britain or her allies do so at their own risk.

IMPERIAL GERMAN EMBASSY
WASHINGTON, D. C., APRIL 22, 1915.

I wanted to hear the tale from the lips of someone who had lived through that most terrible of all the sea tragedies of our time. Last winter, at a Whitehall Club luncheon in New York City, I was introduced to C. W. Bowring, a tall, fine-looking, white-haired, broad-shouldered shipping man. Afterward I learned that he was one of the *Lusitania* survivors. So I called on him, thinking that he might be just the man to give me a coherent account. Nor was I wrong in my surmise.

From a drawer he took a yellow strip of newspaper backed on cardboard to preserve it. It was the famous Von Bernstorff advertisement that had appeared in all the New York morning newspapers on May 1, 1915, the day the *Lusitania* was announced to sail. It had been inserted near the Cunard Line advertisement.

"When I was rescued, of course I was wringing wet," said Mr. Bowring. "But I put my hands in my pockets to see what might still be there. This water-soaked ad from the New York *Times* was all that I found. It is my one souvenir from the *Lusitania.*" Then he told me the tale.

"Along about noon on May 7th, as we were skirting the Irish coast, I went up on the hurricane deck to get a bit of exercise, and the purser and I were tossing a medicine ball. Standing alongside me, playing ball with some one else, was Elbert Hubbard. That was the last I saw of him.

"We went down to lunch rather late and were sitting at the table when the explosion came. Shattered glass from the porthole windows splattered all around us. I got up and hurried on deck. The purser rushed off to his office. That was the last that I saw of him.

"When I got on deck the passengers were milling around, running in all directions, but there was no panic, no screaming. The ship had already started to list to starboard and the crew were trying to lower the boats. One boat got halfway down. But one end gave way and dumped all her crowd of passengers into the sea. A second boat got down part way, then something happened to the ropes. Down it fell, right on top of the first crowd—smashing them, of course. Seeing the way things were going, and that not many had on life preservers, I decided to go after mine. As I went down the companionway I passed Alfred G. Vanderbilt. He was sitting calmly on a sofa—just sitting, thinking, not a bit excited. That was the last I ever saw of him.

"I carried seven life belts back on deck and passed them around. Near by stood a gentleman and his daughter who also had been at the purser's table. She had none, so I fastened a belt about her. It saved her life. Then I tried to get over to the port side of the ship. But by then the list was so great that I couldn't make it and slid back. The liner was going over fast. I saw how hopeless it was to attempt to get away in a boat. So I waited until the deck rail was within eight feet or so of the water. Then I jumped.

"I had always been keen about sports and was a fair swimmer. But never before had I tried swimming with my clothes on. I struck out, but kept glancing back, keeping one eye on the ship. In another moment or two she would be flat on her side, and I saw that unless I made more speed I would be crushed by one of the huge stacks. A few moments after that it looked as if I might get hit by the main mast. So I slowed up a bit and it fell right in front of me. Clambering over it, I headed for an empty lifeboat. Before I reached it I saw the nose of the *Lusitania* disappear. Her stern rose high in the air. She seemed to poise there for a moment and then, with a lunge, she vanished. Instead of causing a vortex and sucking us down, as I had always heard would happen, the sea seemed to hump up like a big hill. Then, as it flattened out, I was carried farther away.

"One of the ship's officers clambered into the lifeboat with me. She was half full of water, and we tried to bale her out with our hands. Then we spent the next few hours diving in and out of the water, rescuing as many as we could. Most of the people we got hold of were already dead, but we got some twenty safely into the boat. Later, we were picked up by a trawler.

"From her deck we beheld a strange sight that is still a mystery to me. It was of a young woman sitting in a wicker chair, serenely riding the waves. There she sat as though it was always done that way. When we pulled over to her she was stone cold—unconscious. We brought her to, finally. But she seemed to have no recollection of what had happened. Chair and all, she simply had been lifted off one of the decks by the rushing water when the ship went down. To-day she is one of the best-known women in the British Empire—Lady Rhondda, who since the war has gained international fame managing her father's vast coal-mining interests."

Although many of the survivors testified that the *Lusitania* had been hit by two torpedoes, Mr. Bowring agrees with the U-boat commander that there was only one. In less than twenty minutes after the torpedo shattered her hull the *Lusitania* had vanished beneath the surface of the ocean along with 1,152 of her passengers and crew. And there she lies to this day, off Old Head of Kinsale, on the southern coast of Ireland, in 250 feet of water.

A few weeks later the *U-20* tried to torpedo the 15,000-ton *Orduna,* but the liner eluded the missiles and got away. The next big victim was the *Hesperian,* of 10,000 tons, which was sunk on its way from Liverpool to Quebec and Montreal. The following spring the *U-20* sank the liner *Cymric*. The passengers got away in the lifeboats. Three torpedoes were exploded

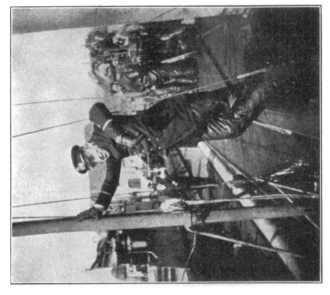

Cheery Rudolph Zentner, watch officer on the U-20.

The man who sank the Lusitania.

*A British trawler setting a snare for submarines—
a net festooned with mines.*

*Between fights. But what would happen if they
had to dive in a hurry?*

against the hull, and then it took five hours before the ship went down.

Another tragic shadow touches briefly the path of the "jolly" boat—the *U-20*—a contact with some of the dark, melodramatic intrigues of our time. In 1916 Sir Roger Casement went to Ireland by the U-boat route to lead a revolt against England there. He was soon caught and hanged. As a quick sequel, the Easter Rebellion in Dublin broke out. It was suppressed with bloody fighting and executions by the firing squad. Out of it came the long, desperate struggle of Sinn Fein and the founding of the Irish Free State. The *U-20* accompanied the boat that took Casement and landed him on the west shore of Ireland. Commander Zentner tells of talking with the ill-starred passenger. One memory lingers with a moody insistence.

The stately, bearded Irishman told the young U-boat officer: "I know I will be hanged." And there was in the exclamation a tone of sombre foreboding and foretelling that looked evil destiny in the face and did not shirk it.

The snow was falling white and windswept in Lübeck. A flame-topped head rested back against two folded hands. Zentner told me of the last cruise of *U-20*.

"We cast off from dock on Friday, October 13, 1916. Friday, the 13th—it promised bad luck. Nothing much happened until, off the coast of Norway on our return trip, we encountered our fellow craft, the *U-30*. She was in distress. Both her Diesel engines had broken down and she was making only three knots an hour. We offered to stay along with her and stand by if anything happened. Sailing on Friday the 13th was bad luck enough—we should have

known better than to have anything to do with the
U-30. She was a Jonah. Almost two years before,
when our submarine fleet had set out on one of its first
trips, the *U-30* sank in Emden Harbour in 120 feet of
water, with all except three of her crew. We passed
that way a couple of days later. The tapping of the
men in the sunken hull was just ceasing. It was three
months before the boat and its dead were brought to
the surface. After that the *U-30* had been overhauled
and refitted. It seemed a staunch enough craft, but
was always getting into trouble. It was a Jonah boat,
surely. And now it was struggling with broken engines
to get back to harbour.

"The boats were running on the surface near the
Danish coast next day when both went aground in a
bad fog. Our compass was off and we had steered
too far to the east. Between the wind, the tide, and
the waves, we were lodged tight on a sand bar. When
we found we could not back off we began to lighten
ballast. That worked with the *U-30*. Throwing
overboard about thirty tons of weight, in a couple of
hours they had her free and in deep water again. But
our boat stuck fast. Although we struggled all night
to get her off, it was hopeless, and when morning came
we were still sitting there. In fact, the last I heard
of her, ten years later, she was still sitting there.

"We were in Danish territorial waters, of course,
and knew that if discovered by the Danes we should
be interned. So the commander lost no time in sending
an SOS to the nearest German base. A rescue squadron set out at once—not just one or two boats, but a
whole fleet of torpedo boats and even our big men-
of-war. You see, we were afraid the British might
have picked up our SOS and despatched some fast
cruisers of their own to spoil the party. If they could
have broadcast to the world that they had destroyed

the U-boat that sank the *Lusitania* it would have had almost the same moral effect as a real naval victory. German headquarters knew this—hence the big rescue force.

"Some of the smaller boats at once began to tug and haul and try to pull us off, while the big fellows stood watch. But it was no use. The tow ropes and chains broke three times. We waited for high tide at eleven o'clock. Still no use. The *U-20* refused to budge.

"'We'll blow her up,' Commander Schwieger announced.

"So we took off our ship's papers and personal belongings and planted a few bombs. The rescue boats took us aboard, and we pushed off. There were several loud explosions, and what had been a fine submarine was turned into scrap iron. I suppose the *U-20* still lies there rusting on a shoal off the coast of Denmark.

"With the *U-30* in tow, the rescue ships started back toward their base. Suddenly there were two more terrific explosions. We had been right about the British picking up our message. Two of our battle cruisers had been torpedoed by an enemy submarine. The *Grosser Kurfürst* was hit in her engine room and the *Kronprinz* was torpedoed squarely under the bridge. Crack torpedo shots, both of them, but not quite fatal. It took more than one torpedo to sink those big dreadnaughts. Both somehow managed to stagger back to port.

"Commander Schwieger then assumed command of the *U-88,* a new, big boat of the latest design, and took most of his old crew with him. I made two cruises with him and then missed a cruise, just as I had done when the *Lusitania* was sunk. The boat never came back. It was lost with all on board during September, 1917, probably in the North Channel between Scotland and Ireland. I have never heard what fate befell my comrades. One rumour is that they hit a mine. Another is that they were sunk by a British Q-ship. Schwieger and his men had gone to join the victims of the *Lusitania* on the floor of the sea."

CHAPTER XIII

WATER POURING IN AND DOGGED BY A PATROL BOAT. BUNKING WITH A DEAD MAN.

Back in October, 1914, just after Weddigen had accomplished the destruction of those three British cruisers, and before Germany had dreamed of an offensive warfare on commercial shipping, a slender boyish young submarine commander, with an old prewar type of U-boat, had made a somewhat startling fifteen-day cruise of 1,700 miles. His voyage had been across the North Sea and through British coastal waters and was a record achievement for that time. Naturally, it did much to open the eyes of the German Naval Staff to hitherto unsuspected possibilities. If a fighting crew could make such a long cruise without returning to base for fuel and supplies, there was no reason why this under-sea warfare might not be made to play an important part in naval engagements all around the British Isles and along the French and Belgian coasts.

That young chap was Kapitänleutnant Claus Hansen, soon to become a veteran raider of the deep. For with the inauguration of the first unrestricted campaign in the following spring, Hansen shot up to further prominence as one of the first submarine aces. Given command of the large new *U-41*, he operated during those early months of 1915 in the North Sea, the Channel, and the Atlantic. The sinkings increased. The tonnage he and his colleagues sent plunging to the bottom of the sea grew larger each month. So, more and more submarines were being rushed off the ways, and officers in the regular navy who craved real action were volunteering by the score for the new service.

Hansen is dead, and it was his second officer who told me about his adventures. I met him one day in the smoking room of the luxurious Atlantic Hotel in Hamburg—a short, thick-set man with iron-gray hair who had all the appearance of a veritable human dynamo of efficient energy. He was the former Korvettenkapitän Gustav Siess, now engaged in the development of a new type of Diesel engine. He had been one of that very group of young officers who had volunteered for U-boat service in the spring of 1915, and then subsequently had done far more than his share in the war under sea. Before that fateful November of 1918 he had subtracted almost 200,000 tons from the shipping lists of his country's enemies. Perhaps his most spectacular exploit was the torpedoing of four ships in one convoy. It was for that record beat that he had been awarded the coveted Pour le Mérite.

But first it was of Claus Hansen that we talked, and of those early war days when Hansen ran his brilliant and brief course as a wholesale commerce destroyer. Hansen flashed across the under sea like some demon of the deep. But his career ended abruptly when a tramp steamer he stopped proved to be the newly disguised British Q-ship *Baralong*. So Hansen was caught in the trap of the *Baralong* and he and his men in the *U-41* dropped to the ocean floor, there to remain until the crack-o'-doom.

Now, young Siess had been with Hansen on one of the latter's wildest adventures before his run of luck had taken that last fatal turn. After finishing his course as a cub at the sub school, an officer had always to go on a cruise with an experienced commander. Hansen was the man to expound and illustrate the ways of the game and give the lads their post-graduate course. Also, he was one of Siess's best friends. They had been pals for years.

In a precise, matter-of-fact way, Commander Siess told me his story. It was an example of the kind of thing that had a way of happening in the early days of the submarine war against merchant shipping.

The *U-41* ran on the surface all night. A dim, gray dawn broke on placid northern waters. In the misty light the shadowy form of a steamer appeared, a small one. She was small, true enough, but what they did not know aboard the *U-41* was that she was the fishing steamer *Pearl,* which not long before had been converted into a patrol boat, armed to hunt submarines. In the half light no sign of her guns or other suspicious mark could be seen. A shot across her bows. The U-boat mistook the sub-chaser for a common, harmless vessel.

The warning shot banged, and bang in return. Nothing to scare anybody. A U-boat need not dive precipitately out of a gun fight with a puny craft like that. No doubt she had some kind of foolish popgun aboard. The *U-41* drew ahead to shorten the range and have it out with shell fire. Both sides held their fire for a bit. The steamer became clearer in the morning light. Rather warlike she seemed with her guns and bulwarks. Hansen turned to the serious-faced Siess.

"Seems to be tougher meat than we expected."

"Too tough, you think?" asked Siess.

"Well, let's try her out with a few more shots," replied Hansen.

"Steering gear has jammed," the report came from below.

And the *U-41* was heading straight for the enemy ship. The men below struggled with the rudder. It would not budge. The submarine kept drifting on, unmanageable. With the rudder out of gear, it could not dive.

The *Pearl,* not six hundred yards away now, opened a blast of fire. Shells popped in the water all around. One struck the hull and exploded just at the water line. It looked like a gone submarine for a moment— but no. A savage burst as a projectile hit the conning tower. Lieutenant Schmidt, the watch officer, who was on deck and standing beside Siess, dropped to the steel plating, horribly wounded. Another shell struck the hull close to the water line. The U-boat's guns were replying shot for shot. Two shells burst on the *Pearl's* deck.

"Steering gear's in control again," the word came from below.

At that moment the *Pearl* turned to ram.

"All hands below for diving!" Hansen yelled.

The wounded watch officer was lowered through the hatch as quickly as possible; the other men tumbled in, last of all the slender, alert commander. The *U-41* plunged just as the *Pearl* came rushing over her.

Water poured into the submarine the moment it submerged. The shell that had struck the conning tower had ripped a hole in the steel plates, and through this water spouted as from the nozzle of a fire hose. Pumps banging and pounding—could they keep the boat from foundering right there? No—the water was slowly rising inch by inch, and there above on the surface lay the *Pearl* waiting with guns and ramming prow. Eloquently and with little figure of speech—they were between the devil and the deep blue sea. The *U-41* had sought the safety of seventy-five or eighty feet. The deeper, the greater the pressure of the water, the faster it would geyser through the hole in the conning tower. Up and a little closer to the perilous surface. The water swishing at the bottom of the hold continued to rise, but at a slower rate.

Up somewhat more, inch by inch. At fifty feet the furiously labouring pumps held the water level. Fifty feet, it was clear, was maximum depth for the boat, beyond which she dared not go. Safety for the moment.

The wounded watch officer was lying in a pool of blood. They carried him to his bunk. He had fearful slashes in his back and legs where the shell fragments had cut him. Hansen and the firm-visaged Siess went to his side. They looked at each other and shook their heads.

The boat ran along slowly under water to get away from the vicinity of the *Pearl*. She nosed upward. Water still rushed through the hole in the conning tower, but the pumps were now more than its match. The hold was pumped dry. At periscope depth the asparagus poked its nose above the surface. If they could run above water they would have a chance to plug up the hole in the conning tower—more or less. Siess anxiously studied the commander's face. Its boyish lines were erased now. Hansen's jaw was set, his brown eyes narrowed. He was peering into the telescope-like eye, the nerve centre, the line of communication with daylight.

"She's still there," he exclaimed, and down came the periscope.

It seemed a queer turn of chance. The *Pearl* had happened to take the same course as the U-boat. The *U-41* went to its "floor" of fifty feet, changed course, and for half an hour scurried along under water as fast as it could, making certain to get away from its above-water enemy. The water spurted into the conning tower with a monotonous splashing, and the pumps clanked and rumbled.

"Out periscope." And again Siess screwed up his frowning brow as he watched the profile at the eyepiece. Hansen's mouth twisted incredulously and he spoke in a tone of wonder.

"She's only a hundred feet away."

Then his tone rose with abrupt alarm.

"Dive—quick—quick—she's ramming us!"

Long, tense moments, while with unbelievable slowness the depth gauge showed that the boat had begun to sink. It is strange how slow things can seem when life and death hang balanced. Then a terrible, shattering crash. To the nerve-straining men in the conning tower the illusion flashed that a shell had hit the boat. The frightening impression of the shells that had burst around them was still vivid in their consciousness. But no shell could have struck the submerged *U-41*. The *Pearl* had surely rammed it. The U-boat rocked from side to side.

"We're done for," muttered Siess, and waited for the sound of water flooding the hull.

The only sound of water was that of the fountain spouting in through the hole in the conning tower. Had the ram prow of the *Pearl* swept along a split second earlier it would have smashed the conning tower. It had merely grazed it, though—and torn away the periscope.

It was clear that in some way or other the patrol boat was trailing the submarine. At the depth of fifty feet at which she kept, she surely could not be seen. Something on the surface was marking the path of the big fish below. U-boats occasionally found themselves in that predicament—followed around by a craft on the surface—and surely the imagination can devise nothing better for stringing out a prolonged accumulation of terror. In later days of the war the suspense was likely to be ended quickly with a depth bomb. The enemy on the surface would not merely track its prey, waiting for it to rise, but would search it out with those charges of high explosive set to detonate at various depths.

As it was, the plight of the *U-41* was sufficiently disastrous. With water pouring through the hole in her conning tower, she could only grope along blindly at her shallow fifty feet. At nightfall she might expect the *Pearl* to lose the trail in the darkness. Siess looked at his watch. It was six o'clock. The days were long. Night would not drop her merciful curtain till eight o'clock, fourteen hours later. The *U-41* could not remain under water that long. Her batteries were already partly exhausted, and, with the amount of power that had to be used to keep the pumps going, they could not possibly last till nightfall.

The boat ran along at snail's pace to save power, just fast enough to keep under control. With her periscope torn away she was sightless. She had a small emergency periscope, but to use that she would have had to come so near to the surface as would have been fatal with an enemy near by. It was evident that the *Pearl* was still on the trail. The noise of her propellers could be heard. Previously the hunted men had not noticed the whirring sound—the noise of their own pumps made it indistinct and, not expecting it, they had not listened for it. The telltale hum from above accompanied them like nemesis. Sometimes it was right above, sometimes to the right or left, but always quite near. The *Pearl* could have dropped her anchor, payed out fifty feet of chain, and hooked the U-boat like a big fish.

The morning passed and noon. It became apparent that the game could not go on much longer. The air was unbearably foul. The wounded watch officer gasped for breath as he tossed in agony in his bunk. The batteries were growing weaker and weaker. Soon they would not have enough power to keep down the water that poured in through the hole in the conning tower. Then the *U-41* would have to come to the surface and face the *Pearl*. The sound of propellers above kept following like a pursuing demon.

After ten hours, at somewhat past two o'clock in the afternoon, the whirring noise seemed to grow faint. The men in the U-boat thought their ears must be failing them. No, the sound grew louder and then dimmer again. And now it could be heard no longer. A sense of mystery more poignant than dread.

"Can it be that she has lost us?" Hansen exclaimed to Siess, scarcely daring to hope. Siess passed his hand over his short-cropped head and scowled in pessimistic doubt.

Not for two hours more of torment did they dare to come up for a look through the emergency periscope, and then the *Pearl* had vanished. The sea was deserted. The U-boat emerged—air, pure, seablown air.

The secret of the mysterious pursuit became clear. The shell that had hit the *U-41* at the water line as if it must sink her had, indeed, perforated the steel hull. But the oil tanks were situated just there, and the result was merely an oozing leak of oil. This, floating on the surface, was the trail the *Pearl* had followed. She had lost it in the broad daylight of afternoon because the sea had grown rough and in the churning of wind and white-capped waves the spoor of oil had become obliterated. Then her own engines had begun to give trouble. When they were working again three hours later, the trail was completely lost.

Below in the *U-41* the wounded watch officer lay in his bunk. Consciousness had never left him or even grown dim. He had talked constantly with men beside him, in spite of his agony, asking how things were going and discussing the progress of their nerve-racking adventure. And now that safety had come, no man aboard rejoiced more than he. He remained

*The dread enemy of the U-boat raider. A depth bomb creates
a geyser higher than any in the Yellowstone.*

Hashagen, who tells of a harrowing adventure with chlorine gas in his iron shell under the sea.

What the well-dressed under-sea buccaneer wears in dirty weather

brightly alert until six o'clock, when he fell into a stupor. At seven he died.

The *U-41*, patched up as well as might be, headed south for Heligoland. Siess described that return trip of several days as a nightmare. Quarters were cramped aboard the small boat. The only available room was in the little officers' cabin, and there the body of the watch officer remained. The sturdy-shouldered, strong-faced man to whom I talked in Hamburg was obviously no shuddering soul given to neurotic sensibilities or overblown imaginings, but he told me that at night when he tried to sleep his eyes wandered constantly to the dead man, and even when he turned them away he could see Schmidt's face floating before him.

Even in the presence of death the duties of war could not be forgotten. Off the coast of Scotland the *U-41* sank a Norwegian steamer that had just been transferred to British ownership. The perilous cruise of the *U-41* stands illuminating when regarded as an officer's introduction to the warfare under the sea. It is no wonder that nerves broke down.

CHAPTER XIV.

MUZZLED IN THE NORTH, THEY SEEK NEW FIELDS FOR THE CHASE

With the sinking of the *Lusitania* in May, 1915, the *Arabic* in August of that year, and the *Hesperian* not long afterward, the outcry against the unrestricted warfare grew loud. The German Government, under pressure of protests by the United States and fearing that the Western republic might declare war, called it off in northern waters. This was in the winter of 1915-16, that time when the British evacuation of Gallipoli was the main topic of the day. The U-boat commanders were ordered to sink no more merchant ships without warning. Attacks were to be made only when warning could be given and the crews could seek safety in the lifeboats.

With that the U-boat warfare practically ceased in the waters around the British Isles. Enemy ships either kept out of the way or were so strongly armed as to be immune from surface attack. Commander Steinbrinck, one of the veterans of the submarine operations off the coast of Flanders, declared that he had let forty ships in the Channel go by which, under the unrestricted warfare, he could have sunk.

The quiet time in the North Sea, though, saw one spectacular U-boat stroke—a rather comic episode. The hero was Ritter Karl Siegfried von Georg, a quiet, capable young Bavarian who was knighted during the war for his U-boat successes. At present he is engaged in importing turpentine and rosin into Hamburg from our own Southern states.

"I always regarded the business of sinking merchant ships," he says, "as disagreeable, but duty was duty and I went about it as efficiently as I could. That night of ship-sinking on the North Sea, though, had elements of humour that made it exceptional. I had picked up a Norwegian vessel and taken her crew aboard my U-boat, when in the dead of night I found myself in the middle of a fleet of ships.

"They were fishing trawlers busy at the task of snaring the denizens of the brine. Now, a trawler is not an important craft, you would say, but really they were an important adjunct to British sea power. The King's Navy relied extensively on Britain's huge fleet of fishing boats. They did all sorts of invaluable drudgery. When they were not fishing they laid mines and swept mines and laid nets to catch the U-boats. They acted as anti-submarine craft, often heavily armed with guns and depth bombs. Sometimes they took the part of Q-ships, trusting to their innocent looks to decoy the unwary submarine commander. And so, a trawler destroyed was an appreciable deduction from Great Britain's defense against the U-boats.

"There we were in the middle of the fishing fleet and quite unsuspected. What good did it do? I couldn't sink a one unless they chose to let me. My orders were to make provisions for the safety of crews, and the moment I gave warning my prospective victim could go scurrying away in the darkness. I resolved to try an experiment. I called the captain of the Norwegian ship I had sunk. He rolled up on his sea legs. Would he do me a service? Yes, he would. I bade him take the small boat with a couple of his men, go over to the nearest trawler and inform the captain of our presence.

" 'Tell him,' I said, 'that he is to abandon ship at

Editor's Note: The use of Q-Ships was an effort to lure U-boats to their end. The British took various types of merchant vessels, large and small, and converted them to powerful, disguised gunboats. From a distance the ship would appear as any other merchant vessel might, vulnerable and tempting. Once the U-boat closed for the kill, the Q-ship would discard the disguise and open fire. Many of these vessels could take a great deal of punishment from a submarine's deck gun without sinking in order to tempt the commanding officer to close for the final stroke, which could well be his last mis-

once and report with his crew to me, as I am going to sink his ship.'

"It was all bluff. If the trawler skipper refused to obey, there was nothing I could do. The bewhiskered Norwegian went his way in the boat. For a time nothing happened. I began to think that my emissary had used his head and was making off with the boat to which I had sent him. No, apparently neither the Norwegian nor the English head were working that night. Soon came the sound of many oars splashing. My Norwegian returned and with him the skipper and crew of the trawler. They drew up alongside the U-boat. The mere word 'submarine' had brought cold chills of apprehension and evoked perfect obedience. The skipper of the trawler had not even attempted to warn the other fishing boats.

"Splendid! Why not carry on the bluff? I now sent the captain of the trawler out and with him one of my officers and four of my men to look after his behaviour. They made the round of the trawlers—there were twenty-two of them—and warned the skipper of each to abandon ship and bring his crew over to the U-boat.

"And now for several hours the splashing of oars resounded on all sides in the darkness. Scores of crowded lifeboats gathered around the black form of the submarine. We gathered the crews aboard one of the trawlers and then set about the work of destruction.

"Dawn was breaking and in the dim light the U-boat slaughtered the fishing smacks. What a massacre of ships that was! We steered back and forth, firing at full speed with our bow gun. One after another, the ships, hit at the water line, listed and plunged, until all had vanished from the surface of the sea save the one on which the survivors were crowded.

"A little Belgian steamer appeared. We gave chase

---

take. In a later chapter, the British *Q-21* nearly destroys *U-93*. The submarine hunter remained afloat under fire, in part because of a large cargo of lumber in her hold intended to provide the ship with greater buoyancy.

and stopped her. The men aboard the remaining trawler were crowded and cramped. The steamer afforded better accommodations. We made the captain take them aboard. The steamer with its swollen passenger list disappeared, while we took a couple of close-range shots at the lone fishing boat that was left, and sent it to join its companions.

"The bluff had worked to perfection, and without endangering a single life we had polished off a neat batch of potential mine layers and sweepers and anti-submarine craft."

I heard from commanders many other tales of how strategy was necessary in the restricted campaign that summer of 1916 if a raider were to bring home any scalplocks. Besides Ritter von Georg, there are many more former submarine commanders in Hamburg, among them a big, jovial, breezy fellow. Lieutenant Commander Ernst Hashagen is now an important figure in the exporting business, but during the war he was one of the most redoubtable of under-sea fighters. Toward the end he gained fame for his dare-devil and unusually successful attacks on convoys. With many a rueful chuckle he told me of the American destroyers that time after time came within an eyelash of getting him. But at the beginning of his career as a U-boat commander there were certain difficulties, he told me.

"Our orders were definite. We were not to sink a merchant ship unless we could save the crew. Well, that didn't leave us much room for action. Often I could tell at a glance that a ship hadn't near enough lifeboats for its crew. Or again we were too far from land and the sea was too rough for them to make it in a lifeboat. Nor could we take them on board. I had a little UB-sub then, and she was already crowded to the decks. So we simply had to let many possible victims go their way.

"There was the little *Fritzoe,* for instance. We met her in the North Sea and sent a shot ripping over her bow. She hove to and I signalled the captain to bring over his papers. He came, but I needed only one look at his battered lifeboats to know that his crew could never make it to the nearest land. The question was, what to do with the ship now that I had her? The expression on the captain's face told me he was wondering the same thing. I had an idea.

" 'Look here,' I turned to him, 'You may take your choice of having your ship sunk here or of taking her to Cuxhaven on your own as a war prize. Which shall it be?'

"You never saw such a look of relief on the face of a man. Without hesitation he agreed to take the *Fritzoe* to Germany.

" 'But how do I know you will do as you say?' I asked him. 'I can't follow you all the time. I must watch out for British patrol boats. There is nothing to prevent you from trying to give me the slip. Then I would have to shoot a torpedo at you. No, perhaps I had better sink you right here.'

"The captain turned a bit pale, but stood his ground.

" 'I am a man of my word,' he said with fine dignity. 'When I say I will go to Cuxhaven, then I will go to Cuxhaven.'

"We parted at that, and I lost sight of the steamer. I really never expected to see it again. But still, according to my orders, I couldn't have sunk her anyway.

"Four days later when I reached Cuxhaven, there was the *Fritzoe* waiting for us. As far as I know, that was the only instance during the whole World War of a captured ship and crew arriving at any enemy port with only the captain's word of honour as an assurance that they would go there. That Britisher knew how to play cricket. All honour to him. His word was his bond."

With the abandonment of the first unrestricted U-boat campaign and the quiet time in the waters around the British Isles, the centre of the U-boat war was transferred temporarily to the Mediterranean. By playing havoc with Allied shipping out there, the results would be the same, and without further arousing the ire of America.

In addition to that dashing fellow Hersing, who torpedoed the battleships *Triumph* and *Majestic,* five more of the ablest U-boat officers were sent around into the Mediterranean between August and October of 1915. These were: Commander Gansser, in the *U-33;* Commander Rücker, in the *U-34;* Commander Kophamel, in the *U-35;* Commander Max Valentiner, in the *U-38;* and Commander Forstmann, in the *U-39.* All of these boats made history in the Mediterranean, and all of their commanders became submarine aces.

It is rather interesting to note that, of the twenty leading submarine skippers, more than half of them reaped their greatest harvest of victims in the Mediterranean. Indeed, the ace of aces among the raiders of the deep bagged practically all of his game out there. This man was Lothar von Arnauld, of whom we shall hear a great deal. He was sent overland from Berlin to Cattaro and there took command of the *U-35,* which had been brought around through the Straits of Gibraltar by Kophamel.

There is another curious fact concerning the undersea war in the Mediterranean. Of the two hundred odd U-boats lost by Germany during the Great War, only seventeen were operating in the Mediterranean. Whether that was because the commanders out there were exceptionally cunning and skillful, or the anti-submarine devices of the Allies less effectual, is a ques-

Editor's Note: Lieutenant Commander Lothar von Arnauld de la Perière was the U-boat ace of aces. He destroyed more ships than any other U-boat commander in either war. To add to the interesting portrait provided by Thomas, Lothar von Arnauld commanded *U-35* and *139* and destroyed 194 merchant ships for 453,716 tons, plus two warships that added another 2,500 tons to his record total. He entered the navy in April 1903 and served just before the Great War at the North Sea Naval Station at Wilhelmshaven. Von Arnauld also served in the Kriegsmarine. Recalled as a vice-admiral, he held

tion. Presumably it was the latter. The perils facing the under-sea raiders out "east of Gib" were certainly less serious than those faced by the submarines in the North Sea, particularly those that had to run the famous "Dover Barrier" in going to and from their Flanders base at Bruges and Zeebrugge.

At any rate, the Mediterranean now became the U-boat raider's Paradise. And where the warships of Greece and Persia, the triremes of Phœnecia, and the galleys of Carthage and Rome once fought for supremacy, the Kaiser's wolves of the deep ran amuck and preyed on the commerce of the modern world. And this brings us to one of the prime figures of our story—the ace of aces of the German submarine commanders.

---

major naval commands ashore in Danzig, Belgium, the Netherlands, and occupied France before dying in an airplane crash on 24 February 1941.

CHAPTER XV

THE U-BOAT ACE OF ACES

Wilhelmshaven lies sleepy, half deserted. Its history gives you its mood. It is a new town, very new for Europe, founded less than a hundred years ago during the reign of the first Kaiser Wilhelm. Its site was originally a swamp on the edge of the Jade Basin, and most of its space is reclaimed land. The town boomed with the German Navy. Jade Basin formed a natural station for the Kaiser's Fleet. From the year 1900, when Wilhelm II saw Germany's future on the sea, Wilhelmshaven flourished and grew bigger, like any mining town of the old West. Tens of thousands of officers and sailors were stationed there, with battleships, cruisers, destroyers, and U-boats lying in the harbour, sailing and arriving. The World War raised Wilhelmshaven to its pinnacle. The harbour was a scene of high pressure industry and warlike swarming. Merchants, hotel keepers, and the other burghers drove a lively trade and laid away profits. New buildings arose and everything bustled.

The port was one of the chief U-boat stations. The others in Germany were Emden, Kiel, and Heligoland. I heard much from the U-boat commanders of the gay casino, the brilliant restaurants, the music, dances, theatricals, and other social festivities. Every leave for the submarine sailor might be his last one. He had just come back from a long cruise among deadly perils. Who could tell whether on the next one he would not leave his bones at the bottom of the sea, securely encased in the iron coffin. Let him be gay while he could. It kept him from thinking.

To-day, with German sea power a vanished dream, Wilhelmshaven is in the doldrums. It is still a naval station, but the German Fleet is but a handful of boats. The great barracks that during the war were filled to overflowing are nearly empty. Only a few ships lie in the harbour. The U-boats are no more. There are empty houses and empty stores. The shops, restaurants, and hotels that are still open struggle for business. In that town of Wilhelmshaven you get a vivid, symbolical picture of the downfall of Germany's glory at sea.

The German Navy of to-day consists bodily of a few inoffensive ships, but as an idea it amounts to something more. After the war the Germans decided that, while they were compelled to surrender their fleet to the enemy, they would preserve the naval tradition which they had built up as one of the world's great sea powers, until some happier day when dreadnaughts and U-boats may again stand as representations of the power of the Reich. To this end they have kept a skeleton of the old officer's corps and the old organization and preserved the old etiquette and ceremony. Thus, when I called at the house of the first admiral staff officer of the Naval Station at Wilhelmshaven I was confronted by a figure that recalled Imperial Germany in its full power and splendour. I found my host in full uniform, resplendent with gold braid, medals, and decorations. A sword clanked at his side and the Pour le Mérite was at his throat. An inspiring nautical figure he made.

The purpose of my visit was simple. Commander Lothar von Arnauld de la Perière ranks as the German U-boat ace of the war. The submarine commanders were rated according to the amount of tonnage they had sunk, just as the aviation aces were according to the number of planes they had brought down. Von Arnauld headed the tonnage list.

The submarine activity in the Mediterranean reached its climax in a prodigious under-sea feat, a cruise that called attention to the possibilities of the Mediterranean as a happy hunting ground for the submarine. Arnauld de la Perière was the German with the ultra-French name who made this spectacular and epochal raid. It was the high spot in his amazing career as the U-boat ace of aces. From then on he topped the list both in number of ships and in gross tonnage sunk. His total bag for this one voyage in the *U-35* was fifty-four vessels—91,000 tons of Allied shipping!

War plays strange tricks with names and races. America's foremost raider of the skies answered to the good old German name of Rickenbacker. On the other hand, Germany's U-boat ace of aces was called Arnauld de la Perière.

His great grandfather was a French officer of the Eighteenth Century, who, having a disagreement with his superior, the Duke of Bourbon, offered his sword to Frederick the Great after a fashion quite common among soldiers of fortune of those days. In the service of the *Alter Fritz* he rose to the rank of a general and founded a family which has traditionally stood high in the German Army and later in the Navy. The U-boat ace found a service career a natural and inevitable thing. During the years before the war he was torpedo officer on the *Emden,* which later was to create wartime sensations. Then he was aide-de-camp to Grand Admiral von Tirpitz. When war broke out he was on the Admiralty Staff. He wanted to see action and chose the zeppelins. No zeppelin command was available. He went to the other extreme, the submarine service. He did not take command of a boat until the beginning of January, 1916, almost a

year and a half after the war began. Yet in ten
months he was leading the field in number and tonnage
of ships sunk. Once out in frcnt, he was never headed.
His record stands at more than two hundred ships and
half a million tons. He was given the Pour le Mérite,
Germany's highest war decoration, in the autumn of
his first year in the U-boat service. Then, as he continued to run his record up, there was no further
honour to give him. He was asked what he wanted,
and replied—an autographed photograph of the
Kaiser. He got it, and later, upon his earning further
honours, the Kaiser sent him a letter of commendation
in his own handwriting. Imperial Germany could do
no more!

I found him a tall, slender man in his early forties,
with brown hair and the keenest possible brown eyes:
a good-looking chap whose jaw and chin were exceedingly firm and were rather in contrast to a fine, gay
smile. You caught at first impression a sense of capac-
ity and strong nimble mind, together with a laughing
wit and penetrating humour, a mixture of ancestral
qualities, you surmised, of German energy and precision and French wit and *savoir faire*. He is usually
spoken of as Korvettankapitän von Arnauld, with the
"de la Perière" left off. He was all obliging courtesy
toward the American who wanted to hear stories of
the U-boats. Tea was served, and we were joined by
Commander von Arnauld's charming wife, who was
educated in England, and the two daughters of the
family, proper little girls whose ages were ten and
twelve.

The house was a museum of mementoes of the
U-boat warfare. The Commander showed me the
tattered flag of his first boat, the *U-35*, and its number
plate. His dairy was bound with the gray leather of
his submarine uniform. On a wall hung the broken
end of a large periscope of the giant submarine cruiser

he commanded late in the war. The asparagus had been snapped off like a match stick when a torpedoed ship sank on top of the boat. Much of the furniture of the house was taken from the submarine cruiser. The desk Von Arnauld had in his cabin still serves him, but is now in his study. Doors and mouldings and panels in the house were made of wood ripped out of the submarine cruiser before she was turned over to the Allies after Germany's defeat. The wood was fine, satiny maple. Those giant submarines were luxuriously equipped, quite different from the tiny, stuffy little craft of the earlier type. The chandelier in one room was made of the round steering wheel of a captured ship. Hanging on a wall was a bunch of pretty glass bulbs, about the size of large grape-fruits—buoys that held up a net laid in the Adriatic Sea to trap submarines.

My obliging host displayed typical German thoroughness in seeing that the American who wanted to tell the story of the U-boats got plenty to tell. He showed me his diary and photographs, and related his adventures. He arranged for me to meet other commanders. Nor did he neglect to have me see the sights. The chaplain of the post, a genial, bald-headed gentleman who, I found, was a fan for Jack London and Upton Sinclair, took me to the garrison church, a red brick building with the steeple rising above a grove of trees. It was built during the Franco-Prussian War and now is filled with relics of the once proud Imperial Navy. I saw the war flags of the great dreadnaughts and battle cruisers, and the Imperial flags, which were flown whenever the Kaiser, the Kaiserin, or a member of the royal family came aboard ship. The great chandelier that hung from the ceiling was the giant steering wheel from the Kaiser's private yacht, the *Hohenzollern*. The walls were covered with the figureheads and coats of arms of the various German warships, some of them originals and some copies, and all emblazoned in gold and red. There was the nameplate of the submarine cruiser, *Deutschland,* which visited the United States first as a peaceable merchantman and then as a raiding warship; life buoys from some of the lost U-boats; the coat of arms of the big battleship *Pommern* and that of the giant battle cruiser *Lutzow,* both of which went down at the battle of Jutland: similar remembrances of the cruisers *Gneisenau, Scharnhorst,* and *Nürnberg,* which were sunk off the Falkland Islands, of the famous raider *Emden,* and of the cruiser *Hela,* the first German warship sunk by a British submarine—for the British, too, could play at the submarine game, although they had not as much chance as the Germans. In a thick volume on the altar were the names of all the German navy men lost during the war, from admiral to cabin boy.

From the chapel we went to the naval cemetery. In the shadow of the great dyke that holds back the North Sea is a stretch of reclaimed land, a bit of earth snatched from the sea, which is covered with hedges and gardens and low trees and hundreds of little headstones and war memorial statues and crosses. There lie the German dead from the battle of Jutland, victims of the British shells that burst like popcorn that day. Of submarine men only a few lie among the flowers and trees. Most of those who died in the warfare under the sea found their last rest in the iron coffins.

Commander von Arnauld himself took me to the Naval Officers' Club, where there was much clicking of heels and saluting. The inner sanctum there was the submarine room, the only place of its kind in Germany. It was covered with photographs of submarine commanders—the dead. The number of pictures was a hundred and fifty-one—approximately that many of

Germany's Captain Nemos went down during the war in their boats. There was Weddigen, the first great U-boat hero; Schwieger, who sank the *Lusitania;* Count von Schweinitz and Commander Pohle, who were lost during the first cruise of the U-boats right after the declarations of war; Claus Hansen, who was one of the first to make a mark for sinking merchant shipping; Kurt Beitzen, a fresh-faced youth who laid the mines that sent Lord Kitchener to the bottom; Rudolph Schneider, who sank the British warship *Formidable;* Hoppe, Güntzel, and Rosenow, each of whom took his last dive when he matched his wits against Gordon Campbell, the sensational British Q-ship commander; eighty-five commanders who went down in the U-boat operations off the coast of Flanders; and others who sank in the iron coffin all the way from the tropical Azores to the tip of the Orkneys and the Murman coast far up in the Arctic Ocean. In cabinets were models of the various types of craft that were used early in the war, the giant submarine cruisers, the UB-boats that were used in the peculiar warfare off the coast of Flanders, and the UC mine-laying boats.

No better setting could be devised for the telling of U-boat stories. Commander von Arnauld gathered a couple of other former submarine commanders who were now in service at the naval station to add their under-sea yarns to his. After a characteristic German dinner in a private room—the *pièce de resistance* was roast hare—the company adjourned to the submarine room. There we sat, the three officers in glittering full naval uniform and myself. I listened to wild tales of periscope and torpedo.

"My friend Von Heimburg," remarked Von Arnauld, indicating one of the other officers, "specialized in bagging fish like ourselves—the U-boats of the enemy."

"A case of submarine eat submarine," I commented, using Americanese.

I had heard of Korvettenkapitän Heino von Heimburg. He was in a professional way the antithesis and complement of Von Arnauld. The latter specialized in merchant shipping; "I just didn't happen to get any large war vessels," he told me. Von Heimburg, though, ran up only a brief list of commercial craft sunk. In Hamburg, Admiral Wilhelm Tägert had mentioned him to me. "He nearly always got transports or warships," the Admiral said; "there was no limit to his courage and audacity." The curious part was Von Heimburg's knack or luck at sinking enemy submarines. For one under-sea craft to sink another was a rare feat, but Von Heimburg contrived to put three or four on his record.

He was a husky big fellow who looked more like an Irishman than a German, black-headed, rather bald on top, with brown eyes and a determined chin. He was quiet and rather diffident, his reticent manner contrasting with the flashing personality that distinguished Von Arnauld. I was later told that he had many relatives in the United States. A sister of his father is the wife of Walter Damrosch, for so many years conductor of the New York Symphony Orchestra.

"Submarine eat submarine," I repeated the phrase; "that must be a nerve-racking kind of fight."

A pennant flown for each ship sunk on a single cruise—3 windjammers and 21 steamers.

The U-boat ace of aces, Commander Lothar von Arnauld de la Perière, who sank more than 200 ships.

The garrison church at Wilhelmshaven, decorated with memorials to lost German raiders and men of war.

The raiders of the deep who never came home. The submarine room at the Naval Club.

CHAPTER XVI

SUBMARINE CONTRA SUBMARINE

"I will tell you about the first one," Von Heimburg began, passing one hand meditatively over his long chin. "I joined up for U-boat service right after the war began, and in 1915 went down to Austria by train to take command of a boat operating in the Adriatic. It was a small vessel which had been knocked down and shipped to the Adriatic as freight. It was not of the U-boat type but the kind of UB craft that we used in the shore waters off Belgium—sewing machines we called them, they were so tiny. These boats were designed for a short cruising radius and to operate at no great distance from their base. They carried small crews. That of my boat numbered only fourteen.

"That sewing machine, the *UB-15*, was lucky. On my first trip out from Pola in June of 1915, I crossed over to the waters in front of Venice. I wonder what the shades of the doges must have thought. We were cruising along under the surface, poking the periscope up now and then to see what was happening, when the picture in the lense showed me an Italian submarine proceeding along above water only a few hundred yards away. It was to the rear of us, and we had no stern torpedoes. It was a simple matter, though, to swing around for a bow shot. Showing the periscope for only brief seconds, I manœuvred the boat. The enemy craft sailed right along where I wanted it.

" 'Torpedo—fire!' I called.

"In an instant I was knocked sprawling as the boat

133

made a wild leap. It took me bewildered moments to figure what had happened. I had never fired a torpedo from that sewing machine before, and had not anticipated what would happen. The boat was so small that when relieved of the weight of the torpedo at the bow she popped up like a jack-in-the-box.

" 'To the bow,' I yelled, 'to the bow!' And every man who could leave his station scrambled to the bow, the combined weight bringing it down level.

"Meanwhile we had heard the sound of the bursting torpedo.

" 'Out periscope!' I gave the order, and peered into the lense. Nothing was to be seen save a cloud of smoke.

"The *UB-15* emerged and we went toward the smoke. Swimming about in the water were half a dozen men. We fished them out. They were Italians. The boat we had sunk was the Italian submarine *Medusa*. The rest of the crew had perished. We took the rescued survivors back to Pola as prisoners of war."

"When those little boats," observed Commander von Arnauld, "started to turn somersaults, it was no fun."

"There was another time," continued Heimburg, "that that sewing machine was almost sucked out of the water. At daybreak we lay on the surface fifteen miles out of Venice. The sea balmy and perfectly calm.

" 'Ship ahoy.' A vessel hove in sight coming out of the harbour.

"She surely would have seen us had we not been lying full in the light of the rising sun. The *UB-15* plunged, and presently the periscope showed not one ship but three, two light cruisers and a big one from which flew an admiral's flag. That big one was our game. We got a perfect shot at it and did not miss.

Just as the torpedo exploded I saw a destroyer darting at us. A quick dive, and the sound of propellers rushed over us. We were deep enough for safety, but the suction as the speeding torpedo boat dashed along jerked our sewing machine almost to the surface. If another destroyer had been following we should surely have been rammed.

"We discovered later that the warship we had sunk was the *Amalfi,* Italy's finest armoured cruiser, which was returning to Venice with its accompanying ships after having made an attack on the Austrian coast defenses near Trieste. Out of a crew of six hundred, four hundred, including the admiral, were saved.

"Another of our victims about that time was a 11,000-ton British transport, the *Royal Edward,* with fourteen hundred British troops aboard. This occurred in the Ægean. When we first sighted her all we could make out were two funnels on the horizon. Then when we crept up on her we saw long promenade decks and high masts and knew that she was indeed a great prize. We let go at her from a distance of 1,600 meters. I watched the path of the torpedo through the asparagus and saw it hit the stern of the transport. A moment later soldiers in khaki were running about on the decks like ants.

"Since there were no destroyers near enough to threaten us, I allowed all of my men to have a look at the spectacle. Last of all came the torpedo mate, the man who had released the missile. He gave a yell.

" 'What is it?' I shouted.

"He turned the asparagus back to me. It was indeed a fearful sight. The giant steamer was now standing almost on end, her bow high in the air. A second later she shot under the waves. All that was left in sight were eight boatloads of men, waving white shirts, trousers, and handkerchiefs, apparently afraid we might destroy them. Shortly after a Red

Cross ship and two French destroyers came to their rescue, but I have since learned that less than six hundred were saved. So with one lone torpedo we not only had destroyed a ship of great value, but we had also wiped out a complete enemy battalion."

After my meeting with Heimburg and his pals at Wilhelmshaven I heard more of the details concerning the sinking of the *Amalfi* while discussing the undersea war with some of my friends in the Italian Navy. It seems that when the *Amalfi* went down the chief engineer was sucked into the still revolving propellers, and one of his arms was cut off almost at the shoulder. Swimming in the water not far from him was the *Amalfi's* surgeon. He saw the bleeding man floundering not far away and swam to him with powerful strokes. There, treading water all the while, he took off his own belt, applied it as a tourniquet to the engineer, and then helped his terribly wounded companion to stay up until help came and they were pulled into a boat.

Heimburg played an important rôle in the U-boat operations around Constantinople, and here again the theme was submarine eat submarine. One of his narrowest escapes was when his boat got enmeshed in the great steel nets that the British had stretched across the entrance to the Dardanelles. Back and forth he drove her, wrenching and tearing against the steel strands in which the U-boat had become entangled. Now and then a terrific explosion would rock them. Bombs attached to the net, placed there for the purpose of demolishing captured steel fish, were going off. Finally, after hours of wild effort, the U-boat was able to rise to the surface with the huge net draped around it. Carrying some of the metal net and dragging the rest of it through the water, the lucky craft just managed to make its base, the little harbour on Gallipoli Peninsula that had recently been named Hersingstand in honour of the conqueror of the *Triumph* and *Majestic*.

"A little while after that," added Heimburg, "we set out again for Constantinople. This time we managed to slip through the Dardanelles, and we came to anchor just this side of the Sea of Marmora, at a place called Chanak where the Turks had their headquarters. No sooner had we anchored than we had a visit from the Prince of Reuss who came aboard to tell me that a fish had been caught in a Turkish net across the strait—an Englishman no doubt. He had been there since six o'clock that morning and it was afternoon then. Explosives had not been dropped on him simply because the weather was too rough. But a Turkish gunboat had been left on watch.

"The weather was clearing, so off we went to investigate. Everything was quiet. The gunboat had nothing to report. Had Herr Englander gotten away? We sounded for him. I was in a small boat with Herzig, my cook, who was a very capable fellow and a natural-born fisherman to boot.

" 'I have him,' yelled Herzig. His plumbline had struck a sudden shallow.

"A mine attached to a line was let down with the fuse lighted. An explosion, and a column of water shot up. A dark spot appeared on the surface that looked like oil. We were about to let down another mine when a dark form broke the surface. It was the British E-boat. Gunboats around opened instant fire. A shell went through the conning tower, another pierced the tanks. The boat was sinking. Men came scrambling out of the hatch. The shooting ceased.

"That cook Herzig was a crazy fellow. He jumped aboard the slowly sinking submarine and helped drive the Englishmen out. *'Raus mit, raus mit,'* he roared, and even prodded men on as they scrambled up.

"The water was closing over the conning tower

when another figure leaped out of the conning tower and into the water and swam over to a boat. It was the captain, the last man to abandon ship."

"What boat was it?" I asked.

"The *E-7,* under Commander Cochrane."

I thought I had recognized the incident. I had heard of Commander A. D. Cochrane, now a member of Parliament, from my friend, Major Francis Yeats-Brown, associate editor of *The Spectator.* The two men are close friends, and "Y. B." had often spoken to me about Cochrane.

"A little later," Heimburg went on, "the French submarine *Turquoise* got tangled up in the Dardanelles nets. She came to the surface and the crew were taken prisoners. In the excitement they forgot to destroy their confidential papers. From these we gleaned several important bits of information. One was a note about a rendezvous. The French submarine was to meet a British submarine at a point in the Sea of Marmora. The *Turquoise* could not keep the date, but we could. I piloted my submarine to the meeting place.

"Sure enough, as we drew near we spied a conning tower. It took a careful bit of stalking, but finally we got a perfect shot. A tremendous explosion, a cloud of smoke on the water. When the smoke disappeared no submarine was to be seen, only men swimming around in the water. We picked up nine Britishers, including the captain, a young Lieutenant Warren. The craft we had sunk was the *E-20.*

"I had quite a pleasant chat with the English skipper.

" 'I say, that was a neat shot!' he exclaimed.

"I thanked him for the compliment and asked how he got into the Sea of Marmora to begin with, which of course meant a trip through the Turkish series of Dardanelles' nets. You see, the Allies had set nets down near the mouth of the Straits, near the Ægean, while the Turks had their nets a bit farther east, near the narrowest point in the Dardanelles, just off Chanak.

" 'We did get caught in a net,' he responded. 'But full speed, and we ripped right on through. I say, though, old fellow, how did *you* get through *our* nets in order to get in here to "Constant" in the first place?'

" 'Same way,' I responded.

"I was busy about other matters when this young English commander was fished out of the water and pulled on board my boat. So some of my men were the first to hold a conversation with him. I understood afterward that when our torpedo struck the *E-20* this jaunty English naval officer was just brushing his teeth. The explosion knocked him senseless and he was only half conscious when we got him up on our deck. When my men revived him they asked him if there was anything that he wanted. Stunned and half dazed, he repeated the last idea that had been in his mind before the crash wrecked his boat.

" 'Yes, a toothbrush,' he replied. So the toothbrush was brought and he went on and brushed his teeth!

"I'm telling you this last anecdote simply because it's a tip-top yarn whether it's true or not.

"Besides the *E-20*, which we had torpedoed, other German U-boats accounted for at least three other British submarines. Commander Steinbrinck of the Flanders Flotilla got the *E-22* on April 25, 1916, in the North Sea. Then the *C-34* was sent down near the Shetland Islands in July of 1917; and finally the *D-6* off the north coast of Ireland, late in June of 1918."

Then I told Heimburg how the British also sank some of their own latest and finest submarines in an appalling accident a few miles out from the Firth of

Forth. A former officer in the Royal Naval Volunteer Reserve, a Mr. Earle who now lives in Toronto, had related the tale to me a short while before. He happened to be in command of a mine sweeper patroling near by at the time. Three British submarines, of the latest model, were manœuvring together when two of them collided and went down. A destroyer rushing to the rescue accidentally rammed the third and sent it to join its comrades.

Heimburg himself had another harrowing adventure with an enemy submarine. Several months after his victory over the *E-20* he was on his way back across the Black Sea from Trebizond, bound for the Bosphorus. In order to make speed he was travelling on the surface. Himself the destroyer of under-sea men-of-war, Heimburg knew just how much to fear from an enemy of his own kind. So he not only kept a double lookout, but he himself remained on the conning tower all morning. When luncheon time came he ordered his meal brought to the bridge. By four in the afternoon he presumed he had passed through the danger zone and went down to his tiny cabin. He lay there dozing and listening to the one unbroken gramophone record left aboard the *UB-15*. It was a popular Vienna music hall song about a young Gretchen named Paulina who simply couldn't stop dancing.

Suddenly came the shrill sound of the alarm. Sleep and Paulina were dashed from his mind as he rushed up to the conning tower. There he met the entire crew tumbling down the ladder from the deck.

"What's up?" he shouted to the lookout.

"Enemy submarine. Only 500 metres away."

The order to dive had already been given, but in the meantime the other submarine had had a perfect target. As the water closed over the conning tower Heimburg had his eye riveted to the asparagus. As he surmised, there it came, a torpedo speeding straight toward them. It was too late to evade it. He could only watch.

"That was surely our lucky day," added Heimburg. "The thing slid past us within a foot or two of our stern. 'Torpedo missed us by two centimeters,' I called out. The crew breathed again. Then we kept on diving deeper and deeper until we were in safe water, and after that we zigzagged our way back to the Golden Horn.

"Ah, yes, it was indeed exciting business, fighting under-sea boat against under-sea boat," he concluded.

"I'll bet," I exclaimed.

For me there was something eerie and unearthly in that submarine-eat-submarine kind of adventure.

The three officers fell to discussing the fact that little reliance was to be placed on reports either in Allied or German newspapers of sinkings or captures. Reports were apt to be unreliable in the first place, and then the governments used various means to hoodwink the fellows on the other side. The British, for instance, had a deliberate policy of not publishing authentic news of U-boats they had sunk. It was thought that the mere blank vanishing of boats, craft that went out and simply did not come back, would increase terror with mystery and have the greatest effect in breaking down the nerves of the German submarine men; and, indeed, no phase of the U-boat warfare was so appalling as those silent vanishings. Often, too, the British thought they had sunk U-boats when they had not. For a long while oil floating on the surface of the water was thought an infallible sign that a submarine had gone down. Presently, though, the U-boats, upon diving away from an attack by gunfire or depth bombs, occasionally resorted to the trick of loosing a little oil, which, upon coming to the surface, would create the belief that the boat had been sunk. Sometimes that caused an attack to be discontinued.

"Yes," laughed Von Arnauld, "and Kapitän Saalwachter here can tell you how he worked that trick once quite involuntarily."

The officer referred to was a short, stocky Silesian, broad-faced, blond, and smiling, the captain of the battleship *Schlesien,* one of the few men-of-war that Germany was permitted to keep.

"There were depth bombs that day," he said, squinting his eyes and grimacing to show that he meant it; "they were popping all around."

He took a long meditative puff at his cigarette and then went on.

"We were in the *U-94,* off Aberdeen on the east coast of Scotland. All night we took it easy on the bottom, sleeping comfortably while the boat lay on the ocean floor. In the morning we came up to look around. The first look through the periscope—*Gott im Himmel*—a destroyer only a few hundred yards away! She saw the asparagus instantly, and came racing. We plunged as fast as we could. We were at twenty yards depth when the first depth charge exploded—not very near us. We kept on going down. Bang—bang—all around. She was searching for us plenty, spreading her sugar plums all over the water. And some of them popped mighty near us. It is not a cheery thing listening to them bang around. At fifty meters' depth we blew the tanks quickly to keep from going too deep. A bomb hit us. At any rate, it burst near enough to hammer us properly. We were nearly deafened by the terrible report, and the boat shook in that ghastly fashion when you feel everything is breaking. We said to ourselves it was "good-bye," and expected to drop like a lead shot to the bottom. No, we were travelling the other way. The depth gauge went rapidly from fifty to zero. We were popping to the surface. That depth bomb had hit us all right. It had cracked open our hull right where our oil supply was stored, next to the engine room. The oil ran out of one of the tanks into the water, air from the inside taking it place. That lightened the boat considerably and made it rise.

"The *U-94* popped right out of the water. We expected the destroyer to finish us off without any more delay. But there she was, rushing away as fast as she could. We had blown our tanks just after she had dropped her last bomb. The blowing of tanks sends to the surface a great bubble of air. So may a shattered, sinking submarine. Then the contents of our broken oil tank came up. That settled it. The destroyer hurried away, certain she had destroyed us. She reported her supposed victory, and her commander got the V. C. And we were left in peace to limp home."

A broad, hearty Silesian laugh followed the tale and celebrated the narrow escape.

"And another narrow escape," Saalwachter exclaimed, suddenly becoming grave. "It was one of those things you can't explain."

"We were on cruise and got a wireless that the British fleet was out at sea. The position was given, and we thought we might as well see what we could do. We ran on the surface as fast as we could go. When we got to the vicinity described, we spied a zeppelin in the sky.

" 'Have you sighted enemy ships?' we wirelessed.

"No answer from the zeppelin. Probably she hadn't picked up our message. Just then British cruisers appeared on the horizon. We submerged, and crept up on the warships. It looked like a fine stroke. We were just in position to torpedo a big cruiser. I was about to give the order to loose the right-bow torpedo when I saw a fountain of water geyser near the ship at which I was aiming—an explosion. The zeppelin was throwing bombs at our prospective prey. In a manœuvre to avoid the bombs the cruiser abruptly changed course. That spoiled my chance for a shot.

"We didn't get another opportunity for a torpedo shot, which caused some quiet swearing aboard. More bad luck, or what seemed bad luck. We cruised around fruitlessly for something to sink. Not a single target hove in sight. Then one of the under-officers happened to examine the right-bow torpedo tube. A piece of timber was wedged tightly in it. If I had given the order to fire at the cruiser, or at any other mark with that particular tube, the missile would have exploded in the tube. Saved by a miracle was the word—or perhaps by a zeppelin which spoiled a perfectly good shot. How that piece of wood ever got into the torpedo tube was not disclosed by any amount of inquiry nor the most ingenious guesses we could think of."

We talked there till long past midnight, amid those hundred and fifty-one pictures of those raiders of the deep who went down in their boats of steel.

The ace of the U-boat commanders told his story with a quiet thoughtfulness which he varied occasionally, when a point of drama and excitement came, with an abrupt, strikingly expressive gesture. Then his face would light up and his eyes shine, and his voice would rise with a tone of soaring intensity. It was a tale full of lively colour, with a mingling of drollery and breath-taking suspense.

CHAPTER XVII

VON ARNAULD'S TALE OF SINKING SHIPS AND THE MONKEY IN THE FAT MAN'S WHISKERS

I began to run up my list of ships sunk, curiously enough, in what might have been called the dull season, the doldrums. It was that summer which in France began with the Battle of Verdun. The "unrestricted" campaign had been called off, largely because of the protests of the United States. Merchant ships were not to be torpedoed any more, and few ships were sunk in the waters around the British Isles. I was sent down to the Mediterranean, and there found the gunning very good. Those waters were not so well policed against U-boats as the seas around Britain.

Still, there were perils enough. One had to be especially careful of the Q-ships. They were carrying on in high style during those summer days of 1916. In fact, I owe my baptism of fire to one of them. It was on my first cruise, and we had said *wie gehts* to a particularly innocent-looking Dutch freighter with a shot across the bow. The crew got into the boats and started to row away. We slowly approached the seemingly deserted vessel. It looked all right. Still, I was particularly on the lookout for Q-ships. So, to be entirely on the safe side of things, I submerged, drew up close, and looked her over through the periscope. All O. K., I thought. I called Lauenberg, my watch officer, to have his opinion verify mine. "Harmless," he said, looking into the periscope. The boats with the ship's crew were lying eight hundred yards astern of the ship. I steered over to them, and emerged within fifty yards of them, feeling safe in their proximity. If there were any hidden guns aboard the ship, the gun crew would scarcely take so much chance of hitting their own people.

"Come alongside," I called to the men in the boats. I wanted to look them over and make finally sure.

A distant clattering and rumbling from the steamer as gun concealments were run down, and the crack of a shot. A shell went whining overhead. Then men in the boats pulled away for dear life. Those Englishmen had their nerve—no doubt of it. But there was no time to stop and generously admire the enemy's courage. Shells were popping around. We were scrambling through the hatches.

"Dive!" I shouted.

The tanks hissed and we began to sink. Then a frantic yell from one of the sailors.

"Lieutenant Lauenberg is not down."

Lauenberg, ordinarily one of the spryest hands aboard, was still on deck. Now it was nervous work. We remained there in the brisk shell fire, while a hatch was pushed open, and Lauenberg streaked in.

"Dive to twenty metres with all speed," I commanded. We did dive with such speed that we went to sixty meters before we could check our descent.

Yes, those Q-ships were no joke, especially as we had to warn all ships before sinking them—that is we had to approach on the surface and take a chance with a craft that might be an armory of concealed guns. The restriction about torpedoing, though, made little difference to me, because I very rarely torpedoed a ship even when it was authorized. I much preferred the method of giving warning and doing my sinking with gunfire or by placing explosives aboard. In that way I saved torpedoes and, besides, I could accost the lifeboats, look over the ship's papers, and get its name and tonnage. Before a commander had a ship officially placed on his record he had to give its name as proof of sinking. Many officers sank more tonnage than appeared on their records because of their inability to produce names and verification. The fact that I nearly always gave warning may explain why my record ran so high; that and the fact that my cruises were not gauged by the length of time my torpedoes lasted. I stayed out as long as I had shells and food left.

One day I stopped a steamer. The tables on deck were set for luncheon. Too bad I couldn't give the guests time to sit down to their repast. Lifeboats rowed away, and I was about to pop my latest capture with a few shells at the water line. Through my binoculars I saw a tiny figure scampering around the well-set tables. It was a monkey, which was capering in the liveliest way and sampling the dishes to its heart's content. No doubt Jocko had never before enjoyed such an opportunity.

"Go aboard," I called to Lauenberg, "and rescue the monkey."

Lauenberg stepped lively. He was always ready for anything unusual. Away our dinghy went with strong strokes of the oars. I continued to watch. That monkey was amusing.

Lauenberg clambered on deck and went over to the monkey. It was docile enough and made friends with him. He petted it for a moment, then picked it up and started down the ladder with it. That monk didn't seem to like ladders or small boats or something. I saw a kind of struggle. The little beast squirmed loose and jumped back on deck, and Lauenberg shook one hand with pain. The monkey had bitten him. I was delighted. Lauenberg was a smart fellow, but that monk was smarter. Back on deck went Lauenberg. It was fine to watch him chase that monkey, coax it, and then make a grab for it. Finally he had the little beast again, grasping it so that it could not bite, and carried it struggling down the ladder. It was now that Lauenberg demonstrated what a bright fellow he was. He took the fight out of that monkey. He nursed his bitten finger and sucked it, and with the other hand held the monkey firmly by the neck. Down he ducked it into the blue Mediterranean again and again until the little beast was thoroughly cowed. You never saw such a tame, submissive animal as that monkey when it finally came aboard the U-boat.

The monkey became the pet and pampered favourite aboard. Somebody gave her—she was a lady monkey—the name of Fipps. What I saw of her while she scampered around on the deserted luncheon tables of the abandoned ship gave the clue to her character. She was an inveterate thief, with edibles as her favourite plunder. She had a persistent hankering after eggs, and used to stalk the larder with inexhaustible patience and the deepest cunning. The cook was always on the defensive. He had to guard the eggs unceasingly. Unfortunately, he was a big fat fellow, slow-witted and slow-footed, no match at all for Fipps. He would be at work in the galley making pancakes, and the moment his back was turned Fipps would dart in and snatch an egg. If he caught her, she got a beating. But he rarely was able to lay hands on her. She knew that once she had her paws on an egg and got a start she was safe. The cook would chase her, bellowing curses, but she would leave him far behind and scurry to the topmost foot of the wireless mast, where she would suck the egg in peace.

We picked up an Italian steamer loaded with bananas. As the vessel went down hundreds of bananas floated off on the surface. The dinghy went out and collected a boatload. We spread the bananas

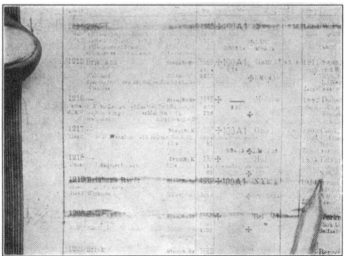

Von Arnauld crosses a British merchantman, the Brisbane River, *out of Lloyds's Register and then chalks up another victim in his own game book.*

*A victim of the U-boat ace of aces photographed
by an Allied airman.*

Towing ashore a boatload of survivors.

out to ripen a bit in the hot Mediterranean sun and prayed that no pestilent destroyer might force us to submerge and lose our precious fruit. We were fortunate and managed to gorge ourselves with bananas. Nothing like Fipps, though. The yellow fruit seemed to remind her of her tropical home. She leaped, chattered, and shreiked with delight, and ate more bananas than I thought her small body would contain.

Fipps was mischievous, too. She used to nibble and ruin my pencils and drink the ink in my inkwells. Once she spilled a bottle of ink over the logbook of the German Imperial Navy. A favourite trick of hers was to play leap-frog over the men asleep in their hammocks. We had a radio operator named Schmidt, who had a majestic round face and ferocious whiskers. When he slept it was like the sound of an airplane motor. His whiskers and his snoring fascinated Fipps. She would watch him for hours while he lay asleep in his hammock, and would jump over him and on him, and sometimes she got tangled in his whiskers. One day there was a frightful commotion below. Fipps had become enmeshed in Schmidt's beard in such a complicated fashion that she nearly destroyed it. That was too much. Schmidt was a patient fellow, but when he had extracted Fipps from his whiskers, he gave her a tremendous beating. From then on the two were bitter, relentless enemies.

With the other men Fipps was on the most cordial terms. She would nose her way into a pocket of the officer on watch and sleep away there for hours at a time. You could never tell whose bunk she would pick for her night's rest, and many a time I woke up with the monkey snuggled up beside me. We were often afraid that we would lose her when we were running awash and she was with the men on deck and when we might have to dive. Several times I sent men out to fetch her in. Once, though, there was no time.

A destroyer was coming at us and haste was necessary. Fipps was outside.

"There goes Fipps," I said to myself regretfully, and gave the order to dive. But just as the hatch was being closed, Fipps dashed in.

We kept her for nearly a year. Then winter came on and she caught a cold. I had heard that monkeys were likely to get tuberculosis and in winter a U-boat is damp, chill quarters. I sent her up to Berlin with a sailor who was going home on leave, and he put her in the zoo there. Several years later, after the war was over, I went to visit Fipps. She was in her cage there, with a plate saying she had been presented to the zoo by the officers and men of our boat. Alas, she had forgotten me, and she gazed blankly at me as if I were any stranger.

"She's a grandmother now," the keeper told me.

Many of the U-boats had pets. Dogs, of course, were common. The strangest case of animals aboard a submarine was that of Commander Kukat's boat, which had two camels. Kukat was one of the commanders who took U-boats to the North African coast to help in a native revolution that was being stirred up against the Italians in Tripoli. He carried a consignment of gold to one of the principal revolting Arab sheiks. The sheik, in grateful return, presented him with two young camels. Kukat put the camels in the mine room, and took them across the Mediterranean back to Pola, where he placed them in the local zoölogical park.

It often turns out that some of the most important events are the least exciting. My record cruise, for instance, was quite tame and humdrum. It lasted for a few days over three weeks, from July 26 to August 20, 1916, and covered a wide sweep of the Mediterranean. We sank fifty-four ships, a record for one cruise. On returning to harbour, I used to fly little flags as scalplocks, one for each ship we had sunk. When the *U-35* put into port at Pola with fifty-four pennants flying, the harbour went wild. Yet we had encountered no spectacular adventures. It was ordinary routine. We stopped ships. The crews took to the boats. We examined the ship's papers, gave sailing instructions to the nearest land, and then sank the captured prizes.

The toughest nut to crack was the British submarine chaser the *Primola,* and I shall never cease admiring her skipper. She was a small craft, scarcely worth a torpedo, but the situation was such that if we did not get her she might possibly get us. The torpedo hit her in the bow, and her foremast went clattering down. We gaped with wide eyes at what that boat proceeded to do. Her engines reversed and she started to back at full speed, coming at us and trying to ram us with her stern. All credit to her skipper for what was a brilliant manœuvre. The *Primola* steamed backward with such speed that it kept the pressure of the water from her shattered fore part, else she would have sunk at once, and at the same time we had to step lively or she would have crashed into us.

I loosed another torpedo. The *Primola,* still with reversed speed, swung around so as to avoid the missile. The torpedo missed, and the damaged boat continued trying to ram us.

"I'll get you yet," I muttered, exasperated.

Another torpedo; that craft with a shattered bow was as slippery as an eel. The torpedo missed. That sort of thing could not go on forever. The fourth torpedo hit, and the *Primola* sank. Four torpedoes for that tiny wasp—I didn't want to come up with any more *Primolas.*

Two important entries on my list were the French transports, the *Provence* and the *Gallia.* The sinking of the *Gallia* was a frightful affair. She was bound with three thousand troops and a large quantity of artillery for the Allied army at Saloniki. Eighteen hundred and fifty-two men and officers were lost. The picture of that foundering vessel sticks in my mind with an undiminished horror.

It seemed so impossible, in the first place, that we should hit her. I had only one torpedo left in a stern tube. With her deck crowded with soldiers, she was zigzagging and making good speed, eighteen knots perhaps. Manœuvre as I would, I could not get a good shot, her zigzagging was so baffling. Then suddenly she turned in such a fashion that I could get an exceedingly difficult and almost impossible shot. It was at a distance of 900 yards and at an almost hopeless angle. It seemed our only chance. The torpedo went its way. We dived to the depths, to avoid being rammed. Nobody believed we would score a hit. Then—ping—the high little sound as the torpedo hit, and immediately afterward the boom of the explosion. Up to periscope depth we went, and I looked through the eyepiece at an appalling sight.

A column of water had shot into the air from the explosion. I witnessed the sight of a great ship moving so fast that it left the column of water behind it. There was a wild panic on the stricken vessel's crowded deck. Lifeboats were being lowered by men too much in a panic to let them down slowly and safely. Hundreds of soldiers were jumping into the water and swimming around. The sea became a terrible litter of overturned lifeboats, overcrowded and swamped lifeboats, and struggling men.

My own men were crowding about me in the conning tower. I let them take a look in the periscope, one after another. Some gazed impassively, others grew pale, some grunted, others cried out in horror. "*Ach Gott!*" a deep guttural cry burst from the throat of the fat cook. The barbaric beard of Schmidt, the radio operator, shook with excitement. A ghastly scene on the surface above—and a strange scene in the conning tower—with Fipps the monkey leaping about from instrument to instrument, infected with the general agitation.

Shadowed against the setting sun, the big *Gallia* plunged stern first. Her bow shot high in the air. She poised like that for an instant and then went down like a rocket. Rescue boats were coming up, and we had to scurry away. With that difficult angular torpedo shot, itself a feat of marksmanship, I had caused one of France's greatest naval disasters. After what I had seen, I did not feel elated.

CHAPTER XVIII

THE TORPEDO THAT JUMPED OVER
A U-BOAT

It was in November of 1917 that the incredible adventure occurred, the one that sounds like a fish story, a whopper. We had been out on a long cruise in the Mediterranean and were on our way back to port. The Italians had a heavy patrol of destroyers across the Straits of Otranto, the mouth of the Adriatic. That was our last danger to surmount, and then a fairly safe run to Cattaro. We slipped through the destroyer net at night without anything exciting happening, and everybody felt fine. After a long, trying submarine cruise, harbour and land are pleasant to think about. We were all eager for shore, and I decided to run the rest of the way to Cattaro above water. With our slow speed, submerged it would take two or three days. With surface speed, we could make Cattaro by nightfall. I had been up all night and was dead tired. I went below for a few hours of sleep, leaving on the bridge my watch officer and with him Prince Sigismund, the son of Prince Henry of Prussia and nephew of the Kaiser. He was a capable young chap, intelligent and full of fine spirit, who had set out to learn something about the submarine business. I had taken him on cruise with orders to see that he got all the experience possible. He got it all right that very day we swung along up the Adriatic toward Cattaro.

Below I saw the crew going about their duties,

154

unkempt and unshaven, dirty. What pigs we were in those submarines! There was never room to carry enough water. The bathing allowance was a few cup-fuls doled out every Sunday morning. We cleaned up once a week, and then we did not get halfway clean. It hurt my eyes to look at my men, they were so like tramps, we were on our way home, and they might as well tidy up a bit, if only very superficially.

"Clean up, men, we'll be in port to-night," and I ordered the last of our water supply to be divided among them.

The amazing thing happened half an hour later, while I was dozing off. Prince Sigismund and Lauen-berg were on the bridge when they saw at a distance of forty yards to the starboard a few inches of peri-scope sticking above the surface of the water. A streak on the water—a torpedo. It was coming straight at the boat. The distance was so short that there was no time to manœuvre to avoid the missile. Nothing could be done, absolutely nothing. The two men stared aghast, petrified, gazing at certain destruc-tion, which was right upon them. The torpedo was perfectly aimed. It was headed straight amidships.

Then the torpedo leaped out of the water. When a dozen yards away it rose from the water like a flying fish. To hit a submarine with a torpedo you have to set the missile for a shallow run. This one had been set for too shallow a run and had done what a tor-pedo in that circumstance is likely to do—popped out of the water. It described a graceful arc and landed on our deck. It slid, with a loud clattering on the steel plates, kept on its way, plunged into the water on the other side, and continued its journey. It had struck the deck just forward of the conning tower, between the conning tower and the forward gun. The space there is only four feet. A little either to the right or the left, and it would have struck its detonating nose against the tower or the gun, and we would have all disappeared from this troubled world right then and there.

The loud banging as the torpedo had struck the deck and rattled across awakened me in my bunk below. I thought one of our masts had fallen down, and scrambled up to the bridge. When I got there I did not ask any immediate questions about the cause of the racket. Prince Sigismund and Lauenberg were as white as a pair of ghosts. Their eyes, wide with consternation, were held spellbound, staring at a point over the side of the bridge. I followed their gaze. There, right beside our boat, was a periscope. I had scarcely spied the periscope when I saw a streak approaching us on the few yards of intervening water—a torpedo.

"Helm hard aport." I gave the order out of instinctive habit. It meant nothing. No earthly power could have swerved the boat in such a way as to get it to one side or the other of the path of the torpedo. The missile was coming directly toward us. Dreadful, agonizing moments. Nothing happened. The torpedo passed under us, but not more than a few inches, I am sure. The enemy, seeing his first torpedo jump over our boat, decided not to set the second one for too high a run. He aimed it too low.

Five seconds later and another torpedo tracked its way through the water, but by now my order 'hard aport' was being obeyed and the *U-35* was swinging around. The torpedo ploughed through the water right beside us. I think I could have touched it with my hand. On its heels a fourth one came, but by now we were zigzagging away.

Prince Sigismund and Lauenberg still stood like a couple of statues, their appalled bewilderment wearing off slowly. When they told me about the torpedo that jumped onto our deck and snaked across—well, it was a good thing I knew them both to be quite sane and truthful men. And there was visible evidence of the truth of it. On the deck was a low rail. It was bent where the torpedo had grazed it.

The crew was in an uproar below. The men did not know what was going on, but something was happening. When they were told about the torpedo playing leap-frog on our deck, they would not believe it. They thought the story was the product of imaginations overwrought by the strain of the encounter with the other submarine. It took the sight of the bent rail to convince them.

My petty officer of navigation was an old submarine man. He was capable, phlegmatic, and had what seemed to be nerves of steel. He knew U-boats from A to Z. He had experienced everything that could possibly happen in the life of a submarine man. Nothing could disturb his stolidity. But this was too much, the last straw.

"When I begin to see torpedoes bouncing up on our deck, then I am through," he said. "The next time I will see a British submarine, periscope, depth rudders, and all come vaulting over us. I'm through!"

And he was through. He refused to go on cruise again, and got himself transferred to shore duty.

In harbour our comrades thought we were spoofing them, but there was still the evidence of the bent rail. I never heard whether the submarine that attacked us was Italian, French, or British. I think it must have been British. I don't believe either the Italians or the French had boats that could have discharged four torpedoes in such quick succession.

Slipping through Gibraltar was always a ticklish piece of business. The British had the straits protected with nets, mines, and patrols of destroyers. I always preferred to go through on the surface at night, rather than take a chance with nets and submerged bombs. The searchlights played across the entire width of the neck of water, but it was possible to sneak through by hugging the African coast. One trip, though, brought us to the point where we were ready to say "hello" to Davy Jones. We had been on a three weeks' cruise in the Atlantic. Incidentally, I had on board five skippers from British ships we had sunk, taking them back to Cattaro as prisoners of war. The sun was sinking behind the jutting rock of Gibraltar as we approached the strait. We nosed our way in the dusk that settled along the African coast. The searchlights of Gibraltar were already sweeping over the water like great pointing fingers of light. Out on deck the men of the crew with the sharpest eyes were peering in the gathering darkness. Those British skippers were seeing war from the other side of the fence.

"Destroyer—port side!" one of the men in front of me exclaimed.

I saw a destroyer bearing down on us at a speed of twenty-five knots. I judged she was trying to ram us. Seemingly she had not seen us, not venturing to show a searchlight with a U-boat around, but was guided merely by the sound of our motors, for she missed us by a hundred yards. As the vessel shot across our bows, one of those wandering, glistening beams from the rock across the strait caught her and illuminated her with a glowing distinctness. She was so near that I could hear the commands of the officers on her deck. We were hidden in impenetrable shadow, and she caught no glimpse of us.

The best policy for us was to press on at our top-surface speed, so we stayed above water. A second destroyer lying at anchor picked us out in the darkness. She could not take up the hunt, but signalled our position both to the first destroyer and to the searchlights. And now ensued a weird hunt. The first destroyer charged around on the black water in the hope of ramming us. Now she was on one side and then on the

other. The searchlights sought us, too. The long
spokes of light moved like great frantic arms. The
streaks of light on the water swept in wide arcs. The
U-35 kept on her way through the infernal net of
charging destroyers and darting beams. The destroyers' blind lunges missed us, and the searchlights did
not pick us out.

It was on this voyage that we had a movie man
along. Poor devil! His face still haunts me. Pea
green it was most of the time. You see, he had never
before gone to sea on a submarine, and he was a suf-
ferer from *mal de mer* in its most virulent form.
Usually he stuck to his camera crank as a real film
hero should. Shells and bullets and oncoming torpedoes could not drive him from it. But sea sickness
did. There were times when he longed for a shell
to come along with his name written on it, to end it all.
Then, when Neptune waved his wand and stilled the
rolling deep, that cinema man was a hero once more.
If we got into a rough-and-tumble gun-fight with an
armed ship he would take his own sweet time and
would coolly refocus his magic box and switch lenses
as though it were a hocus-pocus battle on location
instead of grim reality.

Probably you have had a look at his films. The
final finished product had an adventurous history. A
copy was sent up to German headquarters on the Western Front in April of 1917, so the Kaiser and his generals and even large numbers of the combat troops
might see what we were doing at sea. But the British
somehow captured that copy. They in turn had a
duplicate negative made of it and then, I understand,
had positives shown in cinema theatres all over the
world.

One of the first scenes in that authentic U-boat
film shows our encounter with the 3,000-ton British
steamer *Parkgate,* bound from Gibraltar to Malta.

We sighted her just off Sardinia and sent a shot across her bows. After a hot chase we overhauled her and sent up a signal flag to inform them:

"Send over a boat with captain aboard."

When their lifeboat rowed alongside, fifteen or twenty sailors helped the skipper to his feet. His hat blew off and one of his lads tossed it after him. When he got on deck I noticed that he was slightly wounded and rather more than slightly under the influence of liquor.

"You've had something to drink," I remarked as I glanced over his ship's papers and informed him that he would have to remain and cruise with us as our guest.

"Yes, I have," he responded, "and so would you if you were chased by a U-boat and had shells whistling about your ears, and had nothing under your feet but a ship like mine."

With that he staggered down the stairs. It all shows in that film. Then we sunk a great string of ships, among them the *India,* carrying coal from England to Morocco for the French men-of-war; the Italian *Stromboli* loaded with copper and iron; the *Patagonier,* an Englishman on her way over from Cuba with a precious cargo of sugar, and many others. But we only kept five of the skippers as prisoners. All of these were typical British captains, rather taciturn, now very unkempt, of course, and secretly, no doubt, tremendously interested in the workings and manœuvres of our under-sea raider. When we got them to Cattaro and turned them over to the authorities, one of the captains voluntarily did a very decent thing in writing me a letter of appreciation.

Since the evening I spent with Von Arnauld de la Perière and his U-boat colleagues in Wilhelmshaven I have talked with a number of British naval officers regarding him. All were high in their praise, not only of his remarkable courage, daring, and ability, but also of his sportsmanship. And praise from his

Catarro. Austria
May 6ᵗ 1917

The Captain.
His German Imperial Majesty's
U. 35⁻

Dear Sir
I cannot leave your Submarine without first expressing my gratitude for the kind & courteous treatment I have received at the hands of you, your Officers & in fact the whole of your Crew, during the 23 days I have been Prisoner of War on your vessel.
I Remain
Yours Faithfully
William McLellan Hunter
(Master) S/S Patagonier

adversaries in this case is praise indeed because Commander Lothar von Arnauld wrought terrific havoc to British shipping and played a greater part than any other one U-boat raider in disrupting the vital arteries of commerce that very nearly meant the difference between life and death to the British Empire. He is mentioned in countless British books, official and otherwise. And in not one of them did I find him accused of that brutality in submarine warfare which was laid at the door of some of the other German under-sea commanders. One reason why his enemies had so many gracious things to say about him was that he rarely, if ever, took advantage of the invisibility of his craft by sending torpedoes from a submerged position. He usually came right up to the surface and fought it out.

I might also add an extra little bit of praise of my own to that given Von Arnauld by his adversaries. I was impressed by his modesty. If in recalling an incident he happened to be puzzled about something, or if he got into a tight place through some fault of his own, he never hesitated to say so. Some U-boat commanders almost lead one to believe that no situation was ever too much for them. But not Von Arnauld.

CHAPTER XIX

THE MIGHTY *CORNWALLIS* ZIGZAGS TO ITS DOOM

During the campaign of the raiders of the deep in the Mediterranean there were a couple of incidents that help to explain the odium cast on the U-boat commanders. The feeling was based, first of all, on the practise of torpedoing without warning under the orders of unrestricted warfare. Cases of that sort, with the *Lusitania* as the most startling instance, aroused world-wide protest and brought upon the U-boat commanders the epithets of pirates, murderers, and wolves of the sea.

But, as always happens in every war, there were cases where atrocities seemed to have been done, when the case was not as it appeared. Ships struck mines and went down, when it seemed as if they had been torpedoed. The sinking of S. S. *Britannic* was a case in point and was one of the instances which got the Germans an ugly reputation for sinking hospital ships. I have information of that sinking from Commander Gustav Siess. After his first trip out with Hansen on the *U-41*, he became the skipper of the first big mine-laying submarine, the *U-73*. This was an experimental craft and hard to handle, with engines too small for her tonnage. Nevertheless, she made the voyage from Kiel to the Mediterranean and did some effective mine-laying there.

"On our way to the Austrian port of Cattaro," Commander Siess relates, "we lingered for a while in front of the main British Mediterranean war port at Malta. We laid thirty-six mines about fifty metres apart directly in front of the harbour where British warships would be the most likely to strike them. We did the job at night and were not molested.

"The next morning, as we later learned, the big British battleship *Russell* ran afoul of one of our souvenirs and sank. I understand that she had Admiral Fremantle aboard. He was saved. A patrol boat and a mine layer were the next victims and then a transport with six hundred men aboard.

"Another of the mines laid by the *U-73* off the coast of Greece sank one of England's greatest ships, the 48,000-ton liner *Britannic,* the largest vessel of any kind that went down during the war. Unfortunately, she was a hospital ship, plainly marked and all that—but mines do not choose. It was a part of the fortunes of war that we, the submarine commanders, sometimes had infamy thrust upon us for the work done by mines."

One U-boat commander was listed for a murder trial because of an incident in which he declares that he conducted himself with scrupulous regard for the laws of humanity. He was Commander Kurt Hartwig, who afterward bagged the battleship *Cornwallis* and who had had a career of truly wild romance. He was an officer aboard the cruiser *Dresden,* which was the only German ship to escape from the battle of the Falklands, in which the overpowering guns of British battle cruisers sent Admiral von Spee's squadron to the bottom. The *Dresden* made its way around Cape Horn into the Pacific, only to be sunk by the British in Chilean waters off the island of San Juan Fernandez. The crew escaped to the island. Of them Hartwig was one who contrived to make an adventurous trip back to wartime Germany, where, not content with perils already encountered, he went into the U-boat service.

Kurt Hartwig and his victim, H. M. S. Cornwallis, *the famous British battleship that fired the first shell at the Dardanelles.*

Getting out of the way of the ram bow of an oncoming destroyer.

Raining depth bombs on the unseen foe.

That was just after Von Arnauld had made his record cruise on which he sank 91,000 tons of Allied shipping. The German staff immediately dispatched four more U-boats to the Mediterranean, and Kapitänleutnant Hartwig was in command of one of them.

"I sank the Italian ship, *Porto di Rodi,* in the Ionian Sea," he told me. "The crew took to their boats. Shore was distant and the sea was rough. I doubted whether they could get to land safely. Anyway, it would have been a long hard row in the ugly sea. I took the lifeboats in tow and off we went. The coast finally loomed in sight and everything seemed satisfactory. The lifeboats had only a short pull before them. The Italians were grateful and we parted with a friendly leave-taking. The U-boat headed out to sea and the last we saw of the crew of the *Porto di Rodi* was distant lifeboats pulling lustily for shore.

"A bare few minutes later a vicious storm hit us. It gave us a thorough lashing, but what stuck in my mind was the question of those lifeboats. It was too late to go back to their aid. I doubted if they could weather that violent squall, but there was nothing to do but hope they would get safely to land. I learned it was a vain hope when, sometime later, I saw my name on the 'murderers' list' in connection with the sinking of the *Porto di Rodi.* The boats had been lost. Nothing was known of my provisions for the safety of the crew. It was thought that I had sunk the ship with all on board."

Another prime incident of this period of warfare in the Mediterranean, and one very much within the law, came in January of 1917, when Kurt Hartwig got the big British battleship *Cornwallis.*

Off the cliffs of Malta. A brilliant morning. The sea stretches away with that deep, glowing blue which makes the Mediterranean splendid. A German U-boat

idles along awash.   The lookout on deck shouts a
warning:

"Smoke on the horizon."

There is a dull misty smudge on the skyline.   The
sea closes rippling over steel deck and conning tower.
The distant shadowy blot on the clear blue of sky
magnifies and deepens.   Funnels come into view and
a formidable bulk.   It's a big battleship.   Its guns
point in a menacing series, and it flies the war ensign
of Great Britain.   The huge ship zigzags from side
to side, and around it circles a swift destroyer, searching the expanse of water for the sign of a periscope.

There is a periscope yonder, but it is far distant
now, and it has disappeared before battleship and
destroyer have come near enough to see.   Below the
surface in the conning tower the big blond Hartwig
slaps his broad chest with elation.   The same Commander Kurt Hartwig who had been put on the
"murderer's list" by the Allies after the sinking of the
Porto di Rodi.

"She's coming as if she were catapulted right at us,"
he cries.   "She'll run us down if we're not careful.
We don't have to move ten feet for a shot."

The battleship, indeed, seems bent on its doom.   Its
zigzagging course is carrying it hard upon the submarine.   Hartwig shows his periscope for fleeting instants.
She is the great British battleship *Cornwallis,* the
giant which fired the first shell in the bombardment
of the Dardanelles.   It is too easy.   He has no difficulty in getting into a position where the leviathan
will thunder along across his stern not two hundred
and fifty feet away.   A dead shot for any skillful
marksman with torpedoes.

Two stern torpedoes leave the tubes.   A bubbling
on the surface and the white track of the missiles is
seen.   Two heavy explosions in rapid succession.   The
battleship is hit in the engine rooms.   The U-boat is

plunging to a hundred feet. Hartwig expects the destroyer to come rushing. It does. A crash to one side, and the submarine shakes ominously. A ringing explosion overhead. Another somewhat farther away. The music of the depth charges is not pleasant. The U-boat is scooting away under water as fast as it can and loses the sound of exploding bombs.

Thirty minutes drag on, slowly, blindly under the sea. Then a periscope pops up on the surface. The battleship is lying deep in the water, but not listing. The destroyer is taking survivors aboard. The periscope is spied. Instantly the destroyer is around and charging. She hopes to ram the submerged enemy. She strikes nothing. The U-boat has dived and is clear. As the destroyer passes over the place where the periscope was seen she drops a sprinkling of depth charges off her stern. Again the men in the iron shell a hundred feet below the surface of the sea listen to the menacing rhythm of the bombs. They are lucky— explosions on all sides but none near enough to damage.

"We'll have to hit her again," Hartwig turns to his watch officer. "She won't sink, and they'll take her in tow."

They would, doubtless. Malta is only twenty miles away and the stricken battleship seems in good enough condition to be towed that far.

"If that destroyer would only let us alone," murmurs the watch officer.

But of course the destroyer won't. That would be too much magnanimity.

The battleship is stationary now, a still target, and a long shot is possible. The periscope shows momentarily in the distance and is not seen. Once or twice more it is thrust above the blue water. And now bubbles and a torpedo track from a distance of almost three quarters of a mile. It is seen long before it is near the helpless giant. There is nothing to do. The ship cannot move an inch, much less swing around to avoid the missile. The only thing that can possibly be done is for the destroyer to chase out there where the torpedo track was first seen. It goes, charging like an angry bull.

The sea mammoth, impotent, unmoving, waiting for the deadly blow. The torpedo strikes the engine room again with a sickening explosion. The stricken monster shakes as with a dying convulsion and lists to one side. A mile away and a hundred feet below the placid surface of the Mediterranean men listen to popping detonations. The sounds are weak. The depth bombs are exploding far away. The U-boat is able to get a safe start before the destroyer arrives to drop its affectionate message.

Half an hour later the periscope peeps cautiously. The battleship is lying over on one side. Its crew is aboard the destroyer and in lifeboats lying alongside. In a submerged conning tower a brief colloquy is spoken.

"Shall we get the destroyer?" asks the watch officer.

"No," replies Hartwig, "a battleship is enough for one day."

"*Ja, ja,*" the watch officer assents gladly.

It would be too inhuman, even for the submarine warfare, to torpedo the destroyer crammed with survivors of the battleship—although that swift, buzzing craft had been a pestilential hornet.

The radio operator reports a radio message he has picked up:

"H. M. S. *Cornwallis* sunk by submarine."

CHAPTER XX

VOYAGES OF ILL OMEN AND THE PHANTOM SUBMARINE

In England navy men said to us, "See Spiegel; he's a fine chap." They knew him both as an adversary and a prisoner. And so in Berlin we looked up Adolf Karl Georg Edgar, Baron Spiegel von und zu Peckelsheim, who is very much of the *crème de la crème* of the German titled nobility.

In an apartment at Charlottenburg (everybody in Berlin seems to live in an apartment) we sat and talked and had dinner: Baron von Spiegel, who looks like a young very well-turned-out Englishman, his pretty Baroness, and her nephew, the son of Admiral Tägert, who during the war was German Chief of Staff at Constantinople. It was a lavishly furnished place, with a fortune in pictures and furnishings, the dinner was fit for any epicure, and the talk—well, Baron von Spiegel's career has been sufficiently varied. A social figure in German aristocratic life, he sought adventure in far lands and took part in a native revolution in New Guinea. As a naval officer in the halcyon days before the war, he saw life and gaiety in many a strange port. Then he became a raider of the deep and a prisoner of the British, and finally engaged in the ups and downs of commerce. After the war he started to build a fortune in the shipping business. The German financial collapse hit him hard. He turned to the automobile trade to recoup, and now is making good as the German representative of the

169

American Graham-Paige car. The Baron's narration was woven around a familiar theme, Friday the 13th:

I am a sailor, and a sailor is supposed to be superstitious. I went to sea, not romantically before the mast, but as a cadet officer in the good old days when the life of an officer in the German Navy was a kind of idyll, with a gay social career, fine cruises all over the world, and nothing to worry about. Nevertheless, although I did not learn the tradition of the forecastle among the Jack Tars themselves, I saw enough of the sea and gathered enough of its moody lore to know that Friday the 13th is unlucky. Perhaps you are a landlubber and don't believe it. Go to sea and you'll find out.

The year was 1915, the month January, the date the 13th, and the day of the week Friday. The naval authorities should have known better, but then admirals have a way of not paying much attention to the ideas and preferences of seamen. Three U-boats put out from Wilhelmshaven for a cruise of the North Sea, the *U-22* under Commander Hoppe, the *U-31* under Commander Wachendorff, and my boat, the *U-32*. I will tell you the story of these three craft that stood out to sea that morning of Friday the 13th.

Of my boat there is little to relate. We had merely a straight, consistent run of ordinary bad luck. Our mission was to lie off the mouth of the Thames and see if we could not strike some small blow at Britain's naval might. From the day we left to the day we returned the most terrible storms raged. Our gauge for measuring the force of the wind was numbered from one to twelve. We registered eleven time after time. The waves broke incessantly over our conning tower, and as for the deck, it was the scene of one continual deluge, where every man had to be lashed down. Between that and the unbelievable pitching of the boat we had an epidemic of broken arms, legs, and shoulders. We were at sea for nine days and did not sight one single solitary ship. We put back into port on the 22d, and neither of the two other boats had returned. We worried more and more as day after day went by and no sign of them.

Five days later the news flashed that the *U-22* was coming in. On our boat we all crowded on deck and cheered and waved as the missing craft steered toward the mooring place. Men and officers stood on the deck of the oncoming craft, but no sign of response did they give our hearty greeting. They were like graven images. Their faces were white and drawn. They looked like a phantom crew back from the realm of death. Hoppe, the commander, had unforgettable lines of horror in his face.

The *U-22* docked. Hoppe, moving like an automaton, stepped onto the pier and made his way to the flotilla chief. He saluted with a stiff jerky movement.

"I have to report," he addressed his superior officer in a breaking voice, "I have to report that I have torpedoed the *U-7*. There is one survivor, a member of the crew."

The commander of the *U-7* was George Koenig, Hoppe's best friend. The two men had been inseparable for years. When you saw Koenig you always looked for Hoppe. They ate together, drank together, and what belonged to one belonged also to the other.

It was the custom to inform U-boat commanders by wireless of the presence of other U-boats in their vicinity. Something had slipped up. Hoppe had caught no message that Koenig was operating in his own zone. Submarine ahoy! It was running awash in the distance. All under-sea craft look alike, friend or enemy, when seen from afar. To make sure, Hoppe sent up signal lights, but it was late afternoon and Hoppe was looking straight into the sun. He could not see the answering signals that Koenig sent. Another signal and another response, and again it was invisible to Hoppe. He thought the craft was an Englishman, submerged, and made a perfect torpedo attack. A violent explosion, and an iron hulk dropped to the bottom.

Hoppe hastened to the scene of the sinking. One man was swimming in the boiling sea. The men of the *U-22* hauled him aboard, and instantly Hoppe saw on his cap the insignium *Deutsche Unterseeboots Flottille* of the *U-7,* the boat commanded by his lifelong friend, Koenig.

Two years later Hoppe was killed when his U-boat was destroyed by the Q-ship commanded by the famous Gordon Campbell.

The third boat, the *U-31,* never came back. Weeks and months went by and nothing was heard of her. She had simply vanished, and we supposed she had struck a mine. Six months later she created sensations as "the phantom submarine."

You know the old case of the ship manned by dead men. During the war the instance was known of an airplane rushing around in the sky with a dead man at the stick. And now for the dead men's submarine.

A U-boat above water nosed its way slowly along. Nothing seemed amiss. It looked trim and menacing, as if ready to dive and launch a torpedo at any moment. It was drifting before the wind, though, and finally ran ashore on the eastern coast of England. Astonished fisherman sent out an alarm. Naval men came hurrying. The U-boat lay rocking, aground on a sand bar. They boarded the craft, took her in tow to harbour and dock, and discovered an eerie riddle.

The U-boat, which was the same *U-31* that had left port that Friday the 13th six months before, was in perfect order. She might be on active cruise, save for one thing. Officers and men were in their bunks and hammocks, as if asleep—they were dead. In the log the last entry was dated six months before. The boat, the daily account showed, had steered out of Wilhelmshaven on one of the early U-boat cruises of war. It had encountered no untoward happening. Its voyage had been ordinary and uneventful. The record made humdrum reading, until it suddenly broke off that day six months before, and after that a mysterious blank.

It was a nine day's wonder. This dead man's boat had seemingly been cruising around for six months over the heavily patroled waters of the North Sea. It sounded like a case of spooks. Naval men could find only one explanation for the unearthly phenomenon, and this explanation is no doubt the true one.

The U-boat had gone to the bottom for the night, as was often done. Officers and men had turned in to sleep, while the craft lay securely on the floor of the sea. In that case, one man would very likely have been left on guard, but he may have been tempted to take a comfortable nap, too: a nap from which he never awoke. Poison gases, such as submarines, particularly of the older types, were likely to generate, had crept into the places where the men lay and had suffocated them as they slept. Then the boat lay on the bottom. The compressed air leaked little by little. As month after month went by it gradually blew the tanks, until, finally, the boat was buoyant enough to rise to the surface. Its resting place on the bottom had been near the coast, and in a few hours it had drifted to shore.

That was the prize ghostly episode in the tale of the raiders of the deep.

You would have thought that would have been enough of Friday the 13th. I made a solemn vow never again to sail on that ill-omened day. Nevertheless, in spite of vows, sense, and wisdom, my last cruise began on Friday the 13th. I might have known it would be the last. At any rate, it brought my voyages under the sea to an abrupt close and in a most unexpected and startling way. It was in April of 1917, an eventful month which saw the outbreak of the Easter rebellion in Ireland and the surrender of General Townshend at Kut-el-Amara in Mesopotamia.

Before this cruise I went to a hospital, where I was sent to rest up and be treated for a case of weak heart. Submarine men were likely to break down with nerve strain of some kind or other and were constantly being sent away to recuperate. The ordeal of life aboard the U-boats, with the constant stress of peril and terror, was too much for human flesh to bear for long stretches. Some men went mad. Others, after periods of rest and medication, came around and were, or perhaps were not, fit for under-sea service again. All felt the grinding pressure. I recall receiving a present just before going out on a cruise. It was from a manufacturer of nerve tonic and consisted of a case of his medicine. An appropriate gift it was. My case of weak heart was enough to confine me to a sanitarium for several weeks. It was in 1916. I had been in the U-boat service since before the war and had faced the music, all kinds of music, and most unpleasant music.

The weak heart had not been helped by one particular incident. We were dodging destroyers and sneaking along under water. And then something hit me. A terrible blow on the head, and I lost consciousness. I came to in a few seconds and quickly realized what had happened. We had made the acquaintance of a mine. The explosion had knocked me down and crashed my head on the floor. I was sure we were sinking. A submarine doesn't hit a mine and go se-

renely on its way. But no, the boat was sound and
water-tight. Word came from the helmsman that he
could not steer. I soon realized that we were in a net.
We had not hit the mine directly. We were attached
to the net and the mine had exploded near us.

We tore our way out of the net, and then came the
worst of it. We found ourselves in a predicament of
a sort that had occurred before in the case of other
U-boats. We were swathed in the net and were dragging it along with us. The big, snake-like cork float
that had supported it trailed along behind us on the
surface of the water. Naturally, the destroyers up
there did not miss the interesting sight of the float
running along on the surface of the water. They followed us around, and we knew it from the sound of
their propellers. It was only at nightfall that we
could get rid of those disagreeable bloodhounds that
were sticking to our trail up there.

I came out of the sanitarium feeling quite chipper
and ready for another under-water assignment and
was straightway given command of the *U-93*, a big
modern boat. I took most of my old crew with me.
We knew each other thoroughly, had been in many a
tight corner together, and there was a fine brotherly
feeling among us. We put the *U-93* through several
weeks of practice drills, and then cruising orders came.
We were to stand out from Emden on Friday, April
13, 1917.

The crew were ready for mutiny when they heard
it, and I had to use my best persuasions to quiet them
down.

"Boys," I made them a speech, "you are all wrong
about this. This is all superstition and foolishness.
Only a *Dummkopf* would pay any attention to it. But
even if Friday is unlucky and the 13th is unlucky, why
then one piece of bad luck counteracts the other, just
like two weights in a balance."

They didn't think much of what I said, and neither did I. That Friday the 13th business was bad, and I knew it. I went to our flotilla chief and asked him to phone Wilhelmshaven and beg permission for us to put off our sailing until the 14th. He telephoned. Permission refused. I could scarcely keep the crew from an open outbreak.

We put out from Emden on the 13th, and arrived at Heligoland that evening. We passed the night there, and in the morning I made another address to the men.

"We can consider," I said, "that we are sailing on the 14th. Are we not starting out now? And is this not the 14th?"

They grumbled and muttered and still were not convinced. Neither was I.

We steered through the North Sea, past the Shetland Islands and into the Atlantic. The weather was abominable. Day after day it stormed with shrieking wind and raging sea. On top of that, we had to run submerged most of the time. We had to dodge an unusually large number of patrol vessels, destroyers, and trawlers.

"Yes, yes," I heard the crew growling, "Friday the 13th."

In the Atlantic the weather changed to warm, gentle winds and brilliant sunshine. We cruised back and forth across the shipping lanes, but caught sight of nothing to attack. Five days passed and we spied not a single craft of any description.

"Friday the 13th," grumbled the crew.

On the fifth day we at last met a vessel—a German U-boat. It was the *U-43*, under Commander Juerst, a good friend and quite a paladin among the under-sea skippers. Quite recently he had struck a notable blow against the enemy. The *U-43* raided the waters in front of the Russian Arctic port of Archangel, through which sorely needed supplies were pouring into hard-pressed Russia. Juerst wreaked havoc among the ships loaded with supplies and munitions, sank vessel after vessel, and ran his tonnage list way up. Another exploit of his was the sinking of the *Bistritza* with an eleven-million-dollar cargo of munitions intended for the Rumanians.

The two U-boats held a comradely reunion there on the ocean. Juerst was on his way back to Germany after having had a fine hunting trip.

"Go three hundred miles to the southwest," he told me; "the ships are following a new track. You will find plenty there."

My men listened skeptically, growling their old complaint—"Friday the 13th." I laid a southwesterly course, according to Juerst's directions. Friday the 13th, indeed! The *U-93* promptly found itself in the position of a hunter swamped by partridges or quail.

We got a dozen ships in rapid succession the following week. Some were armed and we torpedoed them, but in nearly every case the crews were able to take safely to their lifeboats. I took aboard five captains and a dozen gunners, British naval men who, according to the rules, were prisoners of war. They were our guests aboard the *U-93* and we got along well enough with them, although, of course, they didn't quite enjoy the perils of the new life they were leading.

Of one ship there were no survivors. She was an armed American vessel. The United States had recently come into the war. I sent a torpedo at her from five hundred yards. In a couple of seconds a frightful detonation rang out and the *U-93* received a heavy blow. We were hurled to the floor and every electric light bulb on the boat was shattered. I thought we had been rammed, and scrambled to the periscope. The 7,000-ton steamer had disappeared.

A vast cloud of smoke billowed on the sea. The air was full of falling débris. The ship's smokestack was falling to the water, whirling like a pinwheel. The ship must have been crammed with munitions.

A fine big steamer hove in sight. It was not armed. We stopped it. The crew took to their boats and we steered over to look at their papers. The ship was bound from Egypt with a cargo of eggs. A cheer went up from the deck of the *U-93*. You can't imagine how tired a man can get of hard tack, pea soup, bacon, and canned stuff. Our foraging party that day worked like the heroes they were. We took ten thousand eggs aboard our craft. Every available bit of space was crammed with eggs. A few thousand went bad in the course of time, and rotten eggs aboard a U-boat are no *eau de cologne*. But for a while we had our fill. I saw one burly mechanic frying twelve eggs for breakfast one morning.

"Now what about your talk of Friday the 13th?" I called.

We had one torpedo left, and were nearly ready to turn homeward. It was sundown of a clear, balmy spring day. A big steamer came along, the British ship *Horsa*. With our last torpedo we scored a clean hit at the bow. She sank very quickly. Her stern rose into the air and she went down like an airplane in a nose dive.

It seemed as if her crew could hardly have had time to take to their lifeboats. Dusk was lowering on the ocean and we could not see much. We came above water and steered over to the place where the vessel had disappeared. Shouts sounded in the darkness, and we could see a black bulge on the water. A lifeboat was floating upside down, and around it men were crowded and clinging desperately to it. We came alongside and dragged them aboard. Some had arms and legs broken by the force with which they had been knocked down when the torpedo hit. The first officer was badly hurt.

We were men hardened by war. Incessant danger and the sight of death had dulled our sensibility to horror. And yet my men were naturally kind-hearted. The sight of those poor fellows battered and broken on our deck touched them sharply. They held a veritable competition of doing things for them. They put splints on legs and arms and administered drugs from our medicine chest. Some gave up their bunks to our injured prisoners.

Strange sounds came from the overturned lifeboat, weak calling and knocking. Two men had been caught beneath it and were holding themselves afloat inside. They were too weak to dive and swim out, and were held there as if in a prison—a rather terrible prison, too. My men got out grappling hooks and tried to turn the lifeboat over. They worked for an hour, but could not make it. We had no facilities for that kind of work aboard. Finally one fellow tied a rope around his waist, dived, and, swimming below water, made his way under the boat. There he took hold of the two men and dragged them out.

The next morning we sighted a Swedish sailing ship. I started toward it. Our forward gun was making ready to drop a shot across her bow when I saw shells falling around her. Somebody had got there before us. Sure enough, on the other side of the ship was a U-boat. It was the *U-21* under Commander Hersing. The crew of the sailing ship were tumbling into their boats. The prize was Hersing's. While he sank it, I stopped the lifeboats and made them take aboard the survivors of the *Horsa*—there were seventeen of them. The *U-21* and the *U-93* drew alongside of each other to pass the time of day, and then each picked up its respective course.

After all is said and done, Friday the 13th means

something. Every man of the crew was sure that we were destined to encounter some mishap or other before we got back to port, and would have been disappointed, I am sure, if everything had gone well. I, myself, could not escape a nervous tingle of apprehension.

We sank the Greek steamer *Phaleron,* bound from the United States to England, and then started for home. But without my knowing it Dame Fortune had decreed that years were to roll by before I saw home and my wife again.

CHAPTER XXI

TRAPPED BY A Q-SHIP, OUR JAUNTY BARON SEES HIS BOAT SINK BENEATH HIS FEET

At sunset I was sitting at supper in our little officers' messroom. From near by came loud, gay talk in English. Our prisoners, the five captains, were having their evening meal. We were running awash.

"Sailing ship ahoy!" the call came.

I hurried to the conning tower and, telescope at eye, scrutinized a little three-mast schooner to our starboard.

A warning shell at a distance of four thousand yards, and the schooner lowered her topsails. The crew took to the lifeboats. Everything looked all right, but I was suspicious. I had heard of sailing ships with British submarines in tow—neat trap. Then when a U-boat drew to fire a few shells at the water line, it was saluted with a torpedo.

"Keep on firing," I called to our gun crew, and then sent the order through the speaking tube: "Half speed ahead."

I wanted to investigate, and we might as well be certain that the ship was abandoned before we drew too near. The sun was sinking below the horizon and dusk was gathering.

We drew up slowly, our shells popping on the deserted deck. "Good shooting," I remarked to my two companions, Lieutenants Ziegner and Usedom. The schooner's deck was a mass of wreckage. The *U-93*

181

circled around the craft while we all scanned it through our powerful binoculars. No, it had no submarine in tow, and was surely deserted. Nobody would stay aboard and take that amount of shelling. We were only eighty yards away, lying parallel with it, when I gave the order.

"Hit her at the water line and sink her."

As our first shell hit just at the water line, there was a loud whistle aboard the schooner. The white war ensign of Great Britain ran up the mast. A movable gun platform slid into view. A roar and a rattling, and 7.5 cm. guns opened at us, and machine guns, too. We offered a fair, broadside target. One shell put our fore gun out of commission and wounded several of the gun crew. Another crashed into our hull.

"Both engines full speed!" I yelled; "helm hard aport!"

The *U-93* leaped forward and swung around quickly, so that it was stern on to the enemy. More shells hit us while she turned the quarter circle.

"Was zum Teufel!" (What the devil!) I felt the vibration of our engines stop. Yes, the engines were cut off. I had given no such command. The only explanation was that the shell fire had damaged them. We were now only five hundred yards away from the muzzles of those large, fire-spurting guns, and were drifting slowly around. Engines stopped and one gun disabled—that was uncomfortable. Shells were striking the boat and exploding with savage pow—pows.

"Man the after gun!" I shouted.

We had one piece of ordnance left, could still put up a fight. Three men responded to the command. I leaped aft with them, and we four worked the gun. A shell burst in our faces. The petty officer of the gun crew fell back with his head blown off. Then I felt a cold sensation about my legs. We were up to our knees in water.

A moment later we were swimming in the Atlantic. The *U-93* had sunk beneath us. I could see her black shadow vanish in the depths of the ocean. A dreadful pang of anguish shot through me at the thought of my fine new boat and my crew going down to their last port on the cold, silent bottom of the sea, and a touch of ironic pity for those five captains who, skippers of prosaic freighters, had never signed any papers with articles about making a last voyage in an iron coffin. "Friday the 13th!" That damned idea flashed into my mind. No time for thinking; I myself was drowning. My heavy leather jacket encumbered me so that I could scarcely move my arms. I tried to work it off, but could not. My thick, warm clothes beneath it were absorbing water and becoming like a suit of leaden armour. My fur-lined boots with thick wooden soles were sodden. They pulled me down as if they were iron weights attached to my feet.

I was sinking when I heard shouts and saw a black shadow in the dusk. I yelled in return and struggled with renewed courage.

"Hello—keep going—we'll be there in a minute," the calls came cheerily. I replied with shouts between gulps of water.

The last thing I remember is seeing a small boat only five yards away. When I recovered my senses I was on the deck of the schooner. They told me I was going down when the boat reached me. The British officer who happened to be at the wheel had to jump into the ocean after me. The boat had also picked up the other two men who were at the gun with me when the *U-93* sank.

The little schooner, which hadn't seemed worth bothering about—I wish we hadn't—was the *Prize*, the British *Q-21*. Those Britishers played that Q-ship game with skill and nerve. The *Prize* was little more than a tin shell filled with wood. She was stuffed with lumber, the idea being to keep her afloat as long as possible as little more than a camouflaged gun platform. Any other species of craft would have sunk a couple of times from the damage our shells did. We had shot her pretty nearly to pieces. The deck was knocked into kindling wood, and below every wall was smashed. You could see through partition after partition into ten rooms. I marvelled at the bravery of these Britishers who in their hiding place could take a shelling like that and then run their gun platform out and start to fight. Some of them had been wounded during the encounter.

An officer took me to his cabin and himself pulled off my sodden clothes and heavy boots. He rubbed me dry with a towel and then gave me some of his own clothes to put on. I was still shaking with cold. He thought it was fright and pointed to a motto on the wall which read: "We are all brothers in Christianity." Those Britishers lived up to the motto in the way they took care of their prisoners. While I was being made comfortable in the cabin the sailors were taking care of my two men.

A little while later I was in the officers' mess, where they gave me cocoa and cigarettes. Suddenly a petty officer reported:

"We are sinking, sir."

"Eh," I said to myself, "evidently I have been saved only to be lost again! Blast this Friday the 13th!"

The *Prize* was in a sinking condition. Our shells had bored some pretty holes at the water line. Men were working frantically, trying to plug them. Others laboured at the furiously rattling pumps. The boat promised to sink at any minute.

"Fire!" the shout rang out.

"Friday the 13th," I groaned.

Our shell fire had destroyed one of the *Prize's* auxiliary motors, and when they started the other one it took fire for some reason or other. I saw an officer go streaking by with a fire extinguisher. He put out the blaze. That was my first glimpse of Lieutenant W. E. Sanders, the skipper of the *Prize.*

A bit later he came into the officers' mess, a tall, slender chap in his twenties with a good-looking English face, fine brown eyes, and blond hair which sprawled all over his head.

"Where is the U-boat captain?" he demanded.

I stood up, and he came to me with a good, friendly smile and grasped my hand.

"My dear fellow," he said, "I am sorry for you. Please feel that you are my guest. But," he exclaimed ruefully, "I'm sorry I can't give you better quarters, especially as we are about ready to sink."

He was a New Zealander, a soldier, a sailor, and a gentleman. I felt it was not so bad to have been defeated by such a fine chap and his nervy crew.

They tried to cheer me, for I looked pretty glum. It was of no use. I couldn't forget my crew, my friends going down out there, drowned like rats in a trap, with some perhaps left to die of slow suffocation. I could imagine how some might even now be alive in the strong torpedo compartments, lying in the darkness, hopeless, waiting for the air to thicken and finally smother them. No, they were not rapping on the iron hull. They knew no help could ever reach them. Aboard the *U-93* we had been like a gang of brothers. Most of my men had been with me from the beginning of the war. In summer the whole crowd had often visited my country place. There was not room in the house for them all, and some of the men slept in the haystacks. At times I took them on pleasure jaunts, and always we laughed and joked together. And then

the prisoners—the British sailors of the gun crews—
well, they had enlisted for warfare; but the unfortunate five merchant captains—those skippers certainly
had been caught in the toils of evil destiny. That
night I could not sleep. I was haunted by the vision of
my boat going down, of that vanishing dark shadow I
had seen while I lay struggling in the water.

The *Prize* was in a bad way. The pumps struggled their hardest against the water that poured in.
All possible weight was shifted from the side where
the shell holes were, so that the gaping rents might be
kept above water. Luckily the ocean was perfectly
calm. If any kind of sea began to run at all she would
sink in a few minutes. Nor could the boat get under
way. The wireless had been shot away and she could
not call for help. There was no wind for the sails
and the motor would not start. The English machinist
had no experience with Diesel engines and was helpless. Sanders came to me in desperation.

"Captain," he asked, "do your men know anything
about Diesels?"

"Why, one of them is an expert," I responded.

Among the two that had been saved along with me
was Deppe, who knew Diesel engines as a parson
knows his Bible. I ordered him to the motor. A few
minutes later I heard the engine start. Deppe came
back strutting.

"They know nothing about motors," he observed
loftily.

The *Prize* was under way now, with the motor
whirring. If she had had to lie there motionless much
longer she would probably have encountered weather
that would have sent her down. We had been able to
lend our captors a lively hand at a time when it
counted, a small return for the handsome way we had
been treated.

The sea remained calm, and for three days and a

half we headed toward the English coast at a rate of two and a half miles an hour. Then a British cruiser hove in sight and took the *Prize* in tow to Kinsale Harbour in the south of Ireland. In port I immediately had a bath and washed my clothes. I found three handkerchiefs in my pockets and was happy. With such trifles can a tragedy of the sea be forgotten for a while.

A steamer took the *Prize* in tow next day and we started across the Bristol Channel to Milford Haven. I sat on the deck of the shell-blasted hulk watching the dim coast of Ireland through a glass.

"Hey, what's this?" I said to myself.

In the distance I saw the conning tower of a submarine. I could recognize the craft as one of those built at the Germania yards at Kiel.

The officer of the deck was near me, scanning the sea with his glass.

"Sailboat over there," he said to me offhand.

From afar the conning tower of a submarine often looks like the sail of a ship.

"Yes, sailboat," I responded in a musing voice.

The U-boat was coming our way. I wondered what its commander some comrade of mine, thought of the steamer towing this stack of lumber which they called the *Prize*.

"Submarine ahoy!" the alarm went around.

All hands scurried about, preparing for a fight.

"And now," said I to myself, "I will learn what it is like on this side of the fence."

The U-boat submerged. Of course, my brother in arms down there was not going to walk right up to anything so strange and possibly suspicious as this steamer towing a battered hulk. Generally speaking, it looked as if somebody might get torpedoed. No, it wasn't amusing on this side of the fence.

It seemed as if the bad luck of that ill-omened

departure was still on our trail and determined to have a finishing go at us. Our steamer with the *Prize* in tow could do nothing to elude a torpedo shot. I expected an explosion at any moment.

A cloud of smoke, and a flotilla of destroyers came rushing along. That eased the situation a lot. The U-boat would attempt no attack with that school of fishes around. The surmise was correct. We saw no further sign of the submarine. I afterward learned that it was commanded by my friend, Commander Ernst Hashagen, and when I saw him again I cussed him out roundly for having given me such a fright.

We arrived at Milford Haven in the morning.

Lieutenant Sanders shook hands with me and wished me godspeed, at the same time asking the officers who were taking me away to treat me well. That was the last I ever saw of the gallant young officer. He was given the Victoria Cross for his brave fight against the *U-93*. Later he carried on in the *Prize*, which had been repaired for further Q-ship duty. One day the *Prize* encountered a U-boat, but this time it was an unlucky day for Sanders and his men. The *Prize* was sunk, and her captain and crew went down with her.

The officers in whose charge I was took me to breakfast, a real British breakfast and not the continental rolls and coffee. We had kippers and eggs and marmalade. They were spick-and-span in their smart uniforms. I felt like a tramp. My uniform was stained with grease and salt water, the gold braid was green, and one trouser leg was a dreadful sight to look at. A deflected machine-gun bullet had ripped it and I had sewed it up with white thread—what sewing!

One of them began to question me. I made it clear that I was disinclined to talk about my boat, but told him of the five captains who were aboard the *U-93* when she disappeared and gave him the names

Adolf Karl Georg Edgar Baron
Spiegel von und zu Peckelsheim.

Ziegner (right) and Usedom, who escaped
in their riddled U-boat.

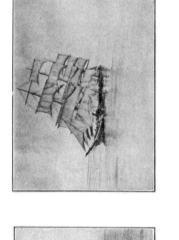

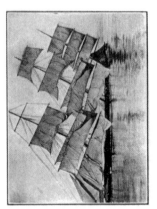

A tragic idyll of the sea. Shelled at the waterline by a U-boat, a fine old windjammer takes her final plunge.

of their boats, so that their relatives might be informed of their loss. The officer understood my reticence and said:

"I have only one more question. Do you know who sank the *Horsa?*"

What the deuce was the matter now, I wondered. Certainly we of the *U-93* had behaved ourselves well and magnanimously in the case of the *Horsa.*

"I sank the *Horsa,*" I replied.

I was scarcely prepared for the effect this statement made. My questioner jumped to his feet and grasped my hand.

"I have wanted to meet the man," he exclaimed, "who rescued and took care of a crew as you and your men did."

The survivors of the *Horsa,* upon getting to shore, had talked to the high heavens of the way we of the *U-93* had used them, especially of our fishing the men from under the boat.

"Strange how destiny works," I mused. I had been in the U-boat warfare for two years and a half—and a cruel iron warfare it was. I had sunk many ships and drowned many men, and never once had I or my command found an opportunity to do anything exceptional in the way of a good, human deed—save in the case of the *Horsa.* And now that one good deed, which had taken place just before I was captured, had come back to me with a swift blessing. I had already been treated well by my captors, and from now on, I knew, would be treated better.

Donnington Hall, I was told, was the best prison camp in England, and if there were any better they must have been de luxe places indeed. It was one of the most beautiful country seats in England, a great gray castle in a perfect setting on green lawns and oak trees. Sheep were grazing on the meadows and birds singing in the trees. The only things to mar the general aspect of sylvan delight was a barbed wire fence, high and formidable around the prison enclosure, and a line of armed guards. There I met a number of U-boat officers, a zeppelin commander, and various military officers. They were a jolly company in a lovely place. The only trouble was that it was a prison.

[In a wartime issue of a British newspaper I ran across an account of a dispute in the House of Commons over the excessive expenditures incurred in fitting up Donnington Hall for a German officers' prison camp. Donnington Hall has long been the most famous country seat in Leicestershire, its history going back to the Tudor period. It was once the seat of the Hastings family. The remodelling of the house for the German officers, and the putting in of bathrooms and billiard tables, brought forth much ironic comment in the House of Commons. "Great idea," one Britisher remarked; "make it so comfortable they won't ever want to go back to Germany!"]

The Commandant was a hook-nosed Britisher with a big, fearful mustache. Lieutenant Piquot he was, a formidable name that I shall never forget. He had fierce ways and a gruff, fierce voice. When he talked at you, you thought he was going to eat you. I was afraid of him at first, but presently I found that Piquot always growled. Growling was his natural language. He growled the most when he was the most pleasantly disposed toward me.

"The Admiralty," he said with his gruffest voice and most forbidding expression, "has sent instructions that we are to see that you are comfortable."

"You will make me comfortable if you will smile— just once," I felt like saying, but prudence persuaded me to confine my remarks to a mere "thank you."

We prisoners were not allowed by the regulations to write more than two letters home each week, but I

was given permission to send any number. I wrote
first to my wife and then to the families of each member of my crew. It was a mournful task. I did my
best to cheer the ones bereft by telling them that their
loved ones had died heroically in the performance of
their duty and for their Fatherland. I did not have
to invent one particle when I spoke of the affection I
had for each man.

Three weeks after my entrance into the prison
camp I heard an astonishing report. The *U-93* had
got back to Germany. It was impossible! Why, I
had seen that boat ripped and smashed by shell fire.
And then she had gone down beneath my very feet.
So I scarcely dared believe the report until I talked to
the tigerish Piquot.

"It's true," quoth he in his most tigerish. "It has
come from the captains you had as prisoners."

Later on I was to learn the story of what had
happened, and that story, I think you will agree with
me when you hear it, is indeed one of the epic tales
of the World War.

CHAPTER XXII

WHEN WE FOUND OUR VOICES IT WAS TO ORDER A BOTTLE OF PORT

Not only did I hear the story of that return trip to Germany from Baron von Spiegel, but better still I got a detailed account of it from the man who had been largely responsible for it—the young watch officer who assumed command and navigated the battered *U-93* over a two thousand mile course back to the naval base at Wilhelmshaven.

Lieutenant Wilhelm Ziegner had joined up for U-boat service at the beginning of 1917, and the trip on the *U-93*, begun on that fateful Friday the 13th, had been his first cruise. The submarine had not gone to the bottom as Baron von Spiegel believed. It had dropped only a few feet below the surface, enough for the sea to sweep him away, and then had bobbed up again some distance off. Although he had had only a few weeks of actual fighting experience, Lieutenant Ziegner, hardly more than a boy, had stepped into the place of his vanished commander and accomplished what both German and English naval men speak of as an epic submarine cruise.

After it had been repaired young Ziegner went on several more cruises on the big *U-93*. Its new captain, after it was put back into service, was Commander Helmuth Gerlach. But in 1918 Ziegner had a siege of tonsilitis that kept him home from one cruise. His luck was still with him, for the *U-93* never returned from that voyage. She was rammed by a British destroyer in the Channel and went down with all hands.

After that, Lieutenant Ziegner was given a command of his own—a little UC-submarine. When the Armistice came he was one of the four German submarine commanders who put into a Swedish port and chose to be interned rather than go back to Germany and turn their boats over to the revolutionists. He remained in active service for another year. Then the throat infection, which had kept him ashore and saved his life two years before, brought about a fatal attack of diphtheria. He died in the naval hospital at Wilhelmshaven in December, 1919. The following account of his return journey in Baron von Spiegel's U-boat was taken from his diary and his letters to his mother:

I was standing on the conning tower when that sailing ship cut loose with her broadside. A murderous fire, a shell bursting seemingly in front of my face, and the next thing I knew I was picking myself up from where I had been knocked senseless. We were half awash; the boat was out of command and leaping about crazily. Faintly visible through the dusk was the sailing ship, still spitting fire.

I sprang up, forgetting my bursting head and the million stars I was counting.

"Hard to starboard!" I yelled to the man at the helm.

At the same moment Lieutenant Usedom rushed up from below, shouting, "Where is the *Kommandant?*"

"He must be below with you," I answered. I was giving all my attention to keeping the boat on a zigzag course to dodge the enemy shells still coming over us. With a 14-degree list to starboard, the *U-93* lay half under water. I expected every moment to see her sink under my feet.

Editor's Note: The UC submarine was a small, 168-ton coastal minelayer. This type carried no torpedoes or deck gun, just cargoes of six to twelve mines, and frequently laid off the French coast between Calais and Dunkirk and off the commercial harbors on England's southern coast.

A couple of wounded men were lying on deck, in the water. Usedom hurried to them, but the captain was not there. Crash! A shell buried itself under the conning tower. Another crash! A deafening detonation. Another shell exploded in the hatch leading to the captain's quarters. I had just given the order to dive, but the second explosion settled that. With those gaping holes, the *U-93* was no longer able to submerge. We could do nothing except stay on the surface and make a last effort to hobble out of range of the British fire. The thickening darkness was our ally there. In a few minutes we were hidden by the dusk and the clouds of shell smoke.

In the meantime, Usedom frantically searched the boat from bow to stern for the Captain. He was not to be found. Two other men were missing, the helmsman Knappe, and the machinist's mate Deppe. The explosion of the shell that had knocked me unconscious and half swamped the boat must have swept all three of them into the sea.

Our beloved Captain! Every man on board worshipped him. Somehow we just couldn't realize that he was lost. We were too helpless even to go back and look for him. For the moment every last ounce of energy had to be concentrated on keeping our crippled and leaking boat above water.

I could only surmise what havoc had been done in our engine rooms. Luckily it was not so bad as I imagined. The chief engineer and all hands below had been working furiously. He was able now to send up the report:

"All clear in the under-water compartments."

Gott sei Dank for that! For we had more than enough to worry us above deck. The *U-93* was a sorry sight, with her upper works shot to pieces and the deck pierced by eight gaping shell holes. The British could well be satisfied with the work their guns had done, even if they had failed to send us to the bottom as they undoubtedly supposed.

We took toll of the damage. One shell had mowed off both our periscopes. Another had torn open two of our starboard compressed-air compartments. For a distance of thirty feet the deck was nothing but a mass of ripped and shredded metal. Five diving tanks were blown open and three oil bunkers were leaking like sieves, leaving behind us a broad shimmering trail of oil. One depth gauge, three compressed air gauges, and a half-dozen other instruments in the central station were utterly useless.

All bad enough, but it was that shell hole in the hatchway that added the last straw. The hatch not only could not be closed for diving; it simply didn't exist any more. Our one really worthwhile weapon of defence—our ability to submerge—had been taken from us. If we tried to dive with that hole unrepaired —and we couldn't repair it—we would simply go straight to the bottom like a rock.

The *U-93* was no longer a submersible. Our one and only chance of escape now lay in our ability to sprint for it on the surface. A night's run at full speed would put plenty of distance between us and that shell-spitting sailing ship. Beyond that? Well, I could see little hope. Even if our luck held and guided us away from British destroyers and patrol boats, there was that tell-tale streak of oil behind us. Any craft could pick up our trail from it. The jinx of Friday the 13th had brought us to this pass. Now nothing but a change of luck could ever get us back to Germany.

We set our course due north, away from the shipping lanes. At last we could give some attention to our men. Six of the crew were wounded, worst of all, the boatswain's mate, a stout fellow named Bay. He had lain torn and bleeding on the steps of the conning tower, his groans and pleadings for help unanswered. Every man still able had joined in our first frantic efforts to get our machinery in order and keep the boat from foundering. Now the most we could do for him was to administer a merciful shot of morphine. He couldn't last long with those frightful wounds.

Two of our petty officers had their legs all but blown off. Usedom and the chief engineer got them and the other wounded into their bunks. They bandaged them as best they could. But they were in frightful agony, poor devils, and begged for opiates. Usedom told me about it afterward. "There I stood," he said, "with a bottle of morphine in one hand and a hypodermic needle in the other, without any idea as to how much I dared give them. I prayed that I was guessing right."

All that night I stayed on the conning tower, while Usedom worked with the wounded men and the chief engineer coddled his damaged machinery. The April night was starry and clear, the sea calm and silvery in the moonlight. It was a night for poetry, for romance. Instead, the tragedies of the hours just passed lay heavy on my mind. What had become of our gallant Captain? How could I, as senior officer now, keep the crew and the boat from further danger? And what would the next day bring?

The first thing it brought was the cook with a cup of hot coffee. My spirits rose fifty per cent. Then came Usedom with the sad news that Bay had died during the night. On our torn and battered deck we held the last rites for the dead. A short service, a prayer, and a body wrapped in the Imperial German war flag was lowered into the blue water that sparkled so gayly. The rest of the crew, excepting the wounded and the few who could not leave their stations, stood with bared heads. One remained below, whence came the steady throb of our Diesel engines carrying

Destroyers sealing the doom of an iron coffin with a depth bomb.

Another snaking torpedo finds its mark.

A U-boat shell hit her squarely amidships. Where the Caprera *had been was now a vast, billowing cloud of smoke.*

During the final years of the war the Germans started building these giant submarines.

us away from the North Atlantic shipping lanes. Above us on the conning tower stood the lookout on watch for that first sight of mast or smoke that might be the forerunner of disaster.

Then a short talk to the crew. With the loss of the Captain, I told them that I, as senior officer, would take command and try to get the boat back to Germany. A cheer went up. Every man stood ready to help to the last gasp. A fine lot were these boys who had been with our Captain so long.

More troubles were piling up. Part of the fresh water supply had been ruined by sea water getting into the tanks. Forty thirsty men and a water shortage! *Herr Gott!* That meant no bathing, no shaves, no cooked potatoes, short rations on coffee, and the smallest possible daily dole to every man.

The next report concerned our fuel oil. We had lost half of it already. While Usedom took over the navigation of the boat, the chief engineer and I sat over the charts reckoning and re-reckoning how far our remaining supply would carry us if we used the least amount possible. The short route home through the Channel was seldom used these days by U-boats in good working condition. Even the regular route around Scotland was out of the question for us. I talked it over with the bandaged and splinted pilot as he lay in his bunk. To avoid the patrol boats that swarmed about the British Isles, we set our course almost to Iceland and the Arctic Circle. By that circuitous route we had a journey of more than two thousand miles between us and Germany. Once off the Skagerrak, we could hope for German torpedo boats to come and tow us in. At any rate, we had to apportion our oil so that it would take us to the nearest German port. To run the slightest chance of doing that meant creeping along at our lowest speed. Two thousand miles at a snail's pace!

Before we went any farther I provided for one more contingency. "Have bombs placed so we can blow up the boat at a moment's notice," I told the engineer.

We couldn't submerge and we couldn't fight, and our chances of reaching Germany were mighty slim. It would be easy enough for an enemy ship to disable the *U-93* completely. We would be helpless to prevent it. But capture was another thing. With our own hands we would send her to the bottom first.

After that, day after day of slow, creeping progress, a double lookout always on watch, right up to the edge of the Arctic Ocean. Then a wide swing across toward the Norwegian coast. And in all this time only one sea-going craft sighted. Perhaps it had the same reason we had for choosing this out-of-the-way course. It was a German U-boat, just visible in the distance. We tried to reach it by radio. No reply. As we waited, the other submarine disappeared from view over the horizon. Our fears about our radio were confirmed. It was not working.

The weather was growing worse and the wind rising. It was a following wind, fortunately, but the waves breaking over our after deck, already lying lower than the bow, were keeping it constantly under water. To raise the *U-93* higher out of the sea, we threw overboard everything we could possibly do without. We were stripped to the bare essentials. Even so, the holes in our outer hull were continually becoming waterlogged and dragging us down. We had to blow our starboard tanks regularly. In good weather once every three hours had been often enough. Now they were re-filling every thirty minutes!

At least, all this kept us busy. I could only pity those poor fellows lying helpless below in their bunks. All we could do for them was administer a shot in the arm now and then to relieve their sufferings. The rest of the crew, when they had time, played the phonograph or read to them from our meager library. It wouldn't have been so bad for them if they could have had a cigarette. That was impossible. The interior of the boat was nearly always filled with gases from the batteries. A lighted match or a smouldering cigarette down there, and pouf—an explosion would have finished what the British hadn't.

"Hard luck," Usedom and I thought as we smoked our own cigarettes on the conning tower. With only two or three hours' sleep snatched out of the twenty-four, we smoked incessantly. Cigarettes and the blackest coffee our cook could brew—those kept us going. I marvelled at the morale of the crew. Every man was thirsty and dirty and nerve-racked and over-worked, but not a one grumbled or shirked.

Five more days passed. The weather grew steadily worse. Rain and snow squalls alternated with fog. Through the mist there hove in sight a fleet of patrol boats, armed fishing steamers. We turned east to dodge them. The manœuvre didn't work. Back to our former course. Again we failed to lose them. Another change of direction, this time to the west. The steamers gradually disappeared astern. Their lookouts must have been asleep not to have seen us. But those same British shell holes were what had saved us. The flooded compartments kept us lying so deep that the high waves almost completely hid us. At times our depth gauge registered as much as twenty-five feet, and water came pouring into the boat. The pumps never stopped.

Even the bridge was awash now. Combers were hurling themselves over Usedom and the petty officer of the watch as they stood lashed to the railing to keep from being swept away. At every roll we feared the boat would founder. The leaking diving tanks were filling up almost faster than we could blow them out. There was no rest for anybody now.

"*Mein Gott,* it is frightful up there!" muttered Usedom as he came down the ladder, blowing like a whale, water streaming from his rubber suit.

Soon we had rigged up a reserve periscope. We needed it now almost as much as though we had been completely submerged. Down below in the central station I took a look into it. I felt my legs go weak under me at what I saw. A couple of miles away was a three-funnelled British destroyer.

"Hard to starboard!" I shouted the command to the helmsman. Could we dodge that Britisher? I watched him through the periscope. He proceeded on his course, cutting the waves at thirty knots, without seeing us.

With a long breath of relief I swung the periscope around to scan the horizon. *Lieber Gott in Himmel!* We had escaped from one destroyer only to run into a half dozen of them, to say nothing of a fleet of armed fishing steamers. I knew how a wounded hare felt surrounded by hounds. I could even see the kettle looming.

We had one opening—to double back on the course from which we had come. I saw all our oil calculations ruined, but it was our only chance. We swung around away from that hornet's nest.

"Full speed on both engines!"

We leaped forward as though we had been kicked from the rear. Even so, the prospects looked black. One of the destroyers had sighted us. It was changing course in our direction, and it could make twice the speed we could.

"Clear for blowing her up," I shouted to the engineer.

Then help came from an unexpected quarter— from the weather we had been cursing so roundly.

Another of those sudden North Sea squalls swept down upon us. We were enveloped in snow, hail, and fog. At the same time, the head wind we had been bucking was now helping us along. We ran on for an hour, blindly and desperately, not able to see more than a few rods in any direction. Then the squall passed as suddenly as it had come. Clear weather again, and not a ship in sight.

It was a sensation such as you have when you see an enemy torpedo coming at you and it misses by a yard. Usedom and I could only shove our caps back on our heads, heave a long breath, and look at each other, speechless. When we found our voices it was to order a bottle of port. We drank to another streak of such luck.

Again on our old course, we moved south all night toward the Bay of Heligoland. The next morning we encountered our first floating mines and sighted a steamer and two sailing ships a long way off. But we missed the mines and the ships missed us.

That night we tried to reach a German station again with our SOS, but there was no answer. Still, we did manage to pick up other radio signals now and then. Our wireless evidently could receive messages but could not send any. We knew that long before this the *U-93* had been given up as lost, and nobody would be looking for us.

The next evening found us hugging the Danish coast.

"We're inside the three-mile limit," Usedom remarked.

To the deuce with the three-mile limit! It was forbidden territory to German U-boats, but this was no time to bother about such rulings. It was the only place where we could be certain to dodge the mine fields. The friendly lighthouses of Bovsbjerg and Lyngwig gave us our bearings. It was bright moonlight besides, and we crept along so close to land we could hear the tinkling bells of the wethers among the flocks of sheep on shore. A pair of north-bound Danish fishing steamers came toward us. Merged against the shadow of the coast, we glided by them unnoticed only fifteen feet away. Usedom and I grinned at each other like two schoolboys.

"Lucky? Yes?" he murmured.

"Lucky. Yes," I returned. "But suppose we take a few soundings. If we get too cocky we may find ourselves sitting on a sand bank."

Two more fishing steamers were sighted the next day. What now? Suppose they were armed. I took a look through my binoculars.

"They're German!" I yelled. "Run up the signals."

The little steamers puffed over to us. Every one of our crew and theirs swarmed up on deck. You can imagine the astonishment, the questions, the excitement. Our rescue was at hand. One of the steamers would take us into the next harbour.

On the conning tower, Usedom and I basked in the sunshine and talked of those nine astounding days through which our luck had brought us. If that luck had but held for our Captain as well. We could only fear the worst as to his fate. I remembered all too well that hell of shell fire in which he had vanished.

We came to anchor at List, alongside the hospital ship, and the wounded men were taken off. Usedom had reason to be proud of the results of his medical experiments. Not a man had fever; not a wound was infected. "I wasn't too far off on the morphine, either," he breathed in relief.

That was the end of Ziegner's story. There was little more to tell. On shore he wired his report to U-boat headquarters and had a square meal and a night's sleep in a comfortable bed. At five o'clock next morning the voyage was resumed, this time in tow. The oil tanks of the *U-93* were empty. The calculations of Ziegner and his engineer could hardly have been closer.

In Wilhelmshaven almost the whole fleet came out to meet the returning U-boat. Admiral Scheer himself went on board to present to Ziegner decorations conferred on him by telegraph. He was the hero of the day, and later was personally commended by the Kaiser.

To the authorities, Ziegner reported that Commander von Spiegel and the other two men were surely lost, but to the Baron's young wife, who went to Wilhelmshaven at once, he and every man in the crew vowed stoutly that her husband had surely been picked up by the British. She immediately had inquiries made through diplomatic channels—the Baron's letter had not yet reached her. Then the news came that Von Spiegel was a prisoner in England. Ziegner and his men gasped to find that their merciful lie was the truth.

One day young Adolf Karl George Edgar, Baron Spiegel von und zu Peckelsheim was called up before Piquot, who was more of a bear than ever that day.

"You must have good friends back in Germany," he boomed savagely, and then went on to say that at the instance of Prince Henry and the Crown Princess of Germany, the King of Spain and the Queen of Denmark had asked for information.

"Life at Donnington Hall was pleasant," according to the Baron. "The food was good and the discipline not too severe, and one learned to grow fond of the ferocious Piquot. Of course, I took part in an attempt to escape. No prison career would be complete without that. Our little party of would-be escapers did not get away, but had a good joke anyway. Day after day we dug a tunnel. The Commandant got word of it, but did not know who the guilty parties were. He stationed a soldier inside of the tunnel to wait and see who turned up for a bit of digging. We, on our part, discovered his little plan. At the entrance of the tunnel was a door. We nailed it up, sealed it up properly—with the soldier inside. He set up a great uproar when he found himself thus buried alive. They had to do quite a bit of carpentering before they got that door open and let him out."

So the Baron and his pals were obliged to continue the enjoyment of the luxuries of Donnington Hall until after the Armistice. In fact, it was not until June, 1919, that he got home to his wife and his Fatherland.

CHAPTER XXIII

NEW TERRORS OF THE UNDER SEA

The raiders of the deep might tell their story by setting down a catalogue of the devices of warfare used against them. The perils they had to encounter changed and developed in heart-breaking succession. At first they had to reckon with nothing more than the conventional weapons used against surface craft— gunfire, ramming, mine fields, and torpedoes of enemy submarines, standard and easily understood dangers from which an alert U-boat could readily dive. Those were the halcyon days for the raiders of the deep.

I talked with Fregattenkapitän Waldemar Kophamel, one of the most distinguished of U-boat commanders. At the time of the outbreak of the war Commander Kophamel had served longer with the U-boats than any other officer in the German Navy. He was a lieutenant aboard the first German submarine, the *U-1*, when that craft made its maiden voyage. Later he became the skipper of the *U-2*. In 1917 he made the longest U-boat cruise on record, from Germany down the west coast of Africa and back. In 1918 he commanded one of the boats that raided the coast of the United States. For a year he was commander of the U-boat flotilla at Cattaro. With sixty ships and a total of 190,000 tons sunk, he stands with the first ten on the tonnage list. Among the experiences he related was one that he told in a tone of reminiscent wonder. It was truly a tale of the halcyon days.

Editor's Note: Although German U-boat operations off the American east coast were more ambitious during World War II, the Imperial Navy sent its raiders of the deep to American waters during the Great War. After the entry of the United States into the conflict, the German naval command sent U-boats to raid the eastern seaboard from Newfoundland down to Cape Hatteras in North Carolina from May through October 1918. Five large U-cruisers of 1,503 tons displacement and a 12.5-knot surface speed were outfitted to

"We made our way through the Channel," he said. "It was an easy trip, without bother or much danger. There were no nets in that early time, no submerged bombs laid for U-boats. We lay for hours at the entrance of the port of Havre. We were on the surface and there were scores of enemy craft in sight. They were in the shelter of the harbour and we could not get at them. They saw us plainly but merely kept out of our way. They knew they could do us no harm. Before they could approach within range of gunfire or near enough to ram us, we should be away under the water. I stayed there at my leisure, enjoying the scene, peaceably observing the enemy warcraft and peaceably observed by them. With later times of the war in mind, I can look back upon that sunny afternoon as if it were some fantastic, prehistoric period, an almost forgotten Golden Age."

Another of Commander Kophamel's experiences of those early days is an instance of the weird, unearthly mood of the submarine warfare.

"We were entering the Channel," he relates, "when we encountered the *U-6* on her way back to harbour. Her skipper was Commander Lepsius, who was afterward lost. The two boats drew alongside. Lepsius had a word of warning for me.

" 'You are heading for a mine field, a new one which the British have just laid. We passed straight through it, but luckily we reached it at low tide. They have placed the mines badly, too high in the water, and at low tide their pineapples lie floating on the surface. Look out for them, and wait till low tide before going on.'

"I took his advice, and timed our course so that we reached the minefield at the last ebbing of the tide. A brilliant sun was setting and a brisk wind was up. A heavy sea was running, choppy and angry—the usual rough, turbulent Channel. The mines, black

carry mines—*U-151, 152, 155, 156,* and *140.* One ocean-going minelayer, the *U-117,* also participated. They proved far less effective than the U-boats the United States and Canada confronted twenty-one years later.

and ugly, lay on the surface on all sides. Between the sun, which glared full in my face, and the white capped waves, which rather concealed the mines, I had to look sharp as we ran along awash.

"The boat had scarcely entered the field when I heard a tremendous pop, and out in the distance a geyser of water spouted. Then another explosion and still another, on this side and that, some afar and some near. In the turbulent sea the mines were detonating. The dashing of the waves against them was setting them off. We were sailing through a field of bursting, roaring mines. As we steered on, the explosions became more numerous, a perfect concerto. There was a ceaseless tattoo of crashes on all sides and a panorama of fountains and spray.

" '*Donnerwetter,*' I thought, 'this is something new and hard on the nerves.' We had to pass so near some of the mines that if one should go off only a few feet away from the boat it might be nasty.

" 'Trim the boat down to a hundred feet,' I ordered.

"We submerged and ran along underneath the field of exploding mines. They boomed on this side and that and straight overhead.

"After an hour the detonations grew faint and disappeared behind us. I brought the boat to the surface.

" 'Helm hard aport!' I yelled.

"Right ahead, about three feet from our bow, lay a big fat mine ready for us to hit. We passed it with about a foot to spare. On all sides were thousands of mines lying on the heaving water. This was another field which had been laid in slightly different fashion, and the big bombs were not exploding.

"We had seen enough mines for that day. I took the boat down to a hundred feet again. We ran under the surface for several hours until we were in less dangerous waters."

The war began with the submarine a primitive and comparatively feeble instrument, and on the other hand, just to keep things even, the weapons for fighting the submarine were equally primitive and feeble.

A submarine's trick of generating poison gases provided the dramatic crisis in a thrilling tale told me by Commander Ernst Hashagen, that day when I talked with him in Hamburg. The burly, jovial Hashagen related how, in the spring of 1916 before he had his own command, he had been on a cruise as a second officer aboard the *U-22*.

"We were off Belfast, Ireland, when out of a dense fog appeared a British cruiser. There was no chance for a torpedo shot. In fact, we were the hunted instead of the hunters. She spied us, opened fire, and rushed at us to ram us. I lost no time in giving orders to trim the boat down to fifty feet.

"We dived quickly and got under water all right, but something went wrong with the depth rudder. The boat seemed to have gone crazy. She tilted up and down like a rocking horse, sinking now by the head and then by the stern—but always sinking. Down we went to a hundred feet—a hundred and fifty—two hundred. If we went much deeper and the terrific pressure increased we should be crushed. The only way to rise was to blow the tanks, but that would have popped us out of the water right under the nose of the cruiser up there. Everything else lost its importance in the presence of one particular sound— coughing. I caught the acrid smell of chlorine gas, and everybody was coughing sputtering, choking. My throat and lungs burned with an intolerable torment. Ever inhale a whiff of chlorine? Don't try it. Often when I remember those frightful moments while we were half strangled with that infernal gas there in the depths I think of the gas waves over the trenches in France—war has become too horrible.

"The fearful pressure was forcing sea water through our seams and it was getting into the sulphuric acid of the batteries. Sea water plus sulphuric acid—any high school student of chemistry will tell you the answer is chlorine. If we stayed submerged we should quickly be strangled by that infernal vapour. I don't think there is anything that will strike such fear in a submarine man as the thought of being trapped in the iron hull while choking gas seeps from the batteries bit by bit. No death could be more agonizing. It is the old devilish peril of the craft that navigates the under sea, a common cause of ghastly disaster in the early days of submarines.

" 'Blow the tanks,' the Captain gasped.

"No hesitation. No thought of the cruiser up there. Anything for a breath of pure unpoisoned air. Better to be shot to pieces and drown in a quiet way than this death by choking torment.

"The *U-22* shot to the surface. Yes, there was the cruiser looming in the mist. Never mind—hatches open—sweet, cool air blows in. We fill our lungs until they almost burst.

"The cruiser is still there. It stays there. It had not seen us. The fog is dense and blinding, and we lie so close to the water that we are invisible. The *U-22* slinks away through the mist."

One of the first of the special anti-submarine devices was the net. Since the under-surface boat does not submerge deeply, never more than a couple of hundred feet, great steel nets extending below the surface will stop it and perhaps catch it. A narrow neck of water may be effectively closed to submarine craft by nets. Important war harbours were thus protected, and that exceedingly vital strip of sea, the English Channel, across which lay Britain's line of military communication with France. At first the nets were plain, then later were garnished with bombs which exploded when the net happened to be struck near them. The nets were effective against the U-boats, and in time closed the English Channel against them. More than one German submersible was trapped and lost in the meshes of steel or sunk by the exploding bombs. U-boats of later and improved types carried at the bow great scissors for cutting their way out of the nets.

The Q-ships were the most brilliant and dramatic weapon used against the raiders of the deep. These craft, inoffensive-looking old tubs with concealed formidable guns, took the Germans by surprise, and many a U-boat commander drew carelessly up to some old tramp to sink it by gunfire, only to find himself staring in the face of a battery of heavy metal. The Q-ships accounted for a number of submarines and had their greatest success during the early years of the war. After a while, though, the U-boat commanders grew so wary of the particular kind of trap that the Q-ships had few successes. Eventually they were practically thrown into the discard.

One of the Q-ships, the *Baralong,* became the centre of an ugly controversy. The Germans complained that some of the decoy vessels, upon sinking submarines, killed survivors struggling in the water. The *Baralong* was cited as a specific case and was made the object of international complaint. Similarly, there is dispute about the treatment of U-boat men taken prisoners. It appears from the stories I was able to gather that some were treated rigorously and others very well indeed.

It was in early 1917 that what was perhaps the most logical weapon against the submarine began to play its part. I can best repeat an account that Commander Spiess gives.

"On May 6, 1917, I sat in at a conference, and a most interesting, although not jubilant, confabulation it was. The officers of the U-boat flotilla gathered to take counsel with the commander of the *U-49*, which had just stood in. He related to us an experience he had had on his recent cruise. It was no mere idle, amusing yarn-spinning in a fo'c's'le. The report was of a new danger we would have to surmount, a new and potent piece introduced onto the chessboard of war under the sea. The *U-49* had been bombed with depth charges. No such thing had been encountered before and the news made quite a sensation. And the more we thought of it, the less we liked it.

"The depth charge was a bomb loaded with two hundred pounds or so of high explosive. It could be set to explode at any desired depth under water when dropped overboard. At any place where a submarine was suspected an enemy ship dumped over its stern quantities of these infernal charges set to go off at verious depths. A U-boat under water was peppered with a shower of them. If one exploded close enough it would sink the craft, or would at least make it leaky by springing the seams, and thus disable it. It was an evil invention and one destined to become part of our daily experience.

"Days later I was out at sea and manœuvring for an attack. A convoy of cargo ships was steaming along escorted by a patrol of destroyers. One destroyer was too near for comfort, but I finally got clear of it and launched a torpedo at it. Missed. Then a tremendous bang. No, it wasn't the torpedo. The boat rocked violently, and the lights went out but flashed on again.

"'Depth bomb!' I exclaimed to my watch officer.

"It was my first experience, and it frightened me thoroughly. I was sure we must be sinking. I did not breathe easily till positive reports came from all quarters that the boat was sound: 'Everything in order below.'

"Another one popped, but it was some distance away. You may be sure we were getting away from there as fast as possible. The destroyer had seen the track of the torpedo and had come charging to give us a taste of the new medicine the enemy had compounded for us. And I never did like the taste of that medicine."

Other U-boat skippers join Commander Spiess heartily in his small appetite for the depth charges. The watery mantle of the ocean was an impentrable armour against gunfire, but the cocoanuts dropped into the sea were an extension of the aërial projectile to the world of the sub-surface. They chased the U-boat into the U-boat's own element. Submarine missiles for submarine boats.

The depth charge was aimed by sundry indicators that indicated the presence of a submarine,—the sight of a periscope, bubbles sent up by the firing of a torpedo, the torpedo's track, the streak of oil on the surface left by leaking oil tanks, and so on. Then the listening device called the hydrophone was brought out, with which the presence of a submarine could be detected at considerable distances.

With the creation of new anti-submarine weapons went a multiplication of craft that acted against the submersibles. Great fleets of destroyers and all manner of patrol craft, from yachts to trawlers, scoured the sea. When the United States entered the war, the American sub chaser was added to the list. Airplanes and dirigibles scouted for U-boats to report them and drop bombs on them.

Merchant ships sailed armed like young cruisers, with formidable guns and trained naval gun crews, and whenever a U-boat made a surface attack upon

A convoy zigzagging through the danger zone.

*A U-boat sights more victims and prepares
to dive for the attack.*

A U-boat crew surrendering to a Yankee destroyer.

The victim of a night attack abandoned by her convoy.

freighter or liner it was likely to have a battle on its hands. Commander Kophamel tells of a melodramatic gun battle with an armed steamer which occurred during the record distance cruise for submarines, his voyage with the big *U-151* from Germany down the west coast of Africa and back, which covered a distance of twelve thousand miles. This occurred in the autumn of 1917.

A month and a half out, the *U-151* sighted a steamer off the coast of Africa. The swift submersible cruiser cut its way through the water at its best surface speed. A shot across the steamer's bow, and a shot in return. The vessel attacked changed its course and ran as fast as it could, firing with its stern gun. It was fast, but the submarine cruiser was fast, too. And now ensued a long, running fight. The U-boat's shells dropped around the fleeing ship in a continuous succession. Still there was no sign of surrender. Game lads aboard that ship—how game will presently develop. The range was long, but at last the raider of the deep scored a clean hit. The shell burst on deck near the stern, right in the middle of the large store of ammunition for the steamer's gun. A fire started, and as the blaze arose the ammunition supply began to explode. Shells popped, one after another like giant firecrackers, and hurtled out over the water.

The crew had no more fight left in them. They jumped pell mell into their boats as fast as they could. No one who knew the real facts of the matter could blame them. They rowed with crazy desperation in their oars. Meanwhile, the U-boat was drawing up.

"All that remained," Commander Kophamel relates," was to slide up to the craft and at a good point-blank range shoot a couple of shells into her at the water line. However, the fire was still burning aboard, a neat little blaze at the stern, and the fireworks made it seem like an old-fashioned American Fourth of July. The shells were zipping here and there over the sea, and it would be just our luck, if we ventured too close, to get nicked by one.

" 'We won't take any chances,' I said to myself, 'We'll stay out here and pop her at good safe range.' That was one of the luckiest decisions I ever made.

"The *U-151* took a comfortable position just outside what seemed to be the maximum carrying distance of the crazily exploding shells, and began a leisurely, enjoyable bit of gunnery. The men at the gun took a good quiet aim and then the shooting began—I mean the fun began. A shell hit the steamer squarely amidships.

"I thought the end of the world had come. Our eardrums were almost burst. Where the steamer had been was now a vast billowing cloud of smoke. The sky darkened and the air became thick and gray. A hailstorm struck us, a hailstorm of débris. The ship had been blown to atoms. In a few seconds our deck was so covered with bits of pulverized wreckage that there was no space where you could put your hand without touching any. We were neither hurt nor endangered by the descending rain. The pieces were all minute, so violent the explosion had been.

"The lifeboats were in the distance. We overhauled them. The men told us that the ship had been the *Caprera*, an Italian vessel bound from the United States for Italy with a thousand tons of dynamite. They explained to us with the vivid expressiveness of Italians that it was enough for them to have conducted a gun fight with that kind of cargo below the decks, and when the ship had caught fire and their ammunition supply began to explode—well, that was too much. They were right.

"It was that explosion of the store of ammunition that had saved us. If it hadn't been for the danger

of those popping shells, the *U-151* would have sailed
right up and pumped a shell into that mountain of
dynamite at close range—and that would have been
our final effort at gunnery."

This brings us to the final and most effective system
of defense against the U-boats, the convoy system. It
stands as the characteristic feature of the climax of
the U-boat warfare, the second unrestricted campaign,
Germany's greatest effort.

CHAPTER XXIV

THE CLIMAX OF THE U-BOAT WAR

The first unrestricted U-boat campaign had been discontinued largely because of the protests of the United States, but now in the beginning of 1917 Germany decided to fly in the face of the opinion of the world and loose the U-boats again without restriction. She planned to win the war by the full weight of submarine attack.

In February of 1917, the first month of Germany's second unrestricted U-boat campaign, a half million tons of shipping were destroyed. Then the figures leaped another hundred thousand during March. And in April, when the United States entered the war, that appalling total had shot up to *a million tons.* England, in desperation, seized every available submarine weapon, and was fighting with her back to the wall. Still she was unable to stop the inexorable rising tide. The fate of the British Empire hung in the balance.

Just how desperate the situation was, the public, of course, didn't know. The British people little dreamed that in April, 1917, they had only enough food in their country to last through a single month or at most six weeks. Then famine! If the U-boats had continued their terrific rate of destruction, British shipping would have been swept from the seas. Germany knew this and feverishly went on building more U-boats.

Our own Admiral Sims in his *Victory at Sea* gives us a graphic picture of that dark hour:—

Could Germany have kept fifty submarines constantly at work on the great shipping routes in the winter and spring of 1917, nothing could have prevented her from winning the war.

Such was the desperate situation when British and American naval men got together and evolved the idea of putting all shipping in convoy, and of rushing American destroyers across at once. So, from then on, instead of solitary vessels, excellent targets for U-boats, all ships entering dangerous waters went in great convoys—well protected by destroyers. They also proceeded on a bewildering, zigzag course, and this made a ship a difficult mark for a torpedo. The accompanying destroyers and armed auxiliary cruisers surrounding them were ever on the alert, ready to ram a U-boat, or drop depth bombs, or open with gun-fire.

Now for a change, instead of meeting say one ship every day during a ten-day cruise, an under-sea raider frequently would sight a group of ten or twenty or even thirty or forty ships. They would be proceeding together in close formation, under strong destroyer protection. Another result of this system was that sometimes a week or two would pass in which Herr U-boat Skipper would sight not a single ship of any kind—not even a windjammer. Then all of a sudden a forest of masts and funnels would appear over the horizon—the liners and freighters all zigzagging, and the destroyers circling and buzzing around their brood. Naturally, with the odds so great against him, Herr U-boat Kommandant had to strike ruthlessly and without warning, or slink off without striking at all.

Commander Hersing of Dardanelles fame was one

of the raiders of the deep who knew only too well the risky game of attacking convoys. After his return from the Mediterranean in 1917 he was operating again in the North Sea and the Atlantic. Here he had eight exciting encounters with convoys. And on each occasion he scattered the convoy and bagged at least one ship.

"Perhaps my closest shave in an encounter with a convoy," he had told me "was in August, 1917, fifty miles off the southwest tip of Ireland. It was one of those rare sparkling days with hardly a ripple on the sea. Suddenly smudges of smoke appeared far off in the sky to the west. Then through my binoculars I made out one funnel and one mast, and then a great lot of them doing a sort of zigzag sea cotillion. 'Ah, ha, here's where we get some excitement,' I muttered to myself as I pressed the button to sound the electric alarm bells. Then the ocean opened and swallowed us while the convoy bore down upon us. We lay just under the surface, but with that glassy sea I hardly dared show our 'asparagus.' For periods of twenty seconds, but never longer, I would run it up for lightning glimpses. Apparently there were some fifteen steamers, and they were formed in three parallel lines, all zigzagging. Around them was a cordon of destroyers, eight hundred yards or so farther out. Six ran in front of the convoy, six behind, and six on either side. Twenty-four destroyers shepherding fifteen ships. You'd have thought that ample protection indeed. When we stole our last hurried look before going into action that nearest oncoming phalanx of destroyers was so close that they could easily have rammed us before we could have plunged to a safer depth—if they had spotted us.

" 'Full speed ahead!' Submerged, we sped right toward the convoy and passed between two of the zigzagging destroyers. Then up with our periscope for a fraction of a minute. Yes, we were in the midst of it and two of the steamers were directly within range—broadside targets.

" 'First and second torpedoes—fire! Periscope down. Dive to forty metres!'

"As the *U-21* pointed her nose toward the depths, I counted the seconds. Ten—twenty—thirty—forty—almost a minute now—perhaps the torpedoes had gone wild. Then two explosions. Both of them had hit.

"The destroyers were after us. The ways of the torpedoes gave them our trail. Every square yard of water was being literally peppered with depth bombs. They were exploding on every side of us, over our heads, and even below. The destroyers were timing them for three different depths—ten metres, 25 metres, and 50 metres. *Himmelherrgott!* they were letting us have them at the rate of one every ten seconds.

"A terrific detonation right beside us. The boat shivered from the impact, and the lights went out. 'Good-bye *U-21*,' I thought.

" 'Report from all compartments,' I shouted into the speaking tube as I switched on my pocket flash. The reports came back. 'All tight below.' *Gott sei Dank!*

"The lights flashed on again. But the rain of depth charges still continued. We were zigzagging now, more crazily than the steamers above us. But turn where we would, we could not get away. The sound of propellers followed us wherever we went, and the bombs continued their infernal explosions. The *U-21* shivered with each detonation—and so did we. No doubt the destroyers were tracing us by a track of leaking oil from our tanks, or with their hydrophones, or both.

"Exactly five hours went by before the hum of that

plague of propellers above us died away. For five hours we had been pestered by those blasted depth bombs. How we managed to dodge them all is a mystery.

"After that I profited by our experience and tried a different way of getting the best of the destroyers. Instead of trying to put as much space as possible between the *U-21* and a convoy, thus giving the destroyers a chance to chase me on the open sea, I dived right under the steamers and stayed there while the destroyers peppered the surrounding waters. Had they known where we were, what could they have done? Nothing! A depth bomb thrown there would have done as much, and perhaps vastly more, damage to their own ships than to us. Of course, there was always the chance that the torpedoed ship might sink on top of us, just as later happened to Von Arnauld. But I preferred that risk."

It was some two months later that Commander Ernst Hashagen, in his *U-62,* overhauled an American steamer lagging nearly one hundred miles behind her convoy.

"I sent a shot across her bow, but instead of stopping she opened up with her own gun. All morning long we had a running fight with the *Luckenbach.* She did no serious damage to us. But a full dozen of our shells found her. One had even set fire to her cargo of cotton. Still those stubborn Yankees refused to surrender. Our gun outranged theirs, but still they kept on firing at us and flashing out SOS signals.

"Three or four hours later we saw a smudge in the distance. '*Was zum Teufel ist da los?*' said I to myself. Yes, it was what I thought. The American destroyer *Nicholson* popped over the horizon hurrying to the aid of the *Luckenbach.* Those Yankee destroyers!" The husky Hashagen smiled ruefully over the memory of them. "Naturally, we commanders had no love for them. This one opened fire on us at once, and her second shell got us in the bow. That was our cue to get away from that place.

"We dived. Quick as a wink that destroyer was after us, sowing the sea with depth charges. We stayed down for about an hour. Then we came up a bit and took a cautious glance through our cyclop's optic to see what had happened to the lucky *Luckenbach*. And what a sight for a U-boat met my eyes! By chance, in groping blindly under the sea, we had stumbled right into the rest of that convoy. Twenty steamers accompanied by ten destroyers had just arrived over the horizon. And leading the second column was a 13,000-ton British auxiliary cruiser.

"I had only one torpedo left. With such a big ship, a vital spot must be hit or one torpedo is not enough. Waiting until the cruiser was almost broadside to us, I aimed for the engine room. Then I ran the periscope up for an instant. Yes, we had made our bull's eye. But there was no time for a second look. The destroyers saw us, wheeled, and charged. We submerged and pushed off amid the roar of depth bombs. A little later we picked up the wireless message:

" '*Orama* sinking.'

"There was only one way to steer clear of those destroyers. That was to waylay a ship before a convoy was made up or after it had scattered. I met the Cunarder *Ausonia* that way—six hundred miles out from Ireland, steering a lone course westward after the dismissal of its convoy. I was that far out myself only because I was on my way to the Azores. A quick dive, a torpedo hit square in the engine room, and the *Ausonia* took her last plunge, while her crew disappeared over the horizon in their life boats."

Six months passed. The U-boats were fighting a losing game now. The convoy system had most of them baffled. Four hundred miles west of Brest a 10,000-ton French cruiser, bearing the name of the famous old naval family of *Dupetit-Thouars,* steamed west to pick up a convoy from America and escort it through the danger zone. An oily sea and a flaming sunset. A hidden U-boat raised its periscope. Looking through that periscope was the same officer who had the year before won his spurs as one of the few to wage successful war against the convoys.

No depth bomb or "ash can," as the American "gobs" called them, had dropped into the ocean with the doughty Hashagen's name written on it. So he still stalked big game at sea. Through the asparagus he saw the black silhouette of the approaching cruiser outlined against the sky. Below in the *U-62* he waited until the torpedo range had shortened.

"First and second torpedoes—fire!"

They left their tubes and raced neck and neck toward the Frenchman. Both were square hits. The cruiser listed, and her five hundred men took to the lifeboats. SOS calls crackled through the gathering dusk. But there were no sub chasers in the vicinity and the only ships close enough to help were forbidden to go. The fate of the *Hogue,* the *Cressy,* and the *Aboukir* had not been forgotten. In twenty minutes it was too late. The *Dupetit-Thouars* had taken her final plunge.

Yes, many ships were still being sunk. But with the inauguration and development of the convoy system the Allied defense tightened. The U-boats no longer had things their own way so much of the time. Even the American destroyer *Nicholson* got quick revenge for the affront it had received from the *U-62.*

One day she steamed out of Queenstown as the flagship of a westbound convoy. Next in line came another member of her squadron, the U. S. S. *Fanning.* The feathery wake of a periscope appeared in the distance. Both the *Nicholson* and *Fanning* wheeled and charged,

Of course, Fritz had vanished from sight before they reached the spot, but they threw their "ash cans" full of TNT in all directions.

Herr U-boat was too slow and hadn't gotten out of range. Two of those Yankee ash cans found their fish and exploded near enough to disable the prowler's machinery. When she started to sink, the German commander knew his one and only chance lay in coming to the top. That might give some of his men a chance to come through alive. So he ordered the tanks blown, and up she popped right alongside the two destroyers. After opening their seacocks the Germans scrambled through the hatches and into the water. The *U-58* went down like a rock, but the Americans fished up Kapitänleutnant Gustav Amberger and his thirty-five men and took them back to Queenstown.

No doubt many naval experts thought of the convoy system as a possible means of getting the best of Fritz at sea, but the lion's share of the credit for bringing about its adoption goes to none other than Rear Admiral Sims, Commander of the American Naval Forces operating in European waters during the war. That alone should insure Admiral Sims of a high place in naval history, for the part he played in the inauguration and development of the convoy system undoubtedly ranks as one of the most valuable of all the contributions that Uncle Sam made toward Allied victory.

If you doubt this, just ask Herr U-boat Commander who was lucky enough to survive those last thrilling months of the war and hear his remarks when you mention convoys. *"Zum Teufel nochmal!"* he'll say. Indeed, if there are no ladies in the offing he will grow even more sulphurous than that and will express his sentiments in language that fairly smokes.

CHAPTER XXV

THE FLANDERS LAIR

It was a sombre winter day, and my wife and I were winging our way from London to Amsterdam. It happened to be the first flight of our 25,000-mile aërial jaunt over the skyways of Europe. The atmosphere was unusually bumpy and fog was driving us lower and lower. We sped across the Channel less than two hundred feet above the white caps and then swung north at Calais. The frontier between France and Belgium vanished astern and a few minutes later we were looking down on the ancient town of Bruges, near where the English Channel widens into the North Sea. An interesting city, Bruges; a famous commercial mart in the days of the Hanseatic League. I remembered reading of days of revelry which that merrie monarch, Charles II of England, passed there during the time of his exile. But Bruges had been through far more exciting times quite recently. For this ancient port of the Belgæ played a particularly sensational rôle in the greatest of all wars. Bruges was the Flanders lair for the German under-sea corsairs.

On the land below us were canals, interlaced like a fine network. Two of those canals, the two leading to the sea, were the lanes along which the raiders of the deep crept on their way in and out of Bruges. The mouth of one is at Ostend and the other a few miles farther up the coast at Zeebrugge. These three towns and the two lengths of canal connecting them constituted the famous Flanders lair of the U-boats during the World War. An invaluable base it was too, because it was many miles nearer England and the vital Channel ports than the main submarine bases on the German North Sea coast. Then, too, from Bruges the enemy submarines could dart out much more quickly and raid the Atlantic shipping lanes. Bruges, apparently, was a perfectly adapted haven for the raiders of the under sea. After an expedition a U-boat could creep along under the surface of the waters of the English Channel and North Sea, slip into the mouths of those canals, and then continue on up to Bruges, with its ideal inland harbour. There they found fairly safe shelter, out of range of the ever menacing guns of the British Fleet. The entrance at Zeebrugge was the one they generally used, and to great renown did that little Belgian watering place rise during the course of the campaign under the sea.

From Bruges we swung west a bit and flew right above the famous Zeebrugge Mole, a semi-circular concrete wall, the purpose of which was to shelter the mouth of the canal from the assaults of storm-beaten waves. Banking a bit, we tilted way over and got a perfect view of the mouth of the canal. Half submerged down there was the shadowy hulk of a sunken ship. A mute witness of war, a monument to a daring band of men. That hulk is what remains of the famous block vessel which the British, during their raid on Zeebrugge, ran into the canal and sank across its mouth in the hope of cutting the line by which the submarines passed back and forth from Bruges to the sea.

This aërial voyage of ours merely brought idle thoughts to me and my fellow wanderer of the skies. But now, with the tale of the raiders of the deep to be told, the Flanders base of the German submarine service is of big and immediate importance. It ranked second, next to the lair along the north coast of Germany. Sixty-seven U-boats, all operating at one time from the bases on the North German coast was the record for that region. Cattaro in the Adriatic was for a time the home of thirty-four. Between these two came Flanders with a maximum of thirty-seven raiders operating out of Bruges simultaneously. The events off Flanders really constituted a separate phase of the campaign of the U-boats, just as did the happenings in the Adriatic-Mediterranean field, and the tale is one of special interest because here there were singular perils and more than the ordinary submarine-warfare dangers to be faced.

Since the U-boats operating from the Flanders base slipped in and out on short forays, an especial kind of under-sea craft was evolved. This craft was dubbed the UB-boat. These UB's were small and stumpy and had a far shorter radius of action than the U-boat. In fact, some were so tiny that they were called sewing machines. Their crews numbered only about twenty, and even then were frightfully crowded in the narrow space. Still another special type of submersible operated off Flanders. These were the UC type of boats. They were the mine layers that stealthily made their way to the main waterways around Britain in order to deposit their floating bombs.

Bruges, naturally, was not only the rendezvous, but it also was the playground for the Flanders' U-boat men when off duty between raids. The under-sea flotilla chiefs had their headquarters in one of the oldest buildings in the ancient Belgian city. The Jesuits had built the place and it looked it; it was a curious, charming old stone building with mullioned windows that overlooked a narrow, crooked, cobble-stoned street. Here the U-boat master minds hatched their plots. But when meal time came they adjourned to another place, a sumptuous private mansion, a place of spacious

Editor's Note: UB-boats were small coastal submarines of from 120 to over 600 tons surface displacement, depending on need and stage of development.

rooms, lofty ceilings, carved woodwork, and crystal chandeliers. For living quarters they scattered about in private houses deserted by their owners.

There was an old rathskeller, a cellar which you entered by arched doorways two feet thick. This was the nightly congregating place for the daring men who voyaged under the sea in ships. Some submarine commander with a leaning toward art and caricature decorated the walls in fantastic and highly imaginative fashion. On one side was a British ship with John Bull himself as a figurehead being towed into Zeebrugge by a group of submarines. Another cartoon pictured a card game. The players were mines and the stake was a German submarine. Rather grim and sharp-pointed humour. Another familiar haunt was a little Belgian restaurant where the oysters were particularly good. It was kept by a Belgian woman whose pretty daughter helped to serve the Captain Nemos when there was a crowd.

On the outskirts of Bruges was a fine old chateau which the submarine officers used as a country club, and on fine days a crowd would drive out. Automobiles were not available; they were reserved for urgent official use. But there were plenty of two-horse carriages to be hired and they were quite imposing equipages. A sailor, temporarily metamorphosed into a Jehu, would take his place on the box, crack his whip, and off they would whirl to the country club in high state.

"Sunday evening was always dedicated to the muse of music," Commander Günther Suadicani of the Flanders Flotilla told me. "I had a tiny house belonging to a Belgian officer at the front and there we gathered, violinists, cellists, and pianists. Fritz von Tvardovski, then in command of a boat and now of the German Foreign Office; Bieber, who was lost on a mine in the North Sea toward the end of the war; Wendrioner, Von Mangoldt, Walther, and others. Trained musicians were we, and we treated Beethoven and Schumann with reverence and perhaps with some skill."

There were gay times in Bruges during those days. Men who went sliding to terror and death in the submarines tried to forget. They needed to, for the mortality in the Flanders Flotilla was particularly high. In addition to the usual destroyers, Q-ships, depth bombs, mines, nets, etc. that they were accustomed to contend with, these men in their little submersibles were hunted by swarms of seaplanes. In fact, Allied birdmen swooped out of the clouds, destroyed six of them in all, and crippled many more. The days ashore were the only compensation for the hardship and peril at sea, and it was only natural for men to make the most of it. There was plenty of roistering, and the British tell tales of scandalous high jinx at Bruges.

The German base at Flanders was a particularly irksome threat to the Allies, a thorn in the side. It was entirely too near the British coast to be comfortable. The Allied measures of defense were elaborate. They had to be, for the Flanders U-boat lair was right at the very door of the Channel. The U-boats were much too small to attempt the long trip around the British Isles via the Shetlands, which was the usual and by far the safest route to the Atlantic for the bigger submarines. So the Flanders Flotilla had to use the route through the Channel in order to raid the waters off the British south and west coasts, and that route was strewn with dangers. The British had special submarine barriers across the Channel. These were for the benefit of all under-sea raiders, but in particular they were directed against the smaller UB-boats that sneaked in and out of those canals at Ostend and Zeebrugge.

Across that narrow channel between England and France three lines of defense were laid. These formed the famous "Dover Barrier," so called. The first line consisted of nets festooned with mines. The nets were laid below the surface of the water so as to be hidden from the unwary U-boat commander, and behind the nets patrol boats kept watch for any U-boat attempting to creep through on the surface. Submarines sometimes dived under the nets, a hazardous proceeding. Sometimes they were lucky and made it. The barrier was laid deep, and a submarine could only dive to a certain depth. The usual way of passing the barrier was to slide right over the nets at night and play hide-and-seek with the patrol boats.

Beyond the nets came the second barrier, consisting of mines anchored in tiers at various depths, so that U-boats on the prowl down there anywhere would be likely to bump into one and in doing so get "bumped off." Here again patrol boats kept watch for submarines making the passage on the surface, and at night the strait from shore to shore was illuminated by burning magnesium cast out upon the water. The U-boat stealing along on the surface found itself confronted by this belt of dazzling flame. But the burning magnesium gave a fickle blaze, and the lighting was not a hundred per cent. efficient, and there were times when a part of the barrier was in darkness. The U-boat would lurk outside of the illuminated belt and wait for one of those periods of darkness and then try to run through, full speed ahead. It was a gambler's chance, a bout hand to hand with death. If the dark spot brightened up before the boat made it through, then there was merely another entry on the list of lost submarines and another two or three million dollar scalp dangling from John Bull's belt.

If the raider passed safely through all of that gauntlet of grief it then came upon barrier number three. This consisted of a pair of giant searchlights, one on either shore of the narrowest part of the strait. They were so powerful that their beams met in mid-channel and illuminated the entire strait. Swarms of patrol boats hovered in readiness on the edge of these beams. At this point also were placed "drifters" with nets, fishing boats that went about their business, not of catching fish but of netting submarines.

In addition to the Channel barrier the British laid a line of defense directly in front of the Flanders base. It was a line of mine-studded nets and patrol boats placed eighteen miles out from Zeebrugge and extending for thirty-five miles along the coast from the shallow water outside of Dunkirk to the shallows of the Scheldt. There was not enough water at the ends for a U-boat to dodge round the barrier. Nor was it possible to dive under the nets. The water along the line was not deep enough. So it had to be a case of slipping through on the surface at night and trying to give the patrol boats the slip. It would take a fertile mind indeed to conjure up a more hazardous undertaking than this. But men did it and most of them seemed to thrive on the excitement of it. Not nearly so many U-boat officers and men went insane as was rumoured. But the perils they survived made nearly all of them prematurely old.

The British began their net barrier system early in the war. They were constantly enlarging and improving it right up to November, 1918. So the history of the Flanders Flotilla is a tale of contending with imperfect defenses that gradually became more and more perfect. Its great losses, an appalling number, took place along the barriers. One day in February of 1918 eighteen German under-sea raiders left Zeebrugge to run the Dover Barrier. Out of the eighteen only two returned.

By the end of the war the Allies, mainly the British, had practically closed the Channel to U-boat passage and so hampered the work of the Flanders Flotilla that it was of little service. The barriers of mines, nets, and patrol boats likewise explain how England was able to throw her millions of troops into France by means of efficiently convoyed transports with scarcely any loss by submarine attack.

There are few phases of warfare and human peril in general that present such a clear and vivid case of a gamble with death as the operations of the submarines based on Bruges and Zeebrugge. It was seldom a case of fighting and of having a chance to fight your way out. Instead, it was a blind game of luck with mines, nets, gunfire, and depth bombs as ever incalculable and mysterious factors. Either you drew the wrong card or you didn't, and if you did, why that was the end, swift and certain and without much chance of complicated play that would give you a chance to work your way out.

CHAPTER XXVI

AIRPLANE FIGHTS SUBMARINE

The Germans placed their submarine base inland at Bruges to be safe from bombardment from the sea. But there still remained the dangers of bombardment from the air. The town was in easy striking distance for planes coming from the British coast, and the Britishers did not neglect the opportunity. Night and day they rained aërial bombs on Bruges.

"We grew so accustomed to air raids," one of the Flanders U-boat commanders told me, "that we took them as a matter of course. No meal was complete without one to punctuate the courses with the whistle of falling bombs and the roar of them when they went off. Rarely did a bright sunny day or a clear night during those final years of the war go by without a British bombing party heading for Bruges. The enemy planes came in flocks, sometimes as many as thirty and forty at a time. There would be a droning hum of many motors off in the distance, and that was the overture, the curtain raiser, letting us know that the show was about to begin. We had an airplane base a short distance away, but our machines always seemed to be far outnumbered, and then when the British sky raiders came at night our planes would have been of no use even if they had numbered a thousand. In the darkness all we could do was to sweep the sky with searchlights and pepper away hopelessly with our anti-aircraft guns. We had more than two hundred of these. But the enemy planes flew high and were almost out of reach. We did bring down two or three from the ground, but for the most part our archies were more of a danger to us on the ground than to the hostile planes above. When those two hundred defense guns opened up and began scattering shells around the sky and the shell fragments came hailing down it surely was time to look out below.

"Not one of those British air raids could have been labelled an important military success. Vital points were seldom hit, although, of course, there was an enormous amount of miscellaneous damage done here and there. All over Bruges buildings were wrecked and holes torn in the streets. Once a bomb hit an open place where a few minutes before the whole staff of submarine officers at Bruges had been collected. Luckily they were gone when the charge of high explosive struck the spot. Had it registered a direct hit, our Flanders Flotilla would have been crippled indeed.

"Our destroyers and torpedo boats lying uprotected in the harbour were frequently hit, though none was ever sunk or wrecked beyond repair. I remember once that I returned from a cruise with my U-boat and looked forward to going to Berlin on leave. Yes, there was a girl waiting there. When I got into port I was told that the commander of one of our destroyers at Bruges was ill and that, instead of keeping the date in Berlin, I would have to take over the command of his destroyer while my U-boat was laid up for repairs. Naturally, I felt pretty glum, but that night there was an air raid and the destroyer was hit by a bomb. What there was left of it of course had to go to the dry dock. And I went to Berlin!

"Our U-boats were safe from sky attack. Small craft, it was possible to build shelters for them. We had regular U-boat stables, quite roomy structures where as many as twenty-five craft could be run in side by side. The shelters were covered with a roof of cement, iron, and gravel more than six feet thick. Bombs which, exploding in soil, would dig a crater nine feet deep would scarcely make a dent in these well-constructed roofs. The main submarine stables were at Bruges, but we also had a few near the mole at Zeebrugge."

But if the submarines in port were sheltered from peril from the sky, it was far otherwise when they were at sea. There is a savour of strangeness and paradox in the conflict of airplane and submarine, and this new type of conflict found its especial field in the waters where the raiders of the Flanders Flotilla were aprowl.

The Flanders under-sea wolves operated in an area within easy striking range of the Allied eagles whose aeries were along the English coast. So whenever a sub set out from Zeebrugge it had constantly to keep a weather eye on the clouds or on that dazzling sun from whence attack so often came. Particularly partial to the trick of coming out of the sun were those huntsmen of the skies. Completely hidden by the blinding glare, they often would swoop down on the enemy unawares, sometimes on a red-nosed Boche plane, or on a zeppelin, or on a submarine. If the under-sea raider had an anti-aircraft gun it might, perhaps, force the plane to keep at a respectful height. Usually, however, the Allied pilot paid no attention to guns or anything else. Down he would pounce, drop his bombs, and then be off in less time than it takes to tell it. The German's safest course was to dive. But even then he had to go down, down mighty deep in the depths to elude the eagle-eyed war bird above. To an aërial scout a U-boat anywhere near the surface, in calm weather, was just as visible in the water as on top of it. In many places off the Flanders coast the water was quite shallow, so shallow that submarines often found it well nigh impossible to sink to a secure depth.

It was during 1917 that half a dozen boats out of Zeebrugge were sunk by aërial attack. One of these was a curious case. German Army Headquarters had been inquiring about several military officers who were missing. It was found that these men had gone out for a submarine cruise with a certain convivial Commander Glimpf on his boat, the *UB-20*. Then it was also disclosed that Glimpf had taken his raider to sea without orders, just to show these skeptical landlubbers what submarine cruising was like. Half of his crew happened to be in hospital with influenza at the time. Hence the UB-20 was sadly undermanned when she set forth on this under-sea joy ride. The *UB-20* never returned. Several weeks later Commander Glimpf's body was washed ashore. The boat must have gone down with the commander on deck at the time. The British tell of ladies being on board that submarine—a wild joy ride indeed. However that may be, the *UB-20* was near shore when a British air plane swooped down. The water was too shallow for the submarine to dive, and, furthermore, its manœuvres were handicapped by its being manned by only half of its crew. The aërial bombs did their crashing work and the *UB-20* went down with all on board.

The ace of the Flanders men and commander of the flotilla was Otto Steinbrinck, who ranks among the first half dozen of Germany's submarine commanders in point of enemy tonnage sunk. He accounted for two hundred thousand tons of Allied shipping. He is now in business in Berlin and doing well. You may see him almost any day having luncheon at the Kaiserhof in Berlin, and you will wonder that this dark, quiet, slender man is the formidable Steinbrinck whom the British tried so hard to get.

The British dreaded him and admired him. The reason for the admiration is not hard to understand. I will tell you a story about Steinbrinck to illustrate the point. It was related to me, not by a German, but by a British submarine commander who figures in the incident.

"It happened in 1916," he said, "in the North Sea near the English coast at Yarmouth. Steinbrinck had a small boat and was submerged to twenty-five feet when he saw through his periscope four British submarines running on the surface. They were heading north toward him at a rate of about twelve knots. They were strung out about a mile apart. I happened to be the commander of one of those British E-boats. Steinbrinck attacked the leader of the oncoming craft, which was commanded by a friend of mine. The British officer saw the German's periscope, put his helm hard over, eluded the torpedo, and rammed. Steinbrinck lowered his periscope in time, but got his bow net cutter—the big saw-edged blade a submarine uses to cut its way out of nets—caught and bent down. He dived under the E-boat and took a periscope peep from the other side. The E-boat turned back at full speed for another ram when Steinbrinck flicked out both bow torpedoes for a fluke shot. One torpedo hit. It blew up the E-boat, which sank at once, leaving two men swimming. Steinbrinck saw the three other enemy submarines which were coming up swiftly. He then saw them submerge at once, almost as though at a single command. Their periscopes cut through the water toward the scene of the explosion. They were approaching at short range and Steinbrinck knew they would let their torpedoes go the moment they got their sights on him. I remember that down in my conning tower I was waiting eagerly with all four torpedoes ready to go as I came along, twenty-five feet down and nine knots speed.

"Steinbrinck came to the surface. I saw him after the war and compared notes with him. He told me he was damned nervous as he brought his boat out of the water. He expected to be blown up at any moment. He kept his stern to our line of fire so as to present the smallest possible mark for us to shoot at. He steered his boat gingerly over. We wondered what he was up to, until we saw. A couple of his sailors hopped out on deck and leaned down to the water. They were picking up the two Englishmen who had been left swimming when their boat had sunk. Then, having rescued the two men, the gallant Steinbrinck dived as fast as he could and got away from there. Well, *I* wouldn't have done it. I take reasonable risks, but—well I'd like to tell a girl I *had* done it."

No wonder English navy men have a considerable regard for Otto Steinbrinck. He was not of the dashing, dare-devil type, but a conscientious, hard-working officer, serious and responsible. Submarine commanders were likely to be of that sort. Mere recklessness was a sure ticket to the other world in the war under the sea. There were flashing, daring temperaments, but along with fiery spirit went cool, heady calculation and the prosy qualities of industry and application.

One of the Flanders stories was of that frightful experience which the world to-day holds to be one of the most terrifying of misfortunes—trapped in a sunken submarine. It was a common enough thing in this war under the sea which was the lot of the raiders of the deep. In nearly every one of the scores of U-boats sent to the bottom were men who found themselves entombed alive in the iron coffin and doomed to slow death by suffocation, unless they chose to end it more speedily. In the case of Lieutenant Wenninger and his men aboard the *UB-55* the miraculous happened—an escape from the sunken coffin.

The night of April 22, 1918, was a memorable one. During the hours of darkness the British made their incredibly daring raid on Zeebrugge. While this prodigious adventure was under way back at the submarine base the *UB-55* was treading its way through the barriers across the Channel, a lone boat lost in the darkness and surrounded by all the perils which the might and cunning of Britain had been able to throw across the narrow strip of sea.

A patrol boat looms in the darkness. The sub dives and runs under water. A sudden ear-splitting crash, and the boat shakes and staggers in a ghastly way. The lights flash out. The craft has hit a mine and is mortally injured. She reels and lists and sinks. She plunges without help or hindrance. A bump, and she has struck the bottom. Inside in utter darkness the men are paralyzed with horror. They are all alive. Compartments have been shattered, and the main body of the boat is leaking. They have sunk in a hundred feet of water. They work the mechanisms frantically. The boat lies still and dead, an inert mass of submerged steel. Any hope they may have had of refloating her vanishes. Water is seeping in through the leaking hull.

Only one hope, the conning tower hatch. They struggle with it, but it will not open. The boat is filling. The air inside is becoming compressed. If they can only get the hatch open! The compressed air will shoot them out like missiles, just as the torpedoes are launched. Like living torpedoes they will be hurled to the surface of the water. Mad efforts, and the hatch slowly opens.

And so that night on the dark surface a huge air bubble broke from the tossing waters of the English Channel, and with it came the forms of men. Twenty men of the sunken submarine, the *UB-55,* escaped from their iron coffin and fooled old Davy Jones. They now found themselves swimming. The British patrol boat, the one that had caused them to submerge just before they bumped into the mine, was now out of sight. It was hours before dawn and not until dawn could they hope that one of the many English boats patrolling the Channel would sight them and pick them up. They swam and floated hour after hour. Some weakened and went down, as if faithful sailors bent on rejoining their ship. The others, six in number, including the commander, kept themselves up until daybreak, when an English boat hove in sight and took them aboard, prisoners.

Lieutenant Wenninger remained in a British prison camp until the end of the war. Upon his return to Germany he continued in the naval service, and now is executive officer aboard the German cruiser *Berlin*.

CHAPTER XXVII

RUNNING THE DOVER PATROL

In rare cases a U-boat might hit a mine or be otherwise smashed up by explosives and contrive to get back to port. Lieutenant Wassner of the Flanders base—his brother officers called him Uncle Fritz—brought his boat in so badly damaged that it seemed a miracle that it could remain afloat. That boat, though, was saturated with bad luck. It was put in the dry dock for repairs, and while there was hit by an air bomb, and that finished its career. Uncle Fritz went back to Germany to get another boat, but before he could reach Bruges the German collapse had begun. The line was forced back in Belgium and the Flanders base at Bruges and Zeebrugge was given up.

Commander Count Schmettow of the mine-laying *UC-26* was rammed by a steamer. The hull at the point where it was struck was little more than a twisted mass of steel with a gaping hole. Still Count Schmettow brought the craft back to port. But miracles don't happen twice. Later on he was rammed by a British destroyer near the mouth of the Thames. Again he might have brought his boat home safely, but the British took no chance of that. He had dived, and they destroyed him with depth bombs.

A melancholy case was that of Paul Hundius. He was awarded the Pour le Mérite, the highest German decoration and the one so rarely bestowed. He was away on cruise when the award was made and never returned to receive the decoration. His boat was attacked by airplanes and fishing smacks and went down shattered by bombs. It was in September of 1918 and his boat was the last one lost in the Strait of Dover before the Armistice.

Then there was Commander von Zerboni di Sposetti of the *UC-21*. He was of an ancient Italian family transplanted to Germany generations before. His father and four brothers were all German officers. His submarine was caught in the nets and mines of the barriers and was lost with all aboard. By an ironical chance one of his brothers was the victim of a British submarine attack. He went down when the cruiser *Prinz Adalbert* was torpedoed by a British submarine in the Baltic.

The blithesome spirit of the Flanders base was Losz, who made fun of the barriers. "Go through on the surface," he always said. "The patrol boats are blind. They can't see a thing. I go through under their very noses." And he did go through again and again, flirting with death. The barriers had their revenge, though. In the *UB-57* Losz hit one of the mines that formed a part of the barrier off Zeebrugge, and that was the end of him and his raider.

No phase of the war under the sea was more curious than that of the fishing boats that dragged for U-boats with steel nets. A fishing boat could make an ugly trap. Often these craft had long nets extended astern. A U-boat might spy such a vessel and decide to sink it by gunfire. Prudently, the stalking boat might take a good look at its prey first from under the water. It would circle around at close range inspecting through its periscope. And then it might get caught in the hidden net extending under the water from the seemingly innocent fisherman.

Commander Fritz von Tvardovski had a rare adventure with the fishing boats that went netting for submarines. He told me of this when we met in Kiel shortly after the Armistice. It was off the east coast of England. Von Tvardovski attacked and sank a small ship between two little harbours. The moment the alarm was given he found himself surrounded by an angry swarm of patrol boats, armed motor launches, and trawlers. He submerged, but before he could get a safe distance from the coast and its shallows they had surrounded him. Most of the attackers could do ten or twelve knots and the submerged speed of his tiny sub was two. It was like the case of a fox in a thicket surrounded by beaters.

He could hear the propellers of the boats closing in nearer and nearer, narrowing the circle. And he was not fast enough to get out of the circle. They were dragging for him with their nets. He got into deep water and dived as deep as he dared. A few feet farther down the boat would have been crushed by the pressure of the water. It was not deep enough. There was a rattling and a scraping overhead. The U-boat was brought up with a jerk that hurled the commander to the conning-tower floor. One of the chains attached to the nets had caught the cigar-shaped body and held it fast.

Ever go fishing and catch a submarine? Just imagine the thrill of it! Well, those British fishermen had a U-boat on the end of their line. All they had to do was to haul it in, or drop a depth bomb on it. Tvardovski knew he was lost unless he could break loose. The boat was quivering and pitching back and forth very much like a hooked fish.

"Full speed ahead!" was the command—every ounce of engine power.

There was a shattering and a cracking and then a loud report. The U-boat lurched forward. It had torn away, just as a big fish with a lunging dart breaks a fisherman's line.

The fish had broken loose, but was blind. In the

struggle with the entangling chain the U-boat's periscope had been snapped off. The craft could only grope in the depths, or rise to the surface and take what was coming to it there. Away it went, sightless under water, and continued groping its way for an hour. Anything to get as far away as possible from that swarm of enemies. Eventually, though, it had to come up, and when it did the thrill was something tremendous.

"Stand by for the surface!" Tvardovski gave the order, and the boat rose. He hadn't the slightest idea where he might be.

As the conning tower broke the water the commander threw open the conning tower hatch swiftly for a look around. A British submarine was likewise emerging only a few yards away. Its commander was just coming out of his conning tower. The two skippers took one look at each other, and neither ever forgot the expression on the other's face. Simultaneously they both leaped back. Those two boats broke records for speed of diving that day.

Tvardovski's voyage back to Zeebrugge was quite a feat of navigation, running blind below water by dead reckoning, with an occasional rise to the surface for a look around, until he reached waters where it was safe to run awash.

The Flanders Flotilla could scarcely have avoided its share of experiences with Q-ships, and here it had something real to brag about. One of the tiny boats out of Zeebrugge, the *UC-71*, had a tremendous fight with the famous Q-ship *Dunraven* under the command of Britain's Q-ship ace, Gordon Campbell. The submarine succeeded not only in getting out of a well-laid trap, but sank its adversary. The victor was the fair-haired boy of the Flanders base, young Reinhold Salzwedel. He was an upstanding chap, blond and blue-eyed, with a fine wide brow, a firm chin, a humorous mouth, and a proud carriage of head—a gallant, laughing, frank-eyed boy, as far as possible from the popular conception of the barbarous Hun. He was the favourite of the base, and when he was lost . . . But before I tell about when and how he was lost let me add that he won the coveted Pour le Mérite, destroyed more than a hundred and fifty thousand tons of shipping, and won his thrilling victory over the daring Gordon Campbell (now Admiral Gordon Campbell, V. C.) on the *Dunraven.*

In the Bay of Biscay a lazy old British merchant steamer pounded innocently along. At least it looked that way. In reality it was the *Dunraven,* armed to the teeth and disguised with all possible cunning as an ordinary humdrum craft. On the after deck it displayed a small gun, which kept up the appearances all the more, as most Allied ships were going armed at that time. At eleven in the forenoon the *UC-71* sighted this seeming tramp. Salzwedel was wary about Q-ships, and went about cautiously. He inspected the ship carefully, and when he had decided it was altogether inoffensive, he opened fire from about 5,000 yards off the starboard quarter. He wasn't taking any chases of rashly closing in. The *Dunraven,* keeping up its bluff, pretended to try to run away, and opened fire with its little gun. Meanwhile, the concealed crew was waiting at concealed guns, ready to throw off the disguise and open a murderous fire the moment the submarine ventured to approach so close that it couldn't be missed.

After a bit of long-range fire, Salzwedel came up at full speed and opened fire at medium range. The *Dunraven's* next bluff was to pretend that its engines had been hit. It stopped and let off a cloud of steam, as if the boilers had exploded. Salzwedel saw the signs of an explosion and lost whatever uneasiness he may have had. On the *Dunraven* a panic party was staged.

Boats put off with an apparently fear-stricken crew. One of the forward lifeboats was allowed to drop and capsize, as if accidentally, that being usually one of the things that happened when a ship was abandoned in the face of a submarine attack. Meanwhile, shells were striking the steamer. The hidden crew kept its place stoically. It all looked so real that Salzwedel drew close to administer the final stroke.

Everything was primed for blowing the U-boat out of the water when misfortune befell the *Dunraven*. A shell penetrated the ship's poop and exploded a depth bomb. The ship staggered under the heavy detonation. Two more shells followed into the poop and the ship caught fire. The ship's store of depth charges were placed aft, and soon they went off. In the tremendous explosion the after 4-inch gun and the boat's entire crew were blown into the air. The gun described an arc and landed on the forward deck, and one man dropped into the water. When Salzwedel saw the gun and several men go skyrocketing from the supposedly abandoned ship he had no trouble in guessing the real state of things. He immediately submerged. With its secret disclosed, the *Dunraven* threw down its disguises, ran up its war flag, and opened fire. The men aboard thought they hit the conning tower as it disappeared beneath the waves.

Gordon Campbell aboard the *Dunraven* now found himself in a ticklish position. His ship was blazing. His main magazine might explode any time. The submarine was below the water. A torpedo would come next. He had a wireless message that a warship was coming to his aid. He radioed in return, bidding the rescuing vessel to keep away. He and his men had chilled steel for nerves, and they still hoped to snare their prey. His deck was getting red hot under the boxes of highly explosive cordite piled there. The British sailors actually held those boxes in their hands, a foot or so above the hot deck, to keep them from going off and blowing the ship and each and every one of them to kingdom come.

The expected torpedo was not long delayed. It struck amidships and nearly broke the *Dunraven* in two. The vessel kept afloat. It had been filled with lumber, so that it would not sink easily. Campbell now launched a life raft with a part of his crew. But he still kept a force of picked men aboard and stuck to his wreck. He was sure that Salzwedel would believe the ship finally abandoned. Indeed, it seemed impossible for anybody to remain aboard. The after deck was burning fiercely. The fire had got into the store of shells now and these were going off in all directions. Besides, the *Dunraven* was now so far gone that its guns could not be used.

The *UC-71*, as expected, broke water and began to shell the derelict vessel at close range to sink it. Campbell awaited his opportunity. He had one resource left. He had torpedoes. He lay in ambush hoping for a shot. No luck. After shelling the *Dunraven* for a while, Salzwedel submerged again. Campbell, with his ship almost uninhabitable now, took a last chance. Salzwedel's periscope came within torpedoing range. The *Dunraven* loosed its torpedoes one after another—and missed. Salzwedel quite obviously saw the last of the two, for the U-boat changed course sharply. It would have been all over with the *Dunraven* right then if Salzwedel had had another torpedo, but the one he had fired was his last. So he simply lurked in the distance, waiting to see what would happen.

Campbell realized that the game was up. So he wirelessed for the patrol vessels that were waiting over the horizon. These came rushing and took aboard the crew of the *Dunraven*. They put out towlines and began hauling the Q-ship to port. But the *Dunraven*

was too far gone. Before she reached port, she capsized and sank.

That fight is described among naval men as the most
thrilling of all the encounters between submarines and
Q-ships during the war, and it was one of the few
times that a submarine succeeded in putting the quietus
on one of those formidable decoy ships. Gordon
Campbell in particular had been spectacularly successful in the fight against U-boats and had sent three of
them to the bottom before he met the *UC-71*. The
exploit gained Salzwedel much credit, and deservedly
so. It went far toward establishing him as one of the
foremost of the Flanders commanders.

In December of 1917 Salzwedel went out in the
UB-81, never more to return. In attempting a night
passage his submarine struck one of the mines of one
of the Channel barriers, which exploded under his
stern. The stern was shattered, but the forward
part of the boat remained intact. The craft was on
its way to the bottom, when Salzwedel blew all tanks.
The descent was checked, and the boat was rising.
The *UB-81* staggered to the surface. The tip of her
bow stuck out of the water. The wrecked stern held
the rest of the body down. The boat lay like that
and could not straighten out. They opened the bow
torpedo tubes. Two men, an officer and a petty officer,
crawled out. A British patrol boat, having heard the
sound of the explosion, was waiting near by, and, seeing a form emerge, a vague form in the darkness,
turned at full speed to ram. The two Germans clinging to the protruding bow waved their arms and
shouted. The patrol boat did not stop. It crashed
into the derelict hull and hurled it under the surface.
The water rushed in through the open torpedo tube
and drowned every one inside. The two men who had
gotten out were the only survivors.

The Flanders base had many an exciting hour,

between air raids and such, but the pinnacle of wild, mad commotion came at midnight on the eve of Saint George's Day, Monday, April 22, 1918, the date of the famous British raid on Zeebrugge. The elements of the strategy were simple. The submarine base at Bruges depended on those two canals previously referred to, the main one opening to the sea at Zeebrugge and the secondary one not far off at Ostend. If the mouths of these two canals were blocked, why then the German naval craft at Bruges would be bottled up and the Flanders base be put out of commission. How could they be blocked? Why, by sinking ships across them. The idea was the same as in the case of Hobson's famous exploit during the Spanish-American War. So, the British naval authorities decided on a couple of daring raids during which block ships would be run into the mouths of the canals at Ostend and Zeebrugge and sunk there.

The problem at Ostend was the simpler. There nothing was to be encountered except a simple coast lined with guns. At Zeebrugge, though, there was the great mole extending in a semi-circle in front of the canal. The mole was heavily armed with guns and was defended by a garrison. The plan was to attack the mole, both to put its defenders out of commission and to give the impression that this attack was the real thing. It was a kind of feint to mask the real work, which was the running in of the block ships. At the shore end of the mole was a viaduct through which the tidal water ran. It was planned to cut off the mole from land communication by blowing up the viaduct. For this purpose a submarine loaded with high explosive was to be run under the viaduct and touched off. While all this was going on the block ships were to be run into the canal and sunk.

It was a daring venture daringly executed. At midnight the British flotilla stole its way to Zeebrugge. When off shore it began a bombardment. This really aided the surprise. The Germans thought it was merely a case of shelling from the sea and took to their shelters. H. M. S. *Vindictive* bore the brunt of the action. She ran in, braving the fire of the German big guns, drew alongside the mole and landed troops. The German defenders were so thoroughly taken by surprise that they at first scarcely resisted the landing. A tremendous explosion. The submarine loaded with explosive had been steered under the viaduct and blown up. The mole was isolated. The Britisher advanced along the narrow arm sticking out into the water, and savage fighting took place. Under cover of this diversion the block ships were run into the canal and sunk. Then the attackers on the mole retreated. The *Vindictive* took them aboard and was off. The raid was a spectacular success, although many lives were lost.

Simultaneously, the similar raid on the canal at Ostend was taking place. It went awry. The block ships failed to find the canal in the darkness and were sunk off shore where they blocked nothing at all. The British displayed the true spirit of the bulldog. A short while later they took advantage of the fact that a repetition of the raids would not be expected and did the same over again. The *Vindictive*, which had covered herself with glory, was used this time as a block ship and sunk across the canal at Ostend.

I talked with a U-boat officer who had played his part during that incredible hour past midnight. He gave me a few vivid touches.

"During the day I got back to Zeebrugge from a cruise with my boat. We were all very tired and decided to rest for a few hours at Zeebrugge before continuing along the canal to Bruges. We lay in a shelter behind the mole, ready to start up the canal at midnight. We had just taken our boat out of its stall and were ready to enter the canal when the raid began and hell broke loose.

"Out there was the *Vindictive* coming straight in. The big guns were roaring at her, but they had not spotted her soon enough. Before there was a chance to do much she was too close to hit and alongside the mole. The guns of my submarine, however, were in a position to bear on her, and we opened fire. We hit her repeatedly and must have killed many men on her decks.

"I have never seen such horrible hand-to-hand fighting as took place on the Zeebrugge Mole. The sailors from the *Vindictive* swarmed down, and many of the defenders, taken by surprise, were unarmed. I saw an Englishman bayonet a German through the body, and then the dying man sank his teeth in the throat of his adversary.

"Everything went wrong that night. As the block ships came in the junior officer of the land battery at one side of the entrance thought they were German torpedo boats and did not fire on them. Even so, it would have made no difference. He did not see them in time. At the speed they were going, even if he had hit them they would not have stopped before they reached the channel.

"It was a brilliant adventure on the part of the British. It cost them many men, but no doubt helped to buck up the morale of their forces and of the Allies in general. Otherwise it did not have much effect. It did not block the Flanders base. The sunken ships did not cover the entrance thoroughly, and on the day following the raid the U-boats were able to pass in and out at high tide by following a course like a letter S past the port side of one of the block ships and the starboard of the other. At the same time we immediately began to dredge a passage at one side of the canal, and in three days it was deep enough for a torpedo boat to pass through at high tide.

"Nor was the Ostend Canal effectively blocked. In the first attempt the block ships went astray. That was caused by a curious accident. They planned to guide themselves by a certain buoy, but on the day before the raid we for some reason or other, just some reason of ordinary navigation, moved the buoy ten miles to the east, and the raiding vessels were completely baffled. The *Vindictive* was later sunk right in the middle of the Ostend Channel, but we were able to pull it to one side with giant grappling hooks, and our vessels were able to pass through freely.

"The results of the raid were not important so far as the movements of the Flanders boats were concerned. But the affair certainly provided an uproarious midnight for a lot of us."

The end of the Flanders base came at the end of September of 1918. The German armies were in retreat. Belgium had to be evacuated. The base was abandoned. The Germans blew up everything military that they could not take away, wharves, shelters, and fortifications, and four submarines that were unfit to make the voyage back to Germany. Twenty left by sea and put out for the German coast, and arrived safely.

The war was at its close when Lieutenant Emsmann, one of the former Flanders commanders, decided to have another try at the enemy. He steered from Wilhelmshaven to Scapa Flow, where the British Grand Fleet was stationed. He wanted to strike one last big blow from under the sea and get an important British warship. On the 28th of October he managed to get through the outer defenses of Scapa Flow. He was scarcely inside before he hit a mine and was blown up. After the Armistice a diver went down and opened the conning tower of the foundered boat. Just inside was the body of Emsmann, his confidential log book still clutched in his hands. It was apparent that the U-boat skipper had died trying to destroy it.

CHAPTER XXVIII

THE KORVETTENKAPITÄN SPINS HIS YARN IN AMERICAN SLANG

Afternoon tea at the Kaiserhof is one of the bright moments of the daily social whirl in post-war Berlin. The hotel is one of the finest, a glittering spacious place. True, I could remember it in a guise somewhat less festive. That was during the revolution in Berlin just after the end of the war, when savage fighting was going on between the soldiery of the republican government and the bolshevist Spartacans. One night we were unceremoniously ousted from our rooms and the Kaiserhof was turned into a bristling fortress, crammed with fighting men and ornamented at every post of vantage with the ugly muzzles of machine guns. From then on the sumptuous Kaiserhof was a central strategic point in the campaign that resulted in the crushing of the red uprising. But the hotel was all very different ten years later. Red Rosa Luxemburg and the fiery Karl Liebknecht are gone to the Valhalla of the nihilists. The Kaiserhof once more is quiet and sleek and very well mannered. At tea you are likely to see half the notables of Berlin, particularly on the diplomatic side. It is a regular habit with the officials of the Wilhelmstrasse foreign office to adjourn to tea at the Kaiserhof. I remember, the day I sat there in the lounge, glancing over occasionally at Stresemann, the Foreign Minister, with his round head as slick as a billiard ball. My companion for tea that day was in no wise a figure of diplomacy, although

253

of a diplomatic family. He was decidedly a personage of war, in fact one of the most formidable of the raiders of the deep, and he was telling me tales of his adventures under the sea.

Korvettenkapitän Robert Wilhelm Moraht was born in 1884 on the island of Alsen, now a part of Denmark. He spent his boyhood in Hamburg and then entered the Imperial Navy in 1901. His career with the U-boats was comparatively brief. He entered the submarine service in 1916 and was captured by the British in 1918, but those two years were packed with adventure and hair-raising experience and a spectacular panorama of exploding torpedoes and sinking ships. Commander Moraht destroyed forty-four merchant ships of a total burden of almost one hundred and fifty thousand tons. He accounted for two men-of-war, one the largest fighting ship ever sunk by submarine torpedo attack. He was awarded the highest decorations the Kaiser could give, including the Pour le Mérite. After the Armistice he retired from the German Navy, and, planning to enter industrial life, went about it in a characteristic German way. He undertook university studies in the science of economy, took a degree of Doctor of Economics, *magna cum laude*, and has many written treatises. He is now an expert connected with various German industrial organizations. I found him an alert, cheery, good-looking chap of about forty, who told his story in a vivid manner spiced with drollery, not with boisterous laughter but with a peculiarly humorous whimsical smile. He talks English very well, in fact like a cultured Englishman, save for the point of American slang. This particular Captain Nemo and learned Doctor of Economics is particularly interested in talking "United States," and to add to his mastery of scholarly English he makes a serious effort to master its latest jazz forms. He really has a finer command of our language than the average American. But our picturesque slang is his present hobby, and it fits him to a "T." When I talked with him he constantly swung into American slang. Sometimes he got it wrong, but more often right—which gave his narration a colour of its own.

And so at tea in the Kaiserhof (yes, there was tea, not cocktails) the days when the terror of the submarine stalked the sea were conjured back in a dramatic pageant:

My first cruise and my last, each one was—the cat's pajamas you Americans say, don't you? *Ach, Gott,* on that first cruise we were nearly sunk, and on the last cruise there was no nearly about it; the *U-64*, limping, lurching, riddled with shell fire, received her death stroke at last and went plunging to the bottom of the sea, to the doom of that last port to which she had sent many other craft. That was the end, one tough luck, as you Americans say, but before it came we had gone through every kind of experience that you could find in the course of warfare under the sea, happenings terrifying and happenings comic, too, I'll tell the world.

The first cruise had a tremendous mood, epic, great stuff. It was the day before the battle of Jutland. Before I returned, the two greatest fleets of all history had met in a gigantic, fiery collision, a mighty conflict of massed steel and high explosive. Huge ships had gone down with thundering explosions. I had recently joined up in the submarines, and had just finished my studies and training to fit me for the post of a U-boat commander. The *U-64* had just been put into service. She was the latest thing in submarines. Her length from nose to tail was a bit more than 200 feet. Her gross weight when plying as a surface vessel was 800 tons, but when she took to her proper element beneath the waves her tonnage shot up to 920. To submerge we simply opened our valves and let the sea flow into the tanks. And when the *U-64* metamorphosed into a fish she drank 120 tons of water in one long gulp. Her speed on top of the sea was fourteen knots and beneath the waves she did six. To put on her magic cloak of invisibility and dive out of sight took exactly sixty seconds. But there are times when sixty seconds are just fifty-nine too many—as you will observe a little later in my yarn. We were equipped with two Diesel engines for running on the surface and with electric motors for running under the sea. So powerful were her batteries that we could carry on for twenty-four hours in the depths without coming up to recharge.

When submarine men or officers bid farewell to this dizzy earthly sphere they should either go direct to Hell or Heaven without changing elevators in Purgatory. The bowels of any U-boat are Purgatory enough. If you never have been in one I'll give you a brief description of what it's like: At each end of the *U-64* there is a trap door leading from the deck to the interior. You can also get down through another in the conning tower, amidship. Atop the conning tower is a cramped space surrounded by a rail called the bridge. The inside of the conning tower itself is barely big enough to accommodate four men—if they stand up and avoid waving their elbows. From the conning tower a ladder leads down into the *Kommando-centrale,* which is the centre of all operations during attack, either submerged or on the surface. There are enough speaking tubes, electric buttons, and other gadgets here to drive the average mortal loony—*nicht wahr?*—in a week. Here the commander sits with one eye riveted to the nether end of the asparagus, ready to give orders to his assistant who operates the electric lift that slides it up and down. Around him are the warrant officer for navigation busy with the charts, the helmsman with his eye on the compasses, and the torpedo officer ready to relay word to the men in the torpedo rooms. A narrow corridor runs right through the steel fish from nose to tail. In the bow is a torpedo room, but so cramped is the space on board that the men and under officers live here together with their slim bunks one on top of another, and with tables and benches that fold up when not in use. As you work toward the bow the next tiny compartment is the warrant officers' messroom and the kitchen with its electric stoves. The next space, hardly worthy to be described as a space at all, is the officers' mess. Then comes a little room for the commander of the U-boat and a miniature wireless room. Just back of that is the *Kommando-centrale* with its wheels, pumps, ventilators, diving and steering machines, etc., etc. Astern of this are the Diesel and electric engines and the stern torpedo room with more sardine-like bunks for the crew. And along the whole length of the submarine, filling the space between an inner and an outer hull, are the diving tanks.

Mixed with my natural pride at having such a spick-and-span new U-boat were a few misgivings. As you would surmise, life on an under-sea raider in war time demands men as stern and inflexible as the submarine itself. Yet the most of these chaps who were going out with me to do battle were mere red-cheeked boys.

Our training days over, we put to sea on our great adventure one balmy spring evening, with our guns, periscope, and wireless masts festooned with birch bows and huge clusters of lilacs in honour of our "coming-out party." It may seem a bit incongruous to hear of a grim U-boat starting on a raid garlanded with lilacs. But that's the way it happened. However, our adventures soon brought thoughts of other things than lilacs.

We were greenhorns anxious to strut our stuff, and it happened that our first assignment was to go out on cruise on the day before the battle of Jutland. While we were out we received orders to scout for British naval vessels that might still be on the prowl after the fight and see if we could pot them with a torpedo or two. So the *U-64* stood out of port and steered for that stretch of sea off the Danish coast where the day after hell was to break loose.

Greenhorns always feel solemn and nervous on their first cruise, and here we were acting in an epilogue to the greatest naval battle in history. Now, if we could just sink three or four British battleships! But beginners always are afflicted with such pipe dreams, I guess. The prow of our iron shell cut the fateful waters off Jutland. It was a clear day on the restless North Sea. A sense of tragedy weighed upon us. There below us, many fathoms under the gray surface of the sea, lay the hulks of great ships newly sunk, giant coffins for the bodies of brave men that had gone down in the fight. Even the stoniest heart could not refrain from a prayer for the heroes who had died the day before. And we felt in a great mood to be avengers of our fallen comrades.

Avengers we were not. The sea was deserted. We sailed far and wide, but nary a British warship did we see. Yes, we were greenhorns. Tender as they come. We exhausted ourselves, as beginners are likely to do on a first cruise, and the solemnity of the occasion made us work all the harder. By nightfall, after our day of industrious scouting about, we were nearly cock-eyed with fatigue—all in. *Ja,* I'll say we were. We sank to the bottom of the sea for the night and got in a session of heavy sleeping.

"Nothing accomplished," I said to myself disconsolately as I fell off to sleep; "no excitement or anything." But before that cruise was ended I was destined to get the thrill of my life. I didn't know anybody could experience such a pang of fear and despair. My first submarine thrill—well, it was an appropriate way to begin a career as a U-boat commander. Yes, thrill is the word that gives the keynote of life in the war under the sea.

We were on our way back to our base at Emden the next day, gliding along on the surface near the coast. At noon I went above to take my turn at watch on deck. The mate, whom I was relieving, told me that he had noticed a "stick" thrust out of the water on our starboard. Greenhorns? *Ach du lieber,* yes. With a little experience no one but a lunatic would mistake a periscope for a stick. I might have made the mistake myself, only I was well enough acquainted with those waters to know that there were no sticks, such as might be used to mark a channel, to be expected in those parts. Sure enough, it was a periscope. And hot dog—is that what you say?—there came the torpedo! The enemy submersible had cut loose at us at short range, and here came a torpedo straight for the bull's eye. Oh, Mamma!

"Hard aport, both engines full speed astern!" I yelled.

The *U-64,* obeying her controls, swung quickly around.

"Jimminy Christmas, but that was close!" I said when I could breathe again.

I was just getting the burden off my mind when suddenly the whole world went into a daze. A deafening explosion crashed out. I nearly passed right out from sheer funk. It seemed like the end of everything, so far as we were concerned.

Then, to my vast relief, nothing further happened.

The boat just rocked and swayed and bucked a bit. I was tickled pink to find a solid deck still under my feet. A cloud of smoke drifted over us. What happened was this. The water was quite shallow in spots. The torpedo had indeed missed us. It had run on past us and hit a shoal and exploded not a hundred feet farther on.

It was a badly shaken crew aboard that U-boat as the craft got away from there, zigzagging as fast as it could. Hot stuff? *Ja!* I'll say. You bet it left us with something to think about—just as much so as if we had bagged a British super-dreadnaught that day after the battle of Jutland.

Soon afterward I took the *U-64* around through the straits, past old "Gib" and into the balmy Mediterranean. But the voyage out there was anything but balmy. By Jimminy, what a storm we bumped into!

CHAPTER XXIX

THE PETTY OFFICERS ATE ALL THE MAR-
MALADE, AND THE SAILORS ATE ALL
THE HAM, AND THE COOK GOT
THE IRON CROSS

We slid out of Wilhelmshaven on November 26, 1916, and turned the iron snout north toward the Shetlands and the Orkneys. We were going by that route because the big idea was to get to the Mediterranean without running any extra risk of being bumped off on the way. But we'd all have preferred destroyers and depth bombs to the gales we passed through.

Two days out from Wilhelmshaven we sighted the dreary hills of the bleak Shetlands. Then a southeaster hit us, and this was only the first of five storms we had to run through. All day this gale lashed us while we wallowed amid the towering waves. Great combers broke over us. Up on the bridge the three men on watch had to lash themselves to the rail with their life belts to keep from being swept away. They were dressed in one-piece rubber garments, a combination of coat, pants, and shoes all in one, which made them look like divers. Over their heads were tight rubber helmets that fit down around the shoulders, leaving only the eyes, nose, and mouth free.

If you have never been on a submarine you can not imagine the strain of keeping watch in such weather. Each wave slapped against the U-boat like a solid body. It seemed as though they would bash in the conning tower. Our dinghy was splintered and even one of the heavy guns was knocked loose so that its muzzle wobbled crazily from side to side.

Below in the stale air of the closed hull I clutched my desk and studied the charts. The sun was hidden so I could only guess at our position. My desk heaved with the bucking lurches of the U-boat until I was dizzy from the motion. Then the men would clamber down from above shaking the salt water from their swollen eyes and wriggling out of their dripping suits. My man Haupt brought in my supper of scrambled eggs. I often forgot meal hours, but he never did. As I sat there amid the roar of the storm I remembered that it was the anniversary of my wedding day. Just a year before I had been attending my own wedding dinner right here at this same Hotel Kaiserhof.

After darkness the storm increased its intensity and at midnight the watch officer came down with the news that he could no longer hang to the bridge because he was certain to be torn loose by the waves. So all that night we had to run blind. I took a gambler's chance, and guessing at our course, I attempted to steer forty miles off the Shetlands. But before morning the wind veered, and when Lieutenant Quesse mounted the conning tower bridge at daybreak there were the Shetlands, hardly five miles away instead of forty.

After reaching the Atlantic we ran through two more storms and then fought our way through the worst weather of all off the Bay of Biscay, where we were forced to dive and remain submerged for forty hours to save ourselves.

Then, during the months that followed in the Mediterranean, until our iron dolphin met its tragic end, we campaigned in that beautiful sea. Save for the duties of war, it was idyllic cruising, beautiful days, blue water, and lovely coasts. It might have been the most perfect pleasure cruise; in fact, it would have been except for the food, and of course the under-surface voyaging. But food, ah that is always the great problem in a submarine. On a long voyage that interminable diet of canned stuff, with peas and bacon as the *pièce de resistance*, becomes unbearable. Since then I've never been able to look a pea in the face. As for the bacon, on that point I'll be a Mohammedan to the end of my days.

In a way the food situation was tougher on the cook than on anybody else. Our chef was a tall, lanky, stupid-faced son-of-a-sea-cook from the banks of the Weser. As a sea cook mebbe he could have gotten by if he'd had decent materials to work with. As it was, he had no chance to dish anything up to the sailors but very poor grub. Nor did the lads like it. Nor did they hold back their spleen. And poor Miedtank, as he was named, had sensitive feelings.

"That Miedtank," they would say loudly, so he would be sure to hear, "what kind of a cook is he? He can't even boil water. Is he not a marvellous chef, the stupid donkey?"

And Miedtank would come to me.

"They do nothing but grouse and ridicule," he would say. "They have no appreciation nor thanks. I won't cook for them any longer. I will ask to be transferred."

Donnerwetter, holy smoke! A U-boat commander has to have many talents. I had to be a diplomat and even skilful enough to pacify an insulted cook, or we might get a worse one than he.

"Oh no, Miedtank," I would say, "we couldn't possibly get along without you. Where could we ever get another cook like you? You must not pay any attention to the men. They merely joke. They are great humorists."

And then I would clinch the argument. I had married just before joining the U-boat service, and to that dumb sea cook Miedtank, my wife had seemed the greatest lady in the world. Whenever she passed him on the street he would come to rigid attention.

"Oh, no, Miedtank," I would say, "you ought to see what I wrote to my wife this morning. I told her that those pancakes you cooked for me were absolutely delicious, O. K. And I told her also that there never was such bacon and peas as you make!"

The dull face of Miedtank would light up with glow. To be praised to the great lady was the height of glory so far as he was concerned. And he would rest pacified for a while.

Sometimes I would encourage him to proud visions.

"You do your best, Miedtank," I would say, "and cook the best dishes you can, and you will see. You won't have to cook always. I will give you a chance to fight, and you will become a great hero. You will get the Iron Cross."

That would straighten him up and he would walk away proudly, and while he worked with can opener and electric stove he would dream about glory and the Iron Cross.

One day we had a long surface fight with an armed merchantman. I needed every man that could be spared so I set Miedtank to carrying shells on deck. He worked like a Trojan, and thought sure he was a hero. Well, he was. Not that he did anything more gallant or thrilling than working his arms sore, but it was the commander of a boat who recommended men for the Iron Cross. I used Miedtank's labours as a pretext, cited him, and he got the Iron Cross. By golly, you should have seen him swell and strut. After that he was content with his labours at cookery and scornfully paid no more attention to the jibes of the men.

We used to plunder captured ships of whatever foodstuffs we could carry away. Our pantry would be filled with the booty, and the sailors would take individually whatever edibles they could get their hands on. It was impossible to control the hungry seamen in the presence of well-filled ships larders. It used to be no uncommon sight to see sailors of the submarine service going home on leave loaded down with parcels of sugar, bacon, ham, and so on, which represented stuff taken from prizes—very welcome presents for their families, which then were bearing the rigours of Germany's wartime shortage.

One of our first prizes in the Mediterranean was the Norwegian steamer *Tripel*, and she had a pantry that would knock your eye out. Her skipper had a face like a wire-haired terrier and jumped about like an angry cricket. We were on the last leg of the long voyage around from the North Sea, and in the Atlantic the weather had been frightful, day after day. We had had nothing decent to eat since we left Germany. The sailors went wild over the goodies aboard the captured vessel, and loaded themselves down with plunder. It consisted largely of marmalade and ham.

Then the trouble began. One of the sailors came to me and respectfully begged to report that the petty officers had eaten all the marmalade and had given the sailors scarcely a smell of it, saying that such food was too good for common sailors. I called the chief of the petty officers, and asked him how come. He was a big fat fellow, and you should have seen his injured innocence. It may have been, he respectfully begged to say, that in the division of the marmalade a larger share had been accidentally allotted to the petty officers, but it was the sailors who were the rogues. They had eaten up all the ham, in fact had crammed themselves with it until they were sick, merely to see that the petty officers got none. So, there you were.

The marmalade-ham controversy nearly resulted

in a free-for-all, a civil war inside the submarine, which wouldn't have done at all. I had to be a diplomat again, and I rendered a decision worthy of Solomon, if I do say so myself. I made a speech to the crew and told them that, to avoid any such misunderstandings in the future, the orders were that no foodstuffs taken from captured ships thereafter should be kept by the sailors individually, but should be deposited in the boat's pantry. At the end of a cruise if anything remained uneaten it should be divided equitably among the men.

One of our most pleasant days in the Mediterranean came not far north of Malta. Another submarine was sighted afar. We sent up a signal, thinking it was a comrade of ours. It was. The two craft drew up alongside, and out of the other boat emerged a tall blond chap clad only in a bathing suit and two golden bangles around one arm, a curious turn of vanity in a U-boat. He was Prince Henry XXXVII of Reuss, who, like Prince Sigismund, the nephew of the Kaiser, had taken to the most dangerous and arduous service, the submarine arm.

"What news?" he asked.

"I have a bottle of extra-fine Brioni on board," I replied, "come over and let's crack it."

He came over. The wine was as good as I had reported, and for a couple of hours the two U-boats lay on the sparkling Mediterranean almost within gunshot of British-controlled Malta, and wine was sipped and gossip of the under-sea service exchanged.

There were times when life was not half bad. The men could go out on deck and drink in the fresh air. We had a dry sleeping place, warm food, time to rest, and even an occasional bath, although we had to be sparing with fresh water. Half the crew were off duty at a time, and then they would gather together and sing while one of them played his accordion. There is little privacy on a submarine, and all of us were thrown together continually. My little cabin was part of the corridor where all must pass, with only a green curtain drawn across. There I would stand in the morning with my face full of lather answering the *Bitte, vorbeigehen zu dürfen?* (May I be allowed to pass?) asked by a man standing rigidly at attention. But soon I eliminated that part of naval etiquette as unnecessary. Then there would be a cloth spread on my desk, while Haupt brought me coffee, hard bread, marmalade, and a pancake baked on the electric stove. The marmalade was a luxury. I remember to this day a heaven-sent ship that I sunk on which we found enough marmalade to last for six months. No, I shall never forget that ship.

Dinner and supper I ate with the other officers in their little messroom next door, and after that, with the strains of the accordion reaching me from the sailors' quarters, I went back to my desk to read. Sometimes I was hungry for novels and sometimes for books more serious. As *U-64* plowed her way back and forth I myself would be transported back to the days of the Hanseatic sea merchants, and to old Lübeck at the height of its power. Of course, I had a copy of *Faust* with me. Occasionally I would dip into one of Strindberg's plays. Then there were some folk stories in low German written by an old Hamburg sailor, which never failed to delight me.

Out here in the Mediterranean we were attempting to cut one of the life veins of England. Those steamers were bringing her wheat from Australia, cotton from Egypt, tea, hemp, oils, and spices from India, Burma, Malaya, and the islands of the seas, and taking back coal, food, and munitions for the British outposts. What a place for an enemy submarine to work! Whenever there were no ships in sight we revelled in the scenery.

Another red-letter day came when I received a quite cryptic wireless message. I had left my newly married wife back in Germany, and presently to our base at the Austrian port of Cattaro came the news that the stork was expected at home. The *U-64* set out on a long cruise, but before leaving I confided in the chief of the flotilla. He agreed to let me know the news by wireless, although the radio was not to be used for any such personal matters. We arranged a code to make the message sound official. Book No. 14 was to mean a boy, Book No. 15 a girl, and, to provide for all possibilities, Book No. 16 twins. We were out in the middle of the Ionian Sea, and I was asleep in my bunk, when at 4 A. M. the chief of our wireless operations aroused me. There was a message for me, he said, and the message read: Book No. 14. But to make it doubly clear he added the word "periscope."

"*Donnerwetter,* hooray!" I yelled at the astonished wireless officer, "I have a son." And right there, just before dawn on the ancient sea of Ionia, I got up and we drank a bottle of champagne to my newly acquired state of fatherhood.

The next day I ordered an especially good dinner on board to celebrate the event. Miedtank, with his German regard for family matters and his reverence for the great lady my wife, did himself proud. In spite of the unfortunate limitations of his galley, he really turned out a presentable meal, and there was fine celebrating aboard the *U-64.*

When we were in port at Cattaro the crew was assigned to sleep in an old barracks on shore. It swarmed with rats. The pests ran races on the floor and did acrobatics on the sleeping sailors in their beds. The last straw came when one of the rats chewed a piece out of a finger of one of the sailors. After that I had the crew sleep on board the boat. A rat followed the men aboard and they could hear the animal chewing away and running around in the nooks and corners of the iron hull. The sailor with the bitten finger set out for revenge. He got himself a hammer and laid for that rat. The whole boat was engrossed with the vendetta of the wrathful seaman. Finally he got in a lick. He hit that rat harder than any rat has been hit since the day when rats were created. The crew cheered and rejoiced as if it had been a great naval victory.

Behind the Bay of Cattaro rises the mountain of Lovzen, on the other side of which was Montenegro, that small Balkan kingdom about which many curious tales were told. There was one that amused us plenty—a big laugh. I don't know whether it was true or not. But the Austrian and German officers told it with great enjoyment.

It concerned a high order bestowed by the reigning Prince of Montenegro. This decoration was a gorgeous-looking medal liberally set with theoretical diamonds, which really were paste. Once the monarch bestowed the second class of the order on a Venetian banker. He was very proud of it and sported it on all occasions. He was a trifle disturbed to note that the diamonds were false, and, to make his decoration all the more impressive, had it reset with real stones. The Prince heard of this. Sometime later he happened to meet the banker at a state function, and the banker was wearing the bejewelled order.

"Ah, my dear sir," the monarch said to him benignly, "I recollect that I presented you with the second class of the order. You are really a distinguished man, and I should like to honour you with the first class. Permit me . . ."

Whereupon he took the second class decoration with the real diamonds from the banker's bosom and replaced it with an order of the first class with its paste brilliants. Some stunt, eh?

Perhaps eggs mean nothing in your young life, but we yearned for them and for a while in Cattaro it seemed impossible to get eggs. In the heat of summer, carrying meat with us was out of the question. That made eggs all the more desirable. Once we had no eggs for a whole month, and vegetables and macaroni were our most substantial dishes. Now a crew of fighting men need better food than that, and I sent one requisition after another to the flotilla chief, asking for eggs. "The Austrians have eggs," I would say, "so that proves that there *are* still hens."

But for some reason the eggs came not. Always word came back that there were none. So I decided to take matters into my own hands. When we returned to port I sent a foraging party into the country behind the Bay of Cattaro, with instructions on no account to return without eggs. Instead of the time-honoured beads and mirrors they took along a supply of sugar and macaroni, of which we had a surplus, to barter for eggs.

Once out of the city they found plenty of hens, and plenty of eggs, on the farms of the Croat peasants. But neither of the men knew a word of Croat, and they made their bargains only when Fischer, a clever fellow, would sit down on an imaginary nest and give his best imitation of a hen cackling and flapping her wings. After that we always had eggs.

Perhaps I have given some idea of the good feeling aboard our boat. There was really too much good feeling. It had to be guarded against. The proper distance between officers and men had to be maintained just for discipline's sake, all the more necessary aboard a submarine, in the narrow quarters of which officers and men were kept so close together. Both officers and men dressed alike, the only distinguishing marks being the shape of our caps. Our uniforms were of leather—coats, trousers and boots—to protect us from the cold and withstand the water and the infernal oil and grease. I, in particular, had to exert myself to keep the aloof poise of a naval officer and not get too friendly, because inwardly I regarded each man as a pal. After all, it could not have been otherwise. We were facing death together, and a horrible death at that. Whenever I called the men together to speak to them I used to take an especial precaution to keep my dignity and not grow too familiar. But it was not easy. Before I uttered a word aloud I would preface my address with a few choice nautical oaths, which might take the place of "men" or "boys" or "my brave lads." That would give me a sense of proper station and I could go ahead with my remarks without any fear of getting too friendly, for the moment, with the men who were really the finest and best of friends.

I suppose I like to dwell overmuch on the droll and personal side of our adventures. I will have to come only too soon to sterner matters, and the way things ended makes me think all the more of the pleasant things that went before.

CHAPTER XXX

THE RING OF SHIPS CONVERGE THEIR FIRE AND THE *U-64* GOES DOWN

We made eight cruises out of Cattaro into the Mediterranean, each lasting three or four weeks. After the unrestricted U-boat warfare was declared in February of 1917 we had orders to sink everything possible. The *U-64* raided far and wide and wrought its share of the general destruction at sea.

On the 19th of March we were off the southwest coast of the island of Sardinia. I was in my cabin reading a magazine article about the economic situation in Mexico when at midday the call came: "Steamer ahoy." I hurried above. The oncoming ship was vague in the mist, but I could distinguish an unusually high wireless equipment—a warship. We took a dive, and presently I saw through the periscope that the vessel had changed its course. I had a side view of it, with its five funnels and great gun turrets. It was a huge French man-of-war. It was zigzagging. A destroyer was patrolling as an escort, also zigzagging. It was all as easy as pie, what you call a cinch, *nicht wahr?* The gray giant, in the course of its zigzagging progress, put itself straight across our bow in good torpedo range.

"Torpedo tubes ready." My orders followed each other in quick succession. "First bow torpedo, fire— second bow torpedo, fire!"

Bang, bang! Two heavy explosions, one right after the other, and both our torpedoes hit. With our

272

periscope drawn in we stole blindly under water for a few minutes, then up with the asparagus for a look, the once-over, no? The warship had two great holes in its side just at the water line. These were death wounds, I knew, and as I peered through the eyepiece I could see that the vessel was listing.

"Donnerwetter, holy smoke!" I exclaimed, as I almost sat down on the floor. My boat was kicking and bucking like one of those "rocky roads" at your Coney Island. The *U-64* had an unfortunate trick which she indulged in every so often of getting unruly and rearing and plunging like a badly behaved horse. That is what had happened now. She popped up and broke water, so that her superstructure showed above the surface.

"Hot dog!" I ordered, "shake a leg there—that's right isn't it?" Fast work was needed, for that destroyer convoying the battleship was certain to be after us like a streak.

It was, and we got our boat in control just in time. As we hurried down to the depths, bang, bang!—depth bombs. Four explosions rang out uncomfortably near us before we had scurried away.

After we had slid along for a couple of miles I put the asparagus up again. The great warship was listing heavily now. The destroyer was busy rescuing survivors. We watched without molestation and looked through our year book of fleets to identify the stricken vessel. We found it belonged to the Danton class of giant vessels of 18,400 tons displacement and forty guns and a crew of eleven hundred men. We steered nearer to be ready with another if it were necessary to sink the giant. But she was going down fast now. Her stern shot high into the air and she plunged and went down bow first.

The destroyer picked up men struggling in the water and there were rafts floating about covered

with survivors.   Presently the destroyer started off
with her burden and the rafts went drifting toward
the horizon.   They were sighted by fishing boats, as
we learned later, and the shipwrecked men rescued.
After the destroyer had disappeared we came to the
surface and picked up a floating box which was full
of letters.   We learned from them that the foundered
ship was the *Danton* herself on her way from Toulon
to Corfu, where a large part of the French Fleet was
helping to blockade the Strait of Otranto.   Later
reports indicated that of the *Danton's* crew 806 were
saved and 296 lost, including the captain.

Back in my cabin I picked up my magazine, but
the economic situation in Mexico was hazy now.
Words and phrases swam before my eyes.   We had
bagged the prize head of game, had sunk the biggest
ship torpedoed by a submarine during the war, and
even now the word was flashing by wireless around
the world.

We sank eight ships on that cruise, and one of
them gave me a surprise.   Ordinarily people don't
smile happily and laugh joyously when they are sub-
marined.   The Norwegian collier *Gratangen* was
bound with 3,500 tons of coal from Newcastle to
Genoa when she happened to run afoul of the *U-64*.
A shot across her bows and the usual command of
"Abandon ship," and the crew took to the boats.   I was
astonished at the expression of pleasure on the faces
of the sailors.   They chuckled to each other and
grinned jovially.   You would have thought that a
U-boat attack tickled them to death.   I asked the
captain what it was all about, whether his men thought
the war under the sea was a picnic.

"Well," he replied, "because of the dangers of the
service they were promised a bonus of five hundred
kronen each if the ship was sunk by a submarine.
That's why they're happy."

You couldn't blame them. The ship was sunk and they were safe and on their way to the kronen. It was O. K., a hundred per cent.

Another of the ships we destroyed provided the greatest spectacle I have ever seen. We attacked the Standard Oil Company tanker, the *Moreni,* and in spite of the fact that she was loaded with 4,500 tons of benzine she gave us a fight. What did they mean with that kind of inflammable cargo below them? That American skipper had what you call guts. The fight didn't amount to much. We scored a hit near the *Moreni's* smokestack, and the flames shot into the air. In a few minutes the ship was a perfect volcano. The crew leaped to the boats. Several men were wounded. The boats pulled over to us and asked for bandages and medical supplies. We gave them all they needed and complimented the captain for his nerve. There were handshakes all around. A big Spanish steamer was approaching, and the lifeboats pulled for it to enlist the services of the ship's doctor aboard.

The *Moreni* had been abandoned so hastily that her engines had not been shut off. They were going full blast and the ship, a perfect inferno of smoke and flame, went careening around madly. We followed along behind, pumping shells at her. The benzine streamed out and spread over the sea, and there it burned. We were as if on a flaming sea and had to be mighty careful. It was a prodigious spectacle, especially when night came on. The blazing ocean was an eerie sight. The *Moreni* finally sank, but the benzine on the surface burned for several days. Ships were warned by radio from Malta to keep away from the locality.

On another occasion we overtook a Dane and overhauled him with a shell across his bow. The skipper lost no time in coming over to us in his jolly boat. His ship was the *Freja,* carrying three thousand tons of coal from Cardiff to Marseilles. He was a cheery soul and avowed that he was friendly toward Germany and had a nephew in our army. When I handed him a receipt for his ship's papers he recognized my name as one that he had seen in war bulletins published in Denmark. It was hard to tell such a fine fellow that I had to sink his ship. I pointed out to him that the Spanish coast was only eight miles away and as the sea was like a mill pond he would have no trouble making it in his small boat. He politely agreed, gave me a hearty handshake, and pushed off while we polished off his ship.

In these days a large part of the Austrian Fleet was stationed at Cattaro and there were a number of other German and Austrian submarines helping us tie up Allied shipping in the Mediterranean. As I have mentioned, unrestricted U-boat warfare had been declared in February and in the waters about England, France, and Italy; it was now up to us to sink every ship, even without warning. The only zone in the Mediterranean remaining open to neutral navigation was in the western part between the Balearic Isles and the Spanish coast.

The Allies met this move by directing all ships to follow a certain course under the protection of armed patrol ships. This was playing right into our hands because we no longer had to hunt for game. We knew just where our victims were sure to pass. Later the Allies tumbled to this and sent each ship on a different course, with orders to zigzag all the time. Then we never knew where to look for them and ships were as scarce as the proverbial needle in the strawstack. We had to keep a sharp lookout from the top of our little mast. We never were too hopeful about the matter, because then Fate, whom we knew was a contrary wench, would be sure to box our ears by leading.

Commander Moraht, whose raider sank beneath his feet.

A mine sweeper ready for a bit of vertical navigation.

In a few seconds the Standard Oil tanker Moreni
burst into a volcano of flames.

*Abandon ship! The captain of a windjammer
brings over his papers.*

us off on a fruitless cruise.   Instead, we adopted tactics that have proven more or less successful with women ever since the fall of Eve.

"I am sure we shall not meet a ship to-day," I would remark to Quesse in the morning.   "I, too," Quesse would reply.   Then we would wait, more on the alert than ever, knowing that if Dame Fate were acting consistently with all feminine tradition she would send us an extra heavy bag of ships.

Sometimes we would cruise for days when it seemed that the whole Mediterranean was empty. Nary a mast would have in sight, nor a funnel, nor a sail, nor even a smudge of smoke on the horizon.   She was as deserted as a phantom sea.   Indeed, there were days when the only craft we sighted were our own German under-sea raiders.   The whole world was our oyster.   Is that right?   Then, suddenly hell would break loose.

Our most stubborn fight with a merchant ship came after just such a lull.   She was the French steamer *Amiral de Kersaint* with a cargo of oats, wine, and general merchandise bound for Marseilles from Oran on the North African coast.   We sighted her immediately after we had sunk the Italian ship *Ausonia,* which went down so quickly that there was no time to launch a boat.   We picked up fifteen men out of the water.   We were plying the survivors with hot coffee when the Frenchman was reported.   A shell across the bows of the *Amiral de Kersaint,* and we got a shell in return.   The battle was on.   After a few exchanges our gun went out of commission.   The Frenchman ran. We kept after him, just out of range, while we worked with our gun.   Finally it was in order again.   We drew up and the fight was renewed.   We scored fifteen direct hits.   We shot away the tricolor from the mast. Those stout fellows tied another to their railing and continued to fire.   Their ship was in flames and about to sink when they abandoned her, last of all the captain.

By way of contrast, there was a British steamer we attacked. She was armed, but made no pretense of fighting. The helmsman told me that the gun crew was so panic-stricken that the captain could not force them to their stations even at the point of his pistol.

Now, as every landlubber knows, every seaman is superstitious. My men were bitten by that bug also. I recall when we were ordered to put out from Cattaro on a Friday. There were mutterings. I sympathized with my lads, but the Cattaro staff officers only laughed. So I told the crew that if the *U-64* was in shape to leave Cattaro, out we must go. But she was *not* in shape when Friday came. The rudder had suddenly developed some mysterious malady. It wouldn't turn. The men worked at it with exemplary diligence. They were earnest and voluble in their explanations of all the possible causes. Afternoon came, and still that rudder stuck. I had a premonition that it was going to continue to stick. And I had to report my inability to put out to sea to our flotilla chief.

Bright and early Saturday morning the men were at work on that stubborn rudder again. In less than thirty minutes the ruddy-faced chief engineer Ammelt reported that the rudder was O. K. again and everything in ship-shape. The miracle had happened just as I knew it would. My crew, innocent-faced as cherubs, were awaiting orders to get under way. Depth bombs, destroyers, mines, nets, and Q-ships they accepted as necessary evils to be regarded merely as incidents of the day. But to start off on a cruise on a Friday was too much even for the most iron-nerved of the lot. And if you think they were dumb just ask some of the other U-boat people who recklessly went to sea on a Friday. They have some tales to tell that will make your hair curl.

1918 came, and with the arrival of spring came Hindenburg and Ludendorf's great drive in France. That drive nearly won the war for us. It would have done so had it not been for the Americans. The war under the sea was tightening. We had inflicted vast destruction on the Allies. For a while it seemed as if we would sweep the seas of commerce. The convoy system, the best system of defense against the U-boats, came into practice, and that made the going harder for U-boats. Nearly every attack now meant the taking of large chances. You had to deal with fleets of merchant ships efficiently protected by convoying destroyers, those little devils which are the natural and most formidable enemies of submarines. The U-boats didn't have any what you call joy rides. Toward the end of January we sank the British troop transport *Minnetonka,* which was proceeding empty to Malta. Of 13,500 tons burden, she was the largest merchantman on my list. During the following week we bagged five other vessels, one of them a small converted Italian cruiser.

Heavy weather was running off the coast of Sicily, and the *U-64* was ploughing along through a welter of white-capped waves. It was late in the afternoon of the following June. "Steamer ahoy!" and we sighted a big convoy. "Dive for an attack!" was my command. The high sea made it a hard job. The waves broke over our periscope and obscured our vision. But never mind. How is it?—the first hundred years are the hardest?

It was hard to manœuvre, looking through that foggy periscope, but finally I had a big ship sighted for a shot. Torpedo loose, and the missile left the tube. Missed, and the steamer turned and charged, ready to ram us or give us a dose of depth bombs. The *U-64* turned her nose down, and along we went, passing under the oncoming vessel. Back to periscope depth again, and we were quite close to the steamer next in line to the former one. That ducking-under certainly had its advantages.

"Torpedo—fire!" If we miss this one we are dubs. Vision through the periscope is poor, but the range is very short. A great explosion. The torpedo hits the vessel amidships, and that's another big one added to our record.

I thought we were on the outside of the convoy and turned the boat to proceed parallel with it. Thus stalking our flock of game, we could swerve in and get another shot. Suddenly, directly ahead, another steamer loomed. We were not on the outside of the convoy, but in the middle of it. Damn that hazy periscope!

"Dive to forty metres," I ordered quickly.

The *U-64* nosed down, but before we were halfway to a safe depth a tremendous explosion deafened us, and blank, utter darkness as the lights flashed out. We had been hit properly, no doubt of that. The waves dashing in the periscope had prevented me from seeing the destroyer right near us and it had jumped right on us with its accursed depth charges.

"Report on all compartments," I called with my heart in my throat. I had my flashlight on the instrument board. We were holding position all right.

In an instant the word came that there was water in our stern compartment, where the bomb had caught us, but that otherwise the hull seemed tight. We put on the emergency light and managed to stop the leakage in our stern.

"The depth steering gear is out of order," the alarming word came abruptly. The explosion had badly damaged all of our steering gear and the boat was out of control. And we were rising.

I shall never forget my agony of fear as I stood there staring at the depth indicator. The finger was moving. We were rising to the surface, rising inexorably, and a swarm of enemy ships was waiting above. There was nothing to do. We popped out of the water.

There were ships on all sides, big steamers and swift destroyers, though none very near us. The moment we broke water they began to shoot. We lay there on the surface in a rain of shells. I gave the order to try to dive. The boat obeyed and we went to sixty feet, and there the depth steering apparatus balked again.

"Engines full speed ahead!" I shouted the order desperately.

The boat lurched. We were rising again. The hand of the depth indicator moved swiftly. We were shooting to the surface. The *U-64* seemed to leap out of the water. I threw open the conning-tower hatch for a good look around. A destroyer was bearing down on us at full speed to ram us. I gave a frantic order to dive. No use. She would not dive. There was a rending crash. The ram hit the conning tower. The boat lurched violently and began to sink.

We sank stern first. I thought our hull had been shattered, but no—it was still water tight. But our diving mechanism was absolutely gone now and we could not steer to check our descent. We were on our way to the bottom. Before long the pressure would crush us. There was but one thing to do—blow the tanks. That would shoot us to the surface again. Only one hope. With our diving mechanism of no use, we were a submarine no longer. We were a surface craft. We would have to take our chances above water. We might be able to fight our way through the convoy. Darkness was coming on, and if we held out for a little while it would cover us.

The conning tower emerged on the surface of the

sea and a cigar-shaped body followed it. A terrible concentric fire broke out from the circle of ships.

"Are we all right? Can we stay afloat?" I called to the chief engineer.

"Yes," he responded.

"Man the guns!" I yelled, and leaped out on deck. The gun crew followed me, and the lone tiny craft started to fight its way out through the circle of armed merchantmen and destroyers.

We steered ahead, our two guns firing as fast as they could. We shot at the ships near us. All the ships in the convoy concentrated their fire on us. Shells burst on all sides in the sea around us. Shells hit us. One exploded forward. Another passed through the conning tower beside me. Our men at the guns were struck. The pandemonium was dreadful. We were as if in a hell on earth. And all around were the looming shapes of huge gray ships with streaks of fire from their guns. More shells hit us.

"She's going down." The wild despairing cry came from the man beside me, and even as he spoke the *U-64* sank beneath us like a stone.

I began to swim mechanically, but only for a moment. I was jerked under water and carried down. The wireless equipment of the sinking boat had caught me. I struggled desperately under water, and freed myself of the snare. Back on the surface again I swam, was dragged under by the waves, and swam again. My leather uniform and heavy boots made it almost impossible for me to keep afloat. I don't remember how long I was out there in the water or much of what happened. One of the men, a petty officer who had been at the guns and had got away swimming, told me afterward that he saw me floating under water and that he swam to me and held me up until he, himself was exhausted. Fischer, another of the gunners, swam to the nearest British ship and climbed aboard on a tow rope. He told the men aboard that the captain of the submarine was out in the water, and the British put out a lifeboat. I remember faintly being fished out of the water, having my clothes stripped off, and being put in the ship's hospital.

It is hard to tell of my boat going down like that, with my crew consigned to the fate of the submerged iron coffin. I don't know how many were carried down inside of the boat. Perhaps a dozen were on deck when she sank. Some of these drowned and others were killed by shell fire. In all thirty-eight were lost, the crew and several men who had gone on cruise with us.

The British kept me in solitary confinement for five weeks while they questioned me about military secrets, first at Malta, then at Gibraltar, and then in London. Nothing doing. Finally they told me that if I did not answer the questions they put to me I would be turned over to the French, who would shoot me for sinking the *Danton*. I knew that was a bluff and told them to go on and shoot. After that I was placed in the Colsterdale Prison Camp near Ripon in England. I waited there as comfortably as a prisoner can until the war was over. After all the peace-making formalities were completed I was released in October, 1919, and sent back to Germany. It was still later that I learned what craft had been responsible for the loss of the *U-64*. The British destroyers *Lychnis* and *Partridge II* were the boats that brought us to grief. The *Lychnis* dropped the depth charge on us and then rammed us, and the *Partridge* fired the shell that had sent us down. Hard luck, boy, hard luck!"

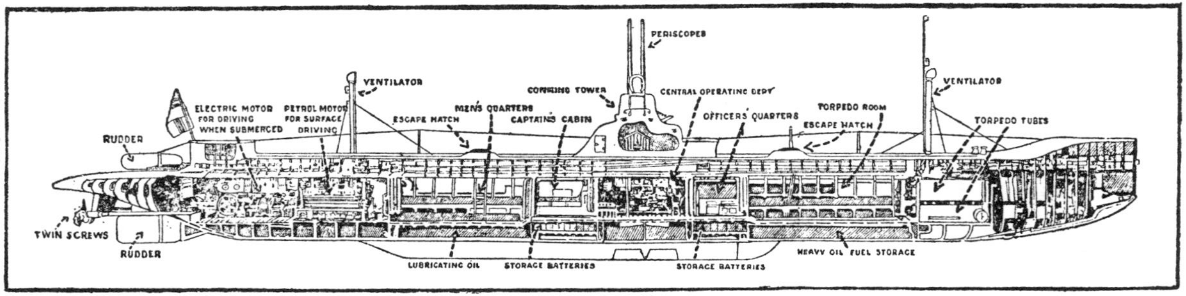
PERISCOPES
VENTILATOR
CONNING TOWER
CENTRAL OPERATING DEPT
VENTILATOR
ELECTRIC MOTOR
FOR DRIVING
WHEN SUBMERGED
PETROL MOTOR
FOR SURFACE
DRIVING
MEN'S QUARTERS
ESCAPE HATCH
CAPTAIN'S CABIN
OFFICERS' QUARTERS
TORPEDO ROOM
ESCAPE HATCH
TORPEDO TUBES
RUDDER
TWIN SCREWS
RUDDER
LUBRICATING OIL
STORAGE BATTERIES
STORAGE BATTERIES
HEAVY OIL FUEL STORAGE

A diagram showing the interior of a modern U-boat

CHAPTER XXXI

HO, FOR A RAID ON UNCLE SAM!

In the early days of June, 1918, the American public got what was undoubtedly its most vivid and immediate war thrill. The Germans were crashing through in France, and our men were getting into it. The great question was whether the Allies would be able to hold out. Then all over the country and particularly along the Atlantic coast, every newspaper carried scare headlines in eight-column streamers:

GERMAN U-BOAT RAID ON AMERICAN COAST.

Ships were being sunk right outside of the principal harbours of the eastern seaboard. The war was being brought home to Uncle Sam, carried to his front door step. The raiders of the deep had indeed struck a blow clear across the Atlantic. They inflicted plenty of damage and raised a vast sensation.

Here was one of the prime exploits of the war under the sea—a phase of it, at any rate, of by far the greatest interest to us Americans. I was keen to find out more about those trans-Atlantic raids of the giant U-boats that had performed the seemingly impossible feat of preying upon American shipping right under Uncle Sam's nose. And from the German Admiralty records I learned that seven of their largest submarines had been ordered to cross the ocean to lay mines and raid shipping from Cape Cod to Key West. These seven were:

The *U-151* under Commander von Nostitz und Janckendorf, which left Germany April 14, 1918, returned late in July, and was off the American coast from May 15th to July 1st;

The *U-156* under Commander Richard Feldt, which left Germany about June 15th, operated along our coast from July 5 to September 1, 1918, but struck a mine in the North Sea barrage on her way home and sank with all on board;

The *U-140* under Commander Kophamel, which left Germany on June 22, 1918, raided American waters from July 14 to September 1, 1918, and then returned to Germany in October;

The *U-117* under Commander Droescher, which left Germany in July, 1918, and returned in company with the *U-140;*

The *U-155* (the former merchant submarine *Deutschland*) under Commander Eckelmann, which left Germany in August, 1918, was off the American coast from September 7 to October 20, 1918, and arrived back in Germany a few days after the Armistice;

The *U-152* under Commander Franz, which left Germany in August, 1918, remained in American waters from September 29 to October 20, 1918, and arrived back in Germany after the Armistice;

The *U-139* under Von Arnauld, which started for America in September but was recalled owing to the impending armistice negotiations.

In Berlin I learned that of all these seven the *U-151* had perhaps the most interesting trans-Atlantic cruise. She was the first and had made the greatest sensation in the U. S. A. But her commander, Von Nostitz und Janckendorf, could not be found. So it was to his boarding officer, Dr. Fredrick Körner, that I went for the story of that astounding voyage. I found him down in Silesia surrounded by his family and his flowers. Körner, by the way, is the man of whom one of his American prisoners, Captain W. H. Davis, master of the *Jacob M. Haskell*, made the remark that "he spoke good English and was so polite that it almost got on our nerves."

He got out his diaries and filled in with bits of vivid description—an epic, a comedy of the raiders of the deep in American waters:

Our U-boat was a sister submarine to the *Deutschland*, which on two voyages had visited America with a peace-time cargo. When you people declared war on us these freight-carrying under-sea cruisers were converted into mine-laying U-boats and equipped for fighting purposes. Originally she had been known as the *Oldenburg*, and during the previous autumn she had made the longest cruise ever undertaken by a submarine when Commander Kophamel took her to the west coast of Africa.

Korvettenkapitän von Nostitz und Jackendorf received orders to pick a crew of dare-devils and equip and provision our giant under-sea boat for a five months' voyage. Nor were we told where we were headed for. Apparently, however, it was to be something on the Jules Verne order. Fine! We were ready for anything in those days. Our great land attack was driving the enemy back in France, and we did not believe the Americans could ever get ready soon enough to turn the tide against us. That was where we guessed wrong. But at that time we all felt certain of victory.

At last the Admiralty order came. It exceeded all of our imaginings. The United States having entered the war against us, we were to raid the American coast. The *Deutschland* had already made the voyage, but then, as a merchantman, she had found the waters of the United States a haven of refuge.

The *Bremen,* another sister ship, had been lost on a similar voyage. But our adventure was sure to be a much stiffer feat than they had tackled, for ours was to be a single continuous cruise, with all the risks of war thrown into the bargain. We set out on Thursday, April 18, 1918, and steered a course north across the Baltic.

It was late afternoon, and night came on quickly. We passed Copenhagen, a distant blaze of lights. At Helsingborg, on the Swedish coast, through our night glasses we could even distinguish the dissipated faces of several late prowlers who lingered under a street lamp near the docks. One of the last houses on the upper side of the harbour was lighted brightly. We passed so near that I could distinctly see the inside of the dining room. A merry celebration was in progress. A gaily dressed crowd sat around a supper table. A rose-coloured lamp shed over them a genial glow. They laughed and clinked their glasses. It was a sight to cause an aching throb in us out there in the dark. The inside of that cozy, luxurious dining room, with its jolly company feasting around the table, was our last glimpse of land.

Under cover of friendly fog we somehow managed to slide through the blockade without sighting a single enemy war craft. Only sea gulls, ducks, and porpoises knew that we were in these waters. After reaching the Atlantic we shaved our heads for coolness and let our beards grow so we wouldn't have to waste any time shaving.

On the second of May the shout arose, "Steamer ahoy!" She proved to be a big armed ship, and our Admiralty orders were not to attack any ship until we had reached the American coast, so that our trans-Atlantic submarine raid might remain a secret until we were in our main field of operations. However, that steamer was too great a temptation, and there are times when orders should not be carried out too strictly. Even if our position were broadcasted now, it could do very little harm. We were not far enough across the Atlantic to give our plan away.

We attacked. Our torpedo missed. Then we tried our guns. She got away. Then we caught her wireless warning:

"The *Port Said.* We have encountered an enemy submarine." She concluded her message by giving the latitude and longitude.

We were not a bit proud. Violating official instructions is sometimes glorious when you score a brilliant success, but not when all you achieve is failure.

When we reached the vicinity of the Azores we were in a semi-tropical latitude. On our low-lying deck we were close to the endless débris of the sea. Driftwood, seaweed, and nettles of all forms and colours floated past. Huge shoals of porpoises went by. Flying fish went darting over our bow. Spearfish rushed at our iron sides, struck vainly against the metal, and then went diving away. Fish nettles that looked like gray bladders and glistened with all the colours of the rainbow sailed proudly along before the wind. We passed a mass of floating wreckage that told of some recent spoil of the sea. At night we gathered around the conning tower for music. There were old songs to the accompaniment of guitars and mandolins. The sky was full of stars and a tropical moon beamed down. The sea was alight, too. It was aglow with millions of tiny phosphorescent organisms. It seemed as though we were travelling through an ocean of glistening molten metal. The waves were silvery, and a silver mist sparkled over our bow.

We could follow the paths of the darting sailfish, like lines in the silver. When they snapped out of the water it made an illuminated fountain. Days passed and no ship came in sight. We were keeping well away from the shipping lanes. We were now past mid-ocean, and if our presence were reported it would be surmised that we were on our way to American waters.

One afternoon clouds of smoke appeared behind us. A 4,000-ton steamer came speeding straight toward us. She had guns fore and aft. Those cannon were a challenge. So, Admiralty orders notwithstanding, we let a torpedo go. Everything was still. We had missed again. The steamer went her way zigzagging. She had seen the torpedo. In a little while we caught her wireless reporting us to the English station at Bermuda. She was the *Huntress* of the British Indian Company. With our presence thus announced, we could no longer hope for our approach to the American coast to remain unheralded. You can bet that we kicked ourselves for our stupidity.

Later on we caught a radio news dispatch from the American coast. To our great joy, it ended with the usual: "No submarine. No war warning." It appeared that no word from the Bermudas about our attack on the *Huntress* had been relayed to the American authorities. We were astonished at this. Apparently there was a lack of coöperation somewhere and luck was with us. Day after day we caught that same reassuring close of the wireless news: "No submarine. No war warning." We had been luckier than we deserved. We sighted another cloud of smoke behind us and also a sail. We gave them both a wide berth. No more attacking until the American coast was reached. We turned north toward Cape Hatteras. The traffic grew livelier all the time, and we kept dodging to right or left or under the water to make sure of avoiding ships.

On the morning of May 21st, a month and three

days since our departure from Kiel, the water turned a dirty gray blue. We sounded, and found a depth of thirty-five metres. We had reached the coast, even though we were not in sight of land. Here was the Western Hemisphere where our serious work was to begin.

CHAPTER XXXII

A U-BOAT ADVENTURE IN DELAWARE BAY

We had, stowed away where we could easily get at them, more than a hundred big floating mines. One of our tasks was to sprinkle these judiciously in the main trails of the munition ships that ran between the United States and Europe. The first batch was destined for Chesapeake Bay for the benefit of the port of Baltimore, America's largest war harbour. A second consignment was intended for the mouth of Delaware Bay to catch ships outward bound from Philadelphia and other inland ports. We headed up the coast.

That afternoon we caught sight of a trim, five-masted American schooner, too far away to catch. She was such a beauty that we were rather glad to see her slip away. Every sailor loves an old-time clipper and I never did relish the idea of sending one to the bottom. The schooner was scarcely out of sight when a man-of-war appeared on the horizon, an armoured cruiser of the Charleston class.

"Oh, for a shot at that fellow!" I mused.

The warship steamed peacefully on, little dreaming how near she was to destruction. We were submerged and ready, but unfortunately could not get quite near enough for a torpedo shot.

A four-master schooner came scudding before the wind on our larboard. Simultaneously, a heavily armed tank steamer appeared on our starboard. We were too near the coast to risk a surface battle, so we stole away. Things were so lively at the surface that we might have stumbled into all sorts of embarrassing complications. So we submerged and went to the bottom to lie on the ocean floor for a few hours. We came up at seven P. M. and found it raining. Lightning flamed and thunder roared. The east and south were gray and threatening and black rainclouds were overhead, but a beautiful sunset was aglow in the west. The sky cleared slowly, and after a while a bright moon shone forth. We reached Capes Henry and Charles at ten o'clock.

Shortly after midnight the alarm went off. We dived to escape a white light that was coming swiftly toward us. A pilot ship with its searchlight. Had it seen us? Apparently not, for afterward we picked up the usual message from the coast wireless stations: "No submarine. No war warning." We continued our way north. At daybreak we settled down again on the bottom. We were approaching Baltimore harbour now, so we followed the usual tactics of a U-boat cruising in crowded waters. By day we lay on the ocean floor. By night we came up and continued our voyage. During the day we occasionally rose to periscope height to have a look around.

"What's that?" Commander von Nostitz shouted to me. The periscope disclosed a picture to make one jump. Less than a mile away an American cruiser of the Saint Louis class, steaming swiftly and followed by two destroyers. For a moment we thought surely our position had in some mysterious way become known and the warships were coming to blow us out of the bay with depth bombs. But no—the cruiser was followed by a steam tug towing a target. It all seemed pathetically innocent. The warships were on their way back to harbour from gunnery trials off Newport News. They had gone out quietly for target practice with a U-boat lurking in near-by waters! Von Nostitz stroked his beard and chuckled merrily. It was certainly too bad that we had not been there to witness the shooting. We could have wirelessed the Washington Navy Department a report on how many bull's-eyes each ship had made, and perhaps we might even have scored a bull's-eye or two ourselves! The cruiser and two destroyers were out of torpedo range when they passed us.

It would have been madness to have attempted to lay mines right at the entrance to busy Baltimore Harbour in the daytime. We waited till nightfall. Even then we would have taken a chance of being rammed in the dark if it had not been for the unsuspecting coöperation given us by the Americans themselves. Far from the scenes of the war, they blissfully kept their ships' lights burning during the night, just as in days of peace. At six-thirty in the evening we came to the surface and steered toward Cape Henry. Soon we made out the lights of Cape Henry and Cape Charles and then the Cape Charles fire ship. A number of steamers passed off in the distance, and we could see the coast in the twilight.

"Mines ready on the top deck!" Von Nostitz commanded.

The moon behind us lighted everything as we glided along toward the fire ship. We could easily have been seen from shore. Had the Americans no coast guard patrol? Or did they think us one of their own submarines? Any watcher with a strong pair of night glasses might have observed an interesting sight on our deck as our men brought up the mines and made them ready for launching. They went about the job as if it were a practice drill near Kiel instead of at the entrance to the largest American war port.

"Hey, what's that?" I heard one of the men grunt.

I turned quickly. It seemed as if Cape Henry

were flashing its light off and on. Then I saw the silhouette of an armoured cruiser. In passing the light, its funnels had cut off the beam at regular intervals. It veered suddenly and bore down upon us. Had it seen us, or was its change of course in our direction merely a coincidence?

One mine was ready for launching. "Overboard with it, and lash the others fast!" the Captain commanded. "Quick with it!"

"The men worked frantically. They, too, saw the danger, and before the cruiser was halfway to us we had dived to safety.

The cruiser's change of course had been mere coincidence, after all, else the wireless would have been hot with warnings of our presence. In half an hour we came up for a look. Everything was quiet. By nine-thirty we had our mines laid. What a relief! We felt like shouting with joy. Half of the most troublesome part of our work was done. Mine-laying was easily the most irksome part of a U-boat's wartime routine.

We listened that night with the keenest interest to the radio news from Arlington, Virginia. First came the weather reports, then warning against wrecks and icebergs, then stock-exchange quotations, sport news, boxing, baseball, and finally—music to our ears—"No submarine. No war warning." Our mine-laying had been entirely unobserved.

Now for Delaware Bay where we were scheduled to drop the rest of our horned monsters. Cruising out to sea again in order to get away from the coastwise shipping lanes, we found ourselves alone on the ocean when dawn came. It was not until nine o'clock that we sighted a sail. Submerging, we watched through our periscope. The ship proved to be a three-mast schooner, heading straight in our direction like some lovely fish innocently cruising toward the enemy's maw. It was as if she were bent on being captured.

"And what about this one?" asked Von Nostitz.

"Let's take her!" I replied.

She was less than half a mile away now, so we came to the surface. One of our guns barked, and a warning shot went over the schooner's bow and sent up a fountain of water on the other side. Men were running on her deck, but she held to her course. Another shot and she heaved to and down came her topsail. We lowered our boat and four men went with me. She was the three-mast schooner, the *Hattie Dunn*, bound for Charleston from New York.

By now another ship had appeared, a four-mast schooner. Von Nostitz, on the deck of the *U-151*, shouted across the water to us as we were ordering the crew of the *Hattie Dunn* to their boats:

"Sink her with TNT, take her crew with you, and follow us in the boats."

The second schooner turned and tried to escape. The elements were with the *U-151* though, for the wind was against the fleeing ship. We watched the race from the deck of the *Hattie Dunn* and saw our comrades gaining. Then we all took to the open boats and pulled away. At a range of eight thousand meters Von Nostitz fired a shot at the schooner that was trying to escape. A moment later came a deep boom, and with it down went the *Hattie Dunn*. It was a long chase before the Captain got the other ship, but after four hours she tacked and came around. She was the *Hauppage*, bound in ballast for Portland, Maine, a new vessel just out of the slip. After catching up with them in our small boat and delivering the crew of the *Hattie Dunn* to the *U-151*, I went aboard this second ship with a couple of men to pick up any odd stuff that we might need. We took the hydrographical charts, a few books, and, best of all, a quantity of fresh provisions. Ah, those green vegetables looked good. For weeks now we had been living on canned grub. While we were engaged in searching her, still another vessel, a large steamer, appeared on the horizon.

"Clear the guns!" Von Nostitz called as he clambered down the ladder from his perch in the conning tower.

The steamer, however, remained in the far distance near the horizon and did not discover our presence.

We blew up the *Hauppage* with TNT. Masts and spars and deck rails sailed high in the air. What a sight! Wonderful in a way, but one to make a sailor's heart grow heavy. In this time of ocean liners a fine, trimly rigged schooner is one of the last reminders of the picturesque old days.

Between the crews of our two prizes, we had seventeen prisoners. Of course, we could have towed them in their lifeboats to some point near shore and then left them to row in, but that would have given our presence away before our mine-laying was done. So long as we kept them on the *U-151* they could spread no news. Fortunately, we had enough room for them. They could at least remain as our guests until we unloaded the rest of our mines at the mouth of Delaware Bay.

"Sail ahoy!"

A schooner in the distance was bearing down upon us with all sails set. We got her, an easy capture. She was the three-mast schooner *Edna*, bound from Philadelphia to Santiago with 6,000 cases of oil and 4,000 cases of gasolene. The sailors aboard the *Edna* were negroes, who didn't know whether to tremble or to grin; they did both alternately. One gathered a few pictures, another a phonograph, a third a pile of bedclothes, and scrambled aboard the *U-151* in a panic.

While we were busy with the *Edna* a large steamer passed along the far horizon and stopped. A mass of wreckage had attracted her. It was the remains of the *Hattie Dunn*, parts of which were still afloat. After a few minutes of inspection the steamer continued on her way. She did not see us, and, I suppose, thought the wreck merely another victim of sea and storm.

We blew up the *Edna*, and from her inherited six more men. This swelled our passenger list to twenty-three. The crew of the *Hattie Dunn* consisted entirely of elderly men. The youngest was a man of forty. The oldest, the cook, was seventy-two. He was a jovial fellow, a German by birth. During the first two years of the war he had sailed on ships of various nationalities in British waters. He had been torpedoed twice and once taken prisoner for a short time. So he decided the war zone was too strenuous for a fellow of his age and signed on an American ship to get out of reach of torpedoes and submarines! Now, here in peaceful American waters, he had encountered still another submarine. The crew of the *Hauppage* were all young men, Danes and Norwegians. The *Edna*, in addition to her coloured crew, carried one Portuguese.

The captain of the *Edna* had just been sent below. He seated himself in the messroom and gloomily contemplated his fate in being a prisoner aboard a marauding submarine. The master of the *Hattie Dunn* came in through the narrow doorway. I happened to be near by. The two men shouted when they caught sight of each other, and shook hands with the utmost enthusiasm. They hadn't seen each other for thirty years. They were old friends and had been brought up together in the town of Saint George, Maine. They still lived in that community and were neighbours. Their wives were girlhood friends and saw each other every day. The two men had gone to sea. They had returned home only at long intervals, and their stays with their families were short. For thirty years their home-comings had never coincided. And now they were having their first reunion—in the bowels of a German submarine!

The captains of our three prizes were genuine old sea lions. They assured us that there hadn't even been a rumour afloat of our presence in American waters. So remote had the possibility of a submarine attacking them seemed that they had each of them taken the first sound of our shots for naval gunnery practice off the coast. They were thoroughly familiar with the shore along which we were running and gave us excellent advice about our navigation. You see, their own fate depended on the success of our navigation.

We had no trouble at all with our prisoners. I don't suppose they particularly enjoyed the submarine cruise in which they found themselves compelled to take part. Quarters were close and uncomfortable and danger always at hand. It would, truly enough, have been trying for the nerves of anyone save a hardened submarine veteran. But they took things as cheerfully as possible. At first they were thoroughly uneasy. When, to begin with, we failed to shell their lifeboats, which, they erroneously had gathered from their propaganda-filled newspapers, was the usual custom of the U-boats, they formed a vague apprehension that we had something worse in store for them, possibly a cannibal stew. But when they found that we were doing as much to make them comfortable as our limited resources would allow, our officers sharing their bunks with their officers, our sailors with their sailors, they were thankful and they grew friendly. Some of them took their trip with us as an exciting adventure, and it certainly was all of that! After all, it was a pleasure for us to have them aboard. You see, we of the *U-151* had grown somewhat tired of looking at each other in such cramped quarters. So any new face was a welcome relief. We hoped, for our prisoners' sakes as well as our own, that we would encounter no accident while they were aboard.

We ran toward Cape May and avoided any ship that came in sight, swerving to right or left or submerging. The boat was crowded. Almost standing room only. So we could accommodate no more prisoners. That day and the next passed without incident. At 9:50 P. M. we sighted the lights of Cape May, and dived to avoid traffic running into Delaware Bay. For quite a while now we ran along submerged. The periscope showed that we were two or three miles distant from the Overfall Light Ship. Out of sight we glided slowly into the mouth of the channel.

I happened to be looking through the periscope at the time. Suddenly there was a heavy lurch that took me right off my feet. The boat bumped two or three times against the bottom and then leaped to the surface as though grasped by a giant hand. There was a general pandemonium. The prisoners, faced with some unseen peril in this mysterious world of a craft that sailed below the surface of the sea, fell into a panic.

"She won't stay down, and I can't control her!" the engineer sang out through the speaking tube.

We had struck bottom. And the shock of it had disabled our steering and diving apparatus.

The channel ran with freakish and powerful cross currents and eddies, and these had caught us and were hauling us about. We were as if dragged hither and thither by some unearthly strength. I felt a strange motion. We were going round and round. The currents were spinning us like a top. Up and up we went, and when we reached the surface we were still helpless

Shelled and burning. The last of a Yankee barque.

Körner, of the U-151, in American waters.

During the final year of the war the raiders of the deep crossed the Atlantic and sank ships right under Uncle Sam's nose.

and revolving like a crazy thing in waters where a ship might run us down at any moment.

Lights ahead and a looming form in the darkness. A large steamer came toward us. It passed us a few hundred feet away. Two other steamers passed close by.

"They would be as badly frightened as we," Von Nostitz said to me, "if they only knew how near they are to a U-boat." That was the only consolation he could think of.

The currents pulled us so near the light ship that we could hear its bell. It sounded like the tolling of a death knell. Down below the men worked feverishly, fighting to get the steering and diving mechanism back in order. Above we took occasion to throw overboard the mines stowed on deck. Luckily, we were in the very channel where they were to be placed.

"Close the hatches!" *Donnerwetter!* It was good to hear again that command to dive. The boat was in control.

We scurried down and lay on the bottom. The depths seemed a snug, comfortable place now, after our anxious time of drifting helplessly in the traffic lane on the surface. We utilized the interval to get the remainder of our mines ready for launching.

Up we came at 3 A. M. A heavy fog lay on the sea. We had no idea of our position. The currents had carried us heaven knows where during the time we were disabled. We went along, groping blindly through the fog. Then we came in earshot of that same lugubrious light-ship bell that tolled in dismal monotony. It was as welcome as salvation now. We ran submerged to keep out of the way of traffic. With the earpieces of our under-water microphone on my head, I listened to the bell and we manœuvred the boat until the tolling sound was of the same loudness in each ear. That meant that we were steering straight toward it, or in other words, through the narrow mouth of the channel. A good place to lay the rest of our mines. We had no mind to do any more launching from deck in those waters, so we laid our mines from under water. This is one of the most difficult tasks of submarine manœuvre. Everything went smoothly, though, and soon we were rid of the most burdensome part of our cargo. No doubt the fishes in the channel of Delaware Bay that night heard the sound of a cheer from the inside of an iron hulk thirty feet below the surface of the sea. It was the cheer that went up when we released our last mine.

With that great load off our shoulders, we came to the surface to take a look around. The fog was so thick that you could hardly have seen a light a dozen or so feet away. Our conning tower had scarcely emerged when we heard the hoarse toot of a fog horn right on top of us. It was the siren of a big steamer sounding its raucous cry at regular intervals. Our men gasped. Again the prisoners thought their last hour had come. We ducked as fast as we could and were lucky enough to escape with nothing more than a good stiff fright.

We were afraid to continue our course under water because we had no idea of the lay of the land around us. At last we decided that the fog on the surface would be a shelter. At all events we would not be seen from any distance. So we emerged, and from there on out to the open sea we made an amusing journey. Through the impenetrable mist the sounds of horns came from all directions. Steamers and tugs far and near were singing away with their sirens. We kept as nearly as we could in the middle of the tootings, which meant the middle of the channel. We answered with our own siren, confidently, impudently. Our musical note was high-pitched and shrill, quite different from the deep, bellowing voices around us. It answered its purpose, however. The passing vessels seemed to respect it thoroughly. Several times a bellow came near to us, so near that we were afraid we might be seen. A shriek or two of our siren and the bellow moved off to avoid a collision. The fog continued without a break, but the siren calls grew less frequent. That meant we were getting out of the channel and approaching open sea.

At 10 A. M. we dived again. Submerging to the bottom of the sea, we lay there and enjoyed a nap. Our distraught prisoners hadn't slept a wink during the exciting night. Now they too had a comfortable sleep. We were at the bottom of the sea, to be sure, but all was tranquil, all was peace. Our troubles, for the present at any rate, had been left behind on the surface of Delaware Bay.

CHAPTER XXXIII

THE LIGHTS OF BROADWAY. WE CUT
THE ATLANTIC CABLE.

And now for a fishing trip. We had on board a newly devised implement for cutting cables. Its operation was something like a glorified angling tackle. And with it we were supposed to attack the trans-Atlantic cables outside of New York Harbour.

So "Weigh anchor and raise sail!" (metaphorically speaking in the case of a submarine). Ho! for the waters of the metropolis, where New Yorkers, on holiday, cast lines for blue fish and weak. We, too, must try our luck at deep-sea fishing! We steered for Fire Island, the lighthouse off the South Long Island shore. Our prisoners? They must come too, for we must continue to entertain them and keep our existence secret until this cable-fishing expedition is over.

After sunset a terrific storm set in. In the northeast, the north, and the southwest the horizons were seas of fire. Flash after flash of lightning, from blood red to orange yellow, crackled across the sky, and with each flash the sea was as bright as at high noon. Rain flooded down. Several of us stayed on deck, drenched through and through. The spectacle of the clashing elements both fascinated us and filled us with awe.

On May 28, 1918, we arrived off New York, and now began our angling. We moved back and forth on the surface with a long line played out. Our cable-cutting mechanism dragged on the bottom. We waited patiently for a bite, that feel of the line which would indicate that we had caught hold of the cable. Then our mechanism at the bottom was set going to cut it. Every time a ship hove in sight we would close our hatches and submerge. This happened many times and grew somewhat exasperating.

That night we had our first sight of the bright lights of Broadway, the great glow that hangs over New York City after dark. The glow and splendour of the western metropolis filled us with a restless longing. A wild idea came of stealing into the harbour and up the Hudson, of landing at some obscure place and taking a night off along the Great White Way. But then, we were hardly so romantic as all that, except in fancy. Fire Island Beach, which we could often see in the course of our trolling for the cables, was also a temptation, with its pretty houses, long beach, and white surf. A stroll on the sand and dip in the breakers, wouldn't that have been fine? Ah yes, but there would be no welcome there for us.

For three days we continued our fishing. At last we let our optimism convince us that there was not a single cable left uncut. The weather was growing ugly, and we were only too glad to pull up our big scissors and be away. How many cables had we really cut? Two, as it afterward turned out, one to Europe and one to South America.

From the vicinity of Fire Island we headed in the direction of the Nantucket Light Ship. There we hoped we might be able to pick up a few ships and then visit Boston and the Gulf of Maine. Our captive captains warned us against going farther north at that time of year. They said that fogs and bad weather were all we could expect along the New England coast. We thought we would see for ourselves.

The three grizzlies and I were discussing these

problems of weather one afternoon and having an after-luncheon liqueur—straight whiskey they preferred—when the alarm bell sounded. I hurried into the control room. The boat by this time was on her nose at a sharp angle.

"An American destroyer," the helmsman called.

My glance fell on the depth gauge.

"What's up?" I shouted to Commander von Nostitz.

The gauge showed that we were still on the surface. And with the boat standing on her nose like that! Water was trickling down through the manhole. One wild surmise—we had been rammed by the destroyer.

I shouted wild inquiries. We had been rammed and were sinking—the frantic word went around. Officers and men came running to the control room. Then my glance fell on the second depth gauge. It registered forty-five metres. We were under water and well out of danger. The first gauge still indicated that we were on the surface. It had gone out of order. That was all. The water trickling down the manhole merely meant that we had dived so fast that a bit of the sea had poured in before the hatchway had closed tightly.

I returned to the mess hall. The three captains were as pale as death, and for a moment none could utter a syllable. Finally one spoke up. He said that he had sailed the sea all these years but that this submarine life was too much of a strain for him. His heart was pounding like a trip hammer, and he didn't know but what it was going to burst.

"Come and look at these fellows," one of my colleagues called.

The scene in the room where the other prisoners, the captive crews were, was as comical as a minstrel show. You would have thought it had been staged.

They had caught the word that we had been rammed. They saw the boat sinking and themselves drowned like rats in a trap. When I got there the gramophone was playing a loud jazz tune. A coloured sailor was jumping about with the wildest gyrations I have ever seen. It seemed as if, in the presence of frightful death, he had reverted to the war dance of his Zulu ancestors. He was oblivious of the others and danced himself to exhaustion. Three other negroes were on their knees, now with backs straight, and then touching their foreheads to the floor. One, who seemed to be a self-appointed deacon, muttered every time he drew himself erect: "O Lo'd, come down heah into dis-heah water and save yoah chillun from de Debil." Whereupon the others would moan "Amen." The white men among the prisoners cowered silent and submissive. The Portuguese crossed himself. The others muttered prayers. I suppose they thought they were facing their end like men.

"The danger is over," we called.

The assurance made no impression. They thought we were merely giving them vain encouragement. It took many repetitions before we succeeded in convincing the frantic group that all was well.

It turned out that the captains were quite right in their weather prophecies. As we ran north the fog grew denser all the time, and the wireless reported worse weather farther north. No use, for the present at any rate, to think more about a raid on Nantucket, Boston, and the coast of Maine. So we nosed her south again, and after some hours of travel ran into sunshine. We headed for Delaware Bay once more, hoping to find excellent weather and plenty of ships to prey upon.

June 2d certainly was our lucky day. We were kept jumping. A bright sun shone and the sea was calm. It was early morning. A sail appeared. We submerged and made for it. Conning tower popped out of water. A shot banged. A shell went whizzing over a saucy bowsprit. The ship was not slow in heaving to. She was the schooner *Isabel B. Wiley* outward bound from Philadelphia.

The *Isabel B. Wiley* had turned toward the wind and was waiting for us, and we were making for her when, at 6:50, a steamer appeared. We left the schooner cold and went after bigger game, running awash. The *Wiley* could have easily bidden us a glad farewell, raised canvas, and made off, but she stood patiently still and watched our encounter with the steamer. She was afraid of our guns, although we were soon out of range and couldn't have touched her.

The steamer kept a poor watch and we were close to her before she saw us. A warning shot, and she drew off steam and raised the American flag. She was S. S. *Winneconne* of New York. Our prize crew went aboard. Soon our new prize was steering over to the obedient *Isabel B. Wiley*.

The quartermaster of the *Winneconne* was a German, born in Baden. Our watch officer was from Baden. Two fellow countrymen had a private little celebration of their own and toasted their native province with enthusiasm. The quartermaster told us that the wireless of S. S. *Huntress* informing the Bermuda station of our futile attack on her had been relayed to the American coast and that our presence in the waters of the United States had been known for some time. Several ships in the past few days had spied us. It was hard to believe that he was telling the truth. The official wireless had given no hint of our existence. Still, the Americans had had no experience with submarine warfare before this and had no system of precautions such as the British had perfected.

We had the lifeboats of both our prizes draw

alongside the submarine. The time had come for a friendly farewell, for a parting with the guests of our under-sea hotel. They were pleasant company, but they also were possessed of excellent appetites. In the three weeks they had spent with us they had eaten a large hole in our food supply. Anyway, it was a favour to them to get them out of their dangerous situation, and they all agreed that they had had quite enough of life on a U-boat. The twenty-six men passed out in single file, each with a cordial good-bye to us. The three captains came last. The old lions seemed a bit loath to leave. Certainly they had acquired no taste for the delights of submarining, but they at least seemed to have grown fond of the company of the under-sea privateers among whom they had been thrown so strangely. Their thanks for the treatment we had accorded them were hearty and they expressed the hope that we would get safely home.

Because of my knowledge of English, which happened to surpass that of our commander, I brought to their notice one point which I thought of certain importance.

"You know the American newspaper reporters," I said. "You've got a big story, and they'll be after you in swarms. All we ask you is to tell them everything you know about us. Tell them how we captured you and how you lived on board."

"Skipper," one of them replied, "we give you our word as old and honourable men of the sea that we will give out a full and accurate report of how well you have treated us and of how thankful we are for it."

"And," I responded jokingly, but also in earnest, "send me, care of the Naval Office in Berlin, a few clippings of your interviews, so that I can read them when we get back home—if we ever get back."

They promised that also.

It would be amusing to read accounts in the American newspapers of our doings along the coast. But I also hoped that the stories of how we had captured our prisoners and then treated them would help some small bit in counteracting the opinion generally held in Allied countries of our U-boat warfare. It would be that much gained in fighting against the anti-German propaganda.

We shook hands again, and the captains got into their lifeboat, vowing they would that night drink each a stein of beer to our health. The boats were well equipped with motors and would have no trouble making shore under their own power. They circled around us three times and each time gave us a cheer. With caps waving and parting farewells shouted, they turned their noses toward the coast and started off at a good clip.

We gave our attention to our two prizes. The *Wiley* went down under full sail, bow first. With her trim form and beautiful white canvas, she was like some living thing making a graceful dive. It was a lovely but sad sight, and in striking contrast to the dirty steamer wobbling about in the waves as it slowly sank.

Our next prize was the schooner *Jacob M. Haskell,* bound out of Boston with a cargo of coal. We had no trouble taking her. The crew, as usual, were frightened half out of their wits at the sight of a dreaded U-boat, but when they found they were going straight ashore they became quite happy. They had first-rate motor lifeboats, and they too circled around us cheering. We were getting more hurrahs in the course of our raid than we had bargained for. When the people on our prizes found that we were not going to sink their vessels with all on board, or even shell their lifeboats, they evidently thought we must be part devil and part angel. The *Haskell* was an even handsomer schooner than the *Wiley*. Why did we have to sink these fine old windjammers? Why didn't more steamers come along?

We had just finished our luncheon when number four for June 2d hove in sight. It seemed as if every American schooner along the Atlantic coast had decided to pay us a visit that day. This new ship was a puzzling sight. We examined her carefully, but couldn't see a single soul on board. Was this a trap, or just a sort of Flying Dutchman? We approached so closely that we could see every detail of the deck. The schooner certainly wasn't armed. It was just a ship sailing along without a guiding hand. Everybody below having a comfortable luncheon was the only way we could figure it out. We steered carefully alongside and my prize crew and I climbed aboard. Still nobody in sight.

"Hey there! All hands on deck," I roared.

The captain came out of his cabin yawning. The old fellow had been taking a pleasant after-luncheon siesta.

"How the hell did you get here?" he growled.

Then he caught sight of the submarine alongside and his face became a study. His crew gathered around, their eyes as big as saucers. They gazed alternately at us there on deck and the gray monster that had stolen up on them.

"Captain, your ship will be blown up in ten minutes."

That woke them up in a jiffy. It didn't take them more than five minutes to gather their belongings and lower their boats. The ship was the *Edward H. Cole* with a cargo out of Boston. It was not long before a charge of TNT roared in her hold and she listed and plunged. Her lifeboats were already well on their way to shore.

At 4:30 we spied a steamer. The ship saw us

coming and tried to get away. A warning shot across her bows was not heeded, nor was a second shot past her stern. She kept on at full speed. Well, we might try to show them that we were in earnest. A careful aim, and the third shot took away part of the bridge on the starboard side. The vessel stopped and raised the American flag. The crew abandoned ship while our boat was on its way over. The steamer was the *Texel*, bound for New York with a cargo of sugar from Porto Rico. It may have been rather cruel to help along the sugar shortage in the United States, but a charge of TNT, and the *Texel* and her cargo went down to sweeten Davy Jones' coffee.

The wireless brought what was destined to be the first of an interesting series of messages. The lifeboats of the first two ships we had sunk that day had been sighted by a steamer which had picked up the crews of the two ships as well as all of our former guests. They were on their way to Delaware Bay. All ships were immediately warned of our presence. Now the hunt for us would begin. We depended on the wireless to give us many a hint of its progress. Our two operators were clever fellows. I bade them be on vigilant duty every hour of the day and night and snatch every word out of the air that they could.

At 5:25 a steamer appeared. It tried to run. A few well-placed shots close to its side, and it came to a stop.

"It's a troop ship!" I exclaimed.

By now there was a huge crowd at the railing. The ship was the *Carolina*, bound from the West Indies for New York. The passengers and crew were climbing down into the boats when the steamer got a message which we also caught:

"Make for the nearest port. Great danger of German submarines."

But for them that warning came just a few minutes too late.

The lifeboats were crowded, and a great wailing of women's voices rose. There was praying and pleading. The negroes thought we were going to use them for target practice. That shelling of lifeboats idea was an obstinate canard. It may have been done, but certainly not to my knowledge. We did our best to reassure them, and started them on their way toward shore, which was not far distant. The captain got his boats into a sort of formation, and soon we lost the sound of their chugging motors as they disappeared over the waves. It was growing dark rapidly, and not wanting to send a party aboard the *Carolina* to plant our usual explosives, we sank her with gunfire.

As night fell we eased out to sea to rest up quietly after a strenuous day. We had sunk three steamers and three sailing vessels, of a total tonnage of 14,518. Not bad!

CHAPTER XXXIV

"HUMAN HUNS." WE CAPTURE A BABY.

The wireless provided us with some very pleasant reading in the way of dispatches that came constantly through our radio room. Early on June 3d the warning was broadcast that our submarine had been seen off Cape Hatteras. We were not near Cape Hatteras, but were, in fact, lying in ambush a safe distance out from the entrance of Chesapeake Bay. Another dispatch reported a submarine near Block Island, which was still farther from our actual location. At noon we were said to be twenty-five miles southeast of Barnegat. For a moment we were tempted to believe that other U-boats had been sent across to American waters, but we knew that could not be. The various reports were merely the wild rumours that go around after any exciting event. The many alarms would certainly cause ships to think that many U-boats were along the coast. That would increase the panic in shipping circles, and destroyers would go hunting for phantom submarines. Let them hunt wherever they pleased, so long as they did not come near us.

At 3 P. M. we caught several SOS calls in rapid succession from a ship in Delaware Bay. Instantly we thought of the mines we had planted there. Apparently they were working properly. The sinking steamer was a 6,000-tonner, but we couldn't catch her name. She sank quickly. Her crew got away in their boats and were picked up by passing ships. We could read the whole story in the brief wireless calls. Perhaps the most interesting item of the whole account was the statement that the foundered steamer had been torpedoed by a submarine. Another ghostly U-boat at large!

The wireless indicated that there was great excitement along the coast. All ships were ordered to hurry to the nearest port, and none was to proceed except under convoy. A submarine was supposed to be lurking in front of every American harbour. Ocean traffic was disorganized to a surprising extent. Ships either stayed in port waiting for convoy, or hugged the coast. Freight rates and insurance premiums went up. This was all damage to our adversaries, indirect, but quite as important as the tonnage we were sinking. It was, with its general hampering of over-sea transportation, one of the main objects of our raid. The American Navy began an extensive hunt for the various supposed U-boats, which quite effectively dissipated the hunt for us. According to press reports, hundreds of airplanes and hydroplanes were ordered to patrol the coast.

A morning and an afternoon passed without a vessel coming in sight. The submarine warnings had cleared the sea pretty effectively. In the evening, though, we picked up a four-mast schooner. She was the *Samuel G. Mengel* of Pensacola, running to New York with a cargo of copra from the Gold Coast. She had no wireless, and the captain was greatly astonished at the sight of a German submarine in American waters.

On the following day we had a ticklish encounter. American destroyers were out. We picked up the Yankee schooner, *Edward R. Baird,* loaded with a cargo of lumber, much of which was piled on deck. We packed the sulky captain and his crew off in their boats and planted TNT. Meanwhile, a tanker appeared. So we left the listing hulk of the *Baird* and made after the newcomer. She was thoroughly camouflaged and appeared to be British. She seemed to have had experience in submarine-frequented waters, too, for when she spied us she started off at full speed, zigzagging. We opened fire at long range. She returned the fire and managed to slip away.

The thunder of the guns attracted a very unwelcome visitor, a destroyer. We immediately dived, and kept watch through the periscope to see what the fellow would do. The destroyer zigzagged over to the hulk of the *Baird,* which, with its cargo of buoyant lumber, was still afloat, its back broken by our charge of TNT. Then she zigzagged her way around the sinking schooner, inspecting it. A three-masted schooner appeared. The warship hurried off, still zigzagging, to warn her. We came to the surface. Another destroyer appeared. It was so near dark now that we did not bother to submerge. We ran south unobserved. That sort of thing would have been impossible in British waters, but the Americans had not yet learned the arts of U-boat hunting.

We had scarcely got out of sight of the destroyers when the dark form of a steamer appeared. We stopped her. The captain came over with his papers. She was S. S. *Eidsvold* of Christiania, another sugar ship bound from Porto Rico to New York.

"Captain," her skipper said to Commander von Nostitz, "I have my wife aboard, and she is very much excited. Can you give me time to quiet her and pack our belongings?"

Of course, we granted him his wish. We waited while they took all the time they wanted.

We ran south all night, and at daybreak sighted a sail. An old craft lumbered up. There was a shout, a kind of long howl, as the lookout, a negro, saw a submarine pop suddenly out of the water and fire a shot across the ship's bows. A score of black men and several whites swarmed the deck, tumbled into boats, and rowed frantically toward us.

"You will be sunk in ten minutes," I said to them.

"Well, ain't that the dickens," twanged an old white man, the captain. "What'll we do now?"

He seemed so genuinely downcast that I asked where the craft was from, and what she was doing.

"We're from Mississippi," he replied sorrowfully, "and we're whalin'—leastwise we intended to. We was on our way up around Greenland to do a bit of harpoonin', but now it looks like we ain't goin' to. It sure is tough."

He continued that the ship was owned by several poverty-stricken families in a town on the Mississippi coast. It was all they had in the world. They lived scantily on the proceeds of the whaling. The old skipper plucked up courage as he told his tale.

"You don't have to sink us, Cap'n, do you?" he protested in his slow voice. "If you do it certainly'll be tough on us."

I looked at the ancient tub. She meant little indeed in the affairs of the World War.

"All right, Skipper," I said, "get your men back aboard. You can go on."

"Well, Cap'n, that sure is good of you." His drawling voice remained perfectly even, but you could tell that the words came from the heart.

His crew cheered with joy. A couple of the negroes tried their feet at dancing as well as the narrow quarters in the lifeboat would allow. They put back to their ship with willing oars.

The ancient whaler picked up its course and went limping along to the north. We on the deck of the *U-151* had to smile to each other. We wondered how a German whaling boat would have fared similarly in the hands of its enemies.

S. S. *Harpathian*, 4,855 tons, was bound in ballast

from Plymouth to Baltimore. She was heavily armed, and therefore subject to torpedo attack without warning. We submerged when we sighted her and ran under water to a point along her course where we could get a good shot. Our torpedo went on its way. A thud came with a dull metallic jar. We ascended quickly for a look through the periscope.

The big steamer was sagging, stern down. The crew were already in boats and rowing away from the sinking vessel. We emerged and made for the boats. The men were all Japanese, save the fat captain, the helmsman, the machinist, and two gunners, who were English.

"Anybody hurt?" I hailed them.

"One man cut a little," the ponderous captain, quite a jovial Britisher, responded.

We hauled the injured man, a Japanese, onto our deck, where our surgeon looked him over. He had a couple of cuts, scarcely more than scratches. A bit of iodine and adhesive plaster, and he climbed back into his own boat. We obliged the men in the boats with a tank of water, a few tins of bully beef to keep the edges off their appetites, and a heap of tobacco. They headed to the west quite cheerfully. Meanwhile, the torpedoed *Harpathian* had vanished.

I am sure that Americans who had to sweeten their coffee during the war with molasses, candy, or saccharine, or not sweeten it at all, will bestow a hearty curse on us, particularly the ladies who found that the grocers would sell them a pound of sugar, at an exorbitant price, only when they bought several dollars' worth of something else in addition. We could sympathize with people who had a sugar shortage. We had a devilish one in Germany! Still, war is war, so they say.

Two steamers appeared at sunset. One puffed its cloud of smoke afar and was steaming so fast that it soon disappeared. The other headed straight toward us and was promptly bagged. She was the Norwegian steamer *Vinland* of Bergen, bound from Guantanamo to New York with a cargo of sugar. Our third sugar ship! The captain said he had read warnings against submarines in the Cuban newspapers, but had dismissed them as merely another of those Anglo-Saxon war rumours. His incredulity made him look somewhat sheepish now.

The sea was high when another steamer hove into sight, the Norwegian ship *Vindeggen* loaded with 6,000 bales of cotton and 2,000 tons of copper for the Allies. We caught her after a chase and a bit of gunfire.

The captain came over with his papers. The *Vindeggen* had been launched two years before in Japan and since that time had been working its way around to New York as a tramp. The wife of the helmsman was aboard with her little daughter, two years old.

"It will be hard for them in the lifeboats," said the captain, "the sea is so rough."

Of course it would. The men, all veteran sailors, would find the trip ashore no great hardship, but with a woman and small child it was different. However, we had no intention of sending the people of the *Vindeggen* ashore just now. The steamer's cargo was too valuable; the copper, to be precise.

Copper was very scarce in beleaguered Germany. Our supplies of the metal, so necessary for making shells, had been large at the beginning, but the tremendous demand for projectiles on our various fronts had depleted it sadly. In our roomy submarine we could pack a good supply of the *Vindeggen's* precious ingots.

We were too near land and the path of coastwise ships, to say nothing of destroyers, for comfortable transporting of a cargo from a steamer to our boat.

Farther out, where the ocean was less frequented, would be better.

"Go aboard your ship, Captain," our bearded skipper said to the Norwegian master. "Then put out to sea. But don't try to run away. We have good guns, and we will be close behind."

The steamer started off. The U-boat trailed along behind like a guard. A small steamer appeared coming toward us.

"Stop and wait, and don't forget," the captain of the *Vindeggen* was warned by megaphone.

The Norwegian did as he was told while we captured and sank the 2,504-tonner *Pinar del Rio*, formerly the *Villa Real* of the Oldenburg-Portuguese line. She was another sugar ship.

We took the *Vindeggen* out a hundred and fifty miles, and then the transfer of the copper began. The crew of the *Vindeggen*, Chinese all, lent a willing hand. We jettisoned our iron ballast and replaced it with the more valuable metal.

Meanwhile, an enemy ship might come up, and we had to be ready to dive at a moment's notice. We had to have our men always ready to leap into the hatchways. The copper was brought onto our deck only a few bars at a time. It would have been disastrous to have had to dive with a load of metal on deck. It took two days of the hardest kind of work before we had our plunder stowed away.

The helmsman who had his wife and child aboard was really no helmsman at all, but a dead-head passenger who was getting a free voyage by grace of the captain. Ugland by name, he was a decent, well-bred fellow. Mrs. Ugland was pretty and amiable, but dreadfully frightened at first. At our invitation, she came over to visit our monster of the deep. Her face was pale and her eyes gaped as she climbed from the lifeboat onto our deck, first passing her baby up into the rough hands of our seamen. I assigned the two fair guests to my quarters.

The child became the ship's darling. Her name was Eva. She gazed at the things around her with marvelling eyes. Our sailors tumbled over themselves to please her. The cook felt himself the chief personage in the entertainment given the young lady. He prepared cakes, candies, and dishes of canned fruits with whipped cream. The sailors fed the delicacies to the child with an unflagging delight. The tiny Eva was a very obliging mite. She tried to please her hosts by eating everything they gave her. She persevered in these good intentions until her stomach overflowed, whereupon Mrs. Ugland intervened and carried the tot away until she had recovered from the over-feeding. Thereafter our men were careful about what they gave Eva to eat, and contented themselves with riding her on their knees and such.

The copper stowed away aboard the *U-151*, only a few more formalities remained. The crew of the *Vindeggen* gathered their belongings, and got into their lifeboats. The boats were strung out in a line, and we prepared to take them in tow. The captain of the *Vindeggen* wanted his ship to sink with her flag flying. The Norwegian colours were hoisted to the masthead. The TNT roared out. The steamer sank swiftly on an even keel. The Norwegian flag was the last thing seen. It seemed to hover fluttering for a moment, and then plunged. The old captain stood rigidly at attention. Mrs. Ugland could not suppress her tears. The tiny Eva clapped her hands with glee at the strange sight.

A seaman's best friend is his ship. When his ship sinks it is like the burial of a comrade. Our men understood our guests' sorrow, and tried to comfort them. They rigged up their orchestra and got out on the submarine's deck. We headed for land, towing the lifeboats behind us. On our deck old songs were sung to the accompaniment of guitar and mandoline.

The concert was interrupted at about 5 P. M., when we sighted smoke on the horizon. So we cut loose from our train of lifeboats.

"Head for the smoke" was the order given them.

They obeyed, and we, too, headed for the smoke. A steamer appeared. We submerged and waited. The steamer, as we expected, sighted the lifeboats and made for them. The voyagers in the boats had a good view of the show. At the proper moment our U-boat put in its appearance. Consternation on the steamer's deck, a scramble to lower the lifeboats, and another capture was made. The ship was the *Heinrich Lund* of Bergen, Norway. She was bound from Baltimore for Buenos Aires with a cargo of coal, engines, and engine parts. Her skipper, Captain Kaltenborn, asked for permission to rescue his belongings before the *Lund* was sunk.

"I have," he added, "a few bottles of champagne and beer, and also some newspapers that tell a lot about your boat."

He got instant permission. The champagne and beer were welcome, and still more welcome were the newspapers. We were eager to see whether they carried any of the interviews which our former prisoners had promised to give regarding their cruise with us.

The usual charge of TNT, and the *U-151* started off again with its string of lifeboats, which now was increased in length by the boats of the *Heinrich Lund*.

Toasts of champagne and beer were drunk all down the line. I devoted myself to the beer. We had not brought any of the refreshing liquid along from Germany and had found very little of it in the ships we had captured. The beer was excellent. In Germany, under the pressure of war, the beer had already gone bad, but this was as good as German beer before the war. We had to congratulate the American breweries. It was too bad that prohibition had to come along and ruin them.

Nothing goes together better than drinking beer and reading the papers. We scanned every page of the journals Captain Kaltenborn gave us. Yes, there were the stories about our former guests. The captains had kept their promises, and more. The articles told fairly accurately of our prisoners' stay with us and of the excellent treatment we had given them. One piece of a later date was about the torpedoing of the *Harpathian*. It was headed "Human Huns." We didn't like that term, Hun, but then the account related fully how we had gone to the *Harpathian's* lifeboats and given all the help we could.

Another skipper, Captain M. H. Saunders of the *Hauppage,* had given the gentlemen of the press quite a colourful yarn. Referring to his little holiday cruise on our under-sea yacht, he said: "Their food was tiptop. Why, for breakfast they even gave us delicious hot rolls and fresh butter. That butter was fine! But their bread was black and came in funny loaves about three feet long. We also had cognac nearly all of the time. They had three gramophones on board and there was a lot of singing. In fact, the members of the crew were cheerful and joked with us a lot, especially after indulging in cognac. They nearly all were very young fellows—and they spoke often of their mothers."

Not such a bad portrait of us "Huns" at that, *nicht wahr?*

Captain Kaltenborn told me that we were supposed to have sunk sixteen ships. We had, as a matter of fact, sunk fourteen. Another had struck one of the mines we had laid and was supposed to have been torpedoed. That made fifteen. There remained a sixteenth. I gathered from further conversation with the skipper that it also had fallen a victim of our mine-laying and had been charged off to the account of our torpedoes.

"Your name is Körner," exclaimed the captain suddenly. "Ah, yes, I remember. Weren't you in Stockholm with the battleship *Hohenzollern* in 1911?"

I replied in the affirmative and he went on to relate that he had heard of me through his sister. At a ball in honour of the German officers I had met her and given her a "grand rush." Yes, I remembered her. In those days I was a gay spark, but since then I had transferred my whole allegiance to the German mother of my children. The world was indeed small when in the middle of a trans-Atlantic submarine raid I could run across a reminder of a flirtation at a ball seven years before.

The *U-151* dragged its towline along peacefully in the light of the sinking sun. We were getting into the shipping lane now and thought it would be an excellent idea to rid ourselves of our train of boats. Von Nostitz arranged with the prisoners that as soon as a steamer was sighted we would pull the boats across its course as near to it as we safely could. Then we would cut loose and submerge and watch to see how things went. They were to signal the oncoming ship by shouting, waving lanterns, and setting off rockets that we gave them. If the ship refused to take them aboard they were to inform the captain of our presence in the neighbourhood and say that if he still refused to take them aboard we would torpedo him, as we certainly would.

Soon after dark we sighted a steamer coming very slowly off our port side. We steered across the bow with our line of boats. It was 9:50 when we loosened the towline. We did not submerge. We could see the ship clearly, while behind us was a mass of dark clouds such as to make us almost invisible. The occupants of the lifeboats at once began to make a devil of a racket. The citizens of Baltimore must have heard it! And they waved lanterns and set off rockets. The line of boats made a tremendous spectacle. The ship, as it drew up, seemed to be a coast patrol boat. It stopped and looked things over. Apparently it "smelled" submarine, because it turned as if to run. We trained our guns on the dark form. The occupants of the boats shouted to the ship that it would be sunk if it did not pick them up. Then the captain seemed to spy us vaguely, only a thousand feet away, and probably reasoned that we could undoubtedly shoot him full of holes. The steamer drew up and took the crowd aboard.

We turned and headed north.

CHAPTER XXXV

DEPTH BOMBS—AND THE LIGHTED DINING ROOM

Our supply of oil was awfully low now, and we could not continue our stay in American waters much longer. You know how the old horse pricks up his ears and shakes his weary legs with new life when he comes to the turn that leads homeward to the stable? That was how we felt.

The fisherman always has to indulge himself in one last cast of his line. We ran south for one more day of hunting in the waters off the United States. An interesting guest paid us a visit. A crane that seemingly had been blown around for days by the raging wind alighted on our deck and lay on its back, exhausted. We amused ourselves by administering to the waif. We brought it food and water. It devoured the morsels as though it were nearly starved. Soon it was on its long legs and drying itself in the sun. It stayed with us a day, quite tame and companionable, and then after a final meal, which we provided bounteously, it leaped away on flapping wings and headed swiftly for land.

Our last day in American waters was fruitless in the way of ships sunk. We sighted two big steamers, but both escaped us.

Homeward bound! It was June 13th. We had been off the American coast for three weeks and two days. We steered east, planning to pick up a ship or two on our return trip. At 5 A. M. on the day after our departure from the American coast we caught the three-masted schooner, *Samoa* of Christiania, bound from Walfish Bay, South Africa, for New York with a cargo of copper ore and wool. She had just trimmed her sails and we were making ready to board her when a destroyer appeared, keeping a course that would take her past us a few miles off. We had launched our small boat and could not submerge right away. The destroyer must certainly see us, or, at any rate, notice the schooner lying there with furled sails. A frantic harum-scarum scene as all hands scurried aboard and below. The destroyer did not change her course. Surely they must have a better lookout than that! She kept straight on her way and vanished on the horizon, leaving us quite free to deal with our prize.

The lifeboats of the *Samoa* were equipped only with oars, and the distance from land would have meant a tremendous lot of rowing. After we had sunk the ship we communicated with the nearest American wireless station and asked that a vessel be sent out after the men. A return message came thanking us.

The *Kringsia* of Christiania, bound for New York from Buenos Aires with a cargo of linseed oil, was the victim of her own excessive timidity. We chased her for three hours and a half, while she ran, sails full set. For a long time we gained on her, though very slowly. Then the breeze stiffened. The ship picked up speed and kept her distance. She began to draw away, and we gave up the chase. A couple of parting shots at an impossible range, more for amusement's sake than anything else! We were not at all astonished to see the shells fall far short. We were thoroughly astonished, though, when the ship immediately lowered her top sails. She had run a good race, but the mere sound of shots had frightened her. We sent a wireless message summoning aid for the lifeboats, and then watched the reddish-brown linseed oil spread over the water as the schooner sank.

On June 18th we finished off an ugly customer. A careful aim through the periscope, and we shot a torpedo at an 8,000-ton armed steamer. A hit. Lifeboats launched and the crew got away safely. We drew up to the boats. The ship was formerly the Russian and now the British steamer *Dvinsk*, bound empty for Newport News to bring back a load of American troops. She carried, we were told, a heavy armament of guns, shells, mine apparatus, and depth bombs, all manner of equipment to put the quietus on a submarine. The bottom of the sea was an excellent place for that junk, according to our way of thinking.

"And now, my dear fellow, here is big game at last." Our skipper stroked his beard with a gesture of anticipation.

The lifeboats of the *Dvinsk* could still be seen in the distance when a big four-funnelled fellow appeared, the former *Kronprinz Wilhelm* of the North German Lloyd Line. We manœuvred submerged, ready for a torpedo shot.

"*Torpedo los!*" Von Nostitz gave the command and the missile went its way. We dived and awaited the result.

Seconds passed, and nothing happened. Another miss! Our torpedoes had been stored too long. We returned to periscope level for another shot. And now, two minutes after the torpedo had been launched, came a dull, thudding report. Hurrah! We had made a hit after all. Then another report came louder than the first. Two more sounded in rapid succession, nearer and nearer to us.

"Depth bombs!" The murmur ran through the boat. Our torpedo had missed and been seen, and we were being counter-attacked with depth bombs!

"Dive!" the Captain roared. "Dive!"

Surely it was an unexpected thing in the middle of the ocean. That steamer must have had its nerve. It was a brave effort for a ship far away from land, and without the support of a destroyer, to see a torpedo and try to chase down the submarine to the point whence the missile came. That was what had happened, though. The steamer had rushed in our direction and now was raining its whole supply of depth bombs over us.

In the submarine we had only one thought—down, down. Water let into all the compartments. Engines ran with full power, throwing us into a steep dive. Bombs exploded incessantly, some far and some near. The boat trembled from the force of the detonations. All of the crew who had no immediate duty to perform were crowded at the doors of the control room, listening to the commands. They were as pale as death. We sank rapidly. The sounds of the explosions became weaker.

A deafening report crashed out. The boat shook in every joint. We were sure we had been hit. But no, we could see each other. There was still light. The first thing to happen when a submarine is hit is for the electric lights to go out. Now everybody ran around the boat, looking, inspecting. No water was coming into the compartments. The seams were tight and no rivets were loosened. She had not been damaged.

Mein Gott, how good everybody felt!

Then we looked at the depth gauge. Sixty-two metres. Our boat had been tested to only fifty metres. In our eagerness to sink we had just kept on going down and down, and we had sunk too far! Even now I could not understand how our boat had withstood so great an excess of pressure, but I knew that it might be crushed at any moment, its iron sides bent in, its seams opened.

"Air pressure!" the skipper yelled.

The compressed air system was started.

The gauge, instead of registering a lower pressure, showed that we were sinking. We were at sixty-five metres, seventy, seventy-two, seventy-five. The pressure of the water about us was so great that the compressed air could not force the water ballast out of our hull.

"No use." The voice of the quartermaster, as he reported, seemed to come out of the unfathomable depths for which we were headed.

"The pumps!" the Captain yelled, "and air pressure in tanks three and four!"

The pumps got into action and the new blast of air pressure hissed and spluttered. Not enough. Eighty-two metres!

"Air pressure of all tanks!" I could see blank despair in Von Nostitz's bearded face. Even if this expenditure of our last reserve did thrust the water from our tanks it would shoot us to the surface, and on the surface we would have to lie. With no compressed air left we could not submerge again and ever hope to rise. And on the surface what? The depth bombs had ceased their infernal explosions, but the ship above could sink us with gunfire. Nevertheless, we must rise if we could. Better to go to the surface and fight and then be sunk than to be crushed in the depths.

The last reserve of compressed air was flowing into the tanks with its sibilant, surging sound. We were sinking. Eighty-three metres! It seemed impossible that the boat could survive. Then we were stationary. My heart pounded like a hammer as I watched the gauge. Were we doomed to remain forever at that level? A ghostly thought. At last we began ever so slowly to creep up. The speed of our rise increased. Now we were at fifty metres, in the zone of safety. If we could only stay there for a while, an hour or so. But we could not stop rising. Our upward progress became a horror, and it increased in swiftness with every moment.

We shot to the surface. The light of day blazed in our faces as we looked. The steamer was not in sight. Every man sank onto the nearest support and lay for moments, exhausted.

The lifeboats of the *Dvinsk* were on the horizon. We made for them.

"Didn't that steamer see you?"

"Yes," they replied. "It came right by. They said they didn't dare to stop with a submarine around, but would send a boat for us later."

The ship, having dropped all of its bombs, had made off as fast as it could. That had saved us. The fact that it was out of sight when we came to the surface indicates how long that agonized struggle in the depths had lasted. We were convinced that the ship was the former *Kronprinz Wilhelm* of the North German Lloyd Line, made over by the United States Navy into an auxiliary cruiser.

We were now back into the main steamship lane. Many steamers passed us, but we were unable to bag a single one of them. One morning, with a heavy fog on the ocean, a giant form appeared suddenly in the mist. It was headed straight toward us. We dived at once. A peep through the periscope showed us the *Mauretania* disappearing in the fog at a tremendous speed.

We rounded the northern tip of Scotland and went along, worming and squirming our way through the blockade. After several more days we caught the odour of growing things, and our first sight of European land came when the twinkling lights of Ruyberg and Hirschhals appeared. As we passed Helsingborg in the night I looked for that red hanging lamp in the Swedish dining room, the one I had seen on our way out. Yes, there it was. And, as before, a merry company sat around the festive board, toasting each other, and laughing and little dreaming that a giant submarine cruiser was just outside, slinking by on her return from an historic trans-Atlantic raid across the ocean to the Western Hemisphere. A little later we glided silently through the sound past Copenhagen, as brightly lighted as it had been on our voyage out.

At dawn we cut off our wild-looking beards and shaved and got out our uniforms. Boats came from Kiel with our flotilla chief and his entire staff to welcome us. One brought Prince Adalbert, son of the Kaiser. We made fast to the pier at 9:30 A. M., July 20, 1918. At home we found everyone full of hope. The Allies and Americans had checked our army in France. But in spite of this we little dreamed that defeat was at hand.

Ninety-four days had passed since we had fared forth on our adventurous voyage. And we had covered exactly ten thousand, nine hundred, and fifteen miles. We had definitely sunk a total of 23 ships, of a gross tonnage of something more than 61,000 tons. In addition, four others had gone down on the mines we had planted, two that we already had heard about, and then two others. This brought our tonnage up to an additional 10,000 or 12,000, and our total sinkings to 27 ships. So, in all, between seventy and seventy-five thousand tons of Allied shipping had gone down to Davy Jones carrying our compliments, and we had shown a skeptical world that even the wide expanse of the Atlantic was not enough to keep us from a super-raid to the coast of far-off America. To those who can see into the future, surely this is a warning of what later wars may bring. For the day will come when submarines will think no more of a voyage across the Atlantic than they do now of a raid across the North Sea. In the not far-distant future our giant *U-151* will be succeeded by craft that will operate not only above and under the sea, but up in the air as well. America's isolation is now a thing of the past.

CHAPTER XXXVI

VON ARNAULD, THE ACE OF ACES, STAGES THE LAST BIG FIGHT

The voyage to America that the German ace of aces was to have made but never completed involved a spectacular adventure which stands as the last big fight of the war under the sea. Commander von Arnauld began with a description of his new big cruiser, one of two giants in which the Germans embodied the latest improvements of submarine construction, then he went ahead with a story full of action:

I remained in the Mediterranean until the spring of 1918, when I was recalled to Germany and placed in command of one of these submarine cruisers, the *U-139*. All of these big fellows were named after submarine commanders who had gone down with their boats. Mine was the *Commander Schwieger*, named after the captain who had sunk the *Lusitania*.

The *U-139* was as different from my old boat, the *U-35*, as a battle cruiser is from a destroyer. The *U-35* was less than two hundred feet long and carried a crew of forty men. Its quarters were cramped. My tiny captain's cabin was scarcely more than a cupboard. One cabin sufficed for the three other officers. They had scarcely enough room to turn around. They did not even have individual sleeping places. There were two bunks. As one of them was always on watch, there were never more than two men in the cabin at

one time. The *U-139*, on the other hand, was almost
the size of a small cruiser. She was nearly four hundred feet from bow to stern. Her tonnage was 1,930
above water and 2,480 below. There were two decks
inside of the huge hull. My cabin was as roomy and
well appointed as that of a skipper of a regular naval
vessel, and the other officers and the men were taken
care of in a similarly comfortable way. Instead of
one 10.5 cm. gun, we had two big 15 cm. guns, one
mounted fore and two at the stern. The *U-35* had
two torpedo tubes at the bow and two at the stern.
The *U-139* had four torpedo tubes fore and two aft.
It carried twenty torpedoes and a thousand shells.
The boat made thirteen knots on the surface and had
a submerging time of two minutes. Briefly, she was
a real warship, one capable of conducting a respectable
naval action by gunfire as well as by torpedo. The
defect of these big submarine cruisers, as compared
with the smaller boats, was that they were unwieldy.
In a surface fight they could hold their own with anything short of really big guns, but submerged it was
difficult to manœuvre for a torpedo shot. They were
clumsy and did not swing around quickly, as is necessary for a craft that aims its shot by aiming itself.

No sooner was this giant tested out when she was
ordered to raid the East coast of the United States.
One great attack in France had failed, and our armies
were driven back. We were losing hope of victory.
Defeat was looming black. Nevertheless, the U-boats
were carrying on.

On October 1, 1918, the *U-139* lay off Cape Finisterre on the northern coast of Spain. We had just
come out from Kiel after one of the stormiest trips
I have ever had the misfortune to encounter. For
days we had to keep our hatches closed while the
tempestuous seas swept over us. Now, though, we
were enjoying our first fine day. Everybody was on

deck enjoying the fresh air. At ten o'clock smoke was sighted on the horizon and a forest of masts came into view. It was a big convoy. As it came into clear view we counted ten large steamers guarded by two British auxiliary cruisers, one of which led the procession and the other brought up the rear. On each side of the column were fussy little patrol boats. The entire company was zigzagging.

It is hard to gauge a zigzagging course. We steered to the right and then to the left of the convoy to get into position where we could lie in wait, to allow the convoy to pass in front of us so that we could get a shot. After a lot of manœuvring we got a beeline on one of the freighters. Torpedo loosed, we went to the depths to get away from an expected rain of depth bombs. No sound, either of torpedo or of depth bombs. We had missed, and neither torpedo nor our periscope had been noticed. The silence was soon disturbed by a huge rushing and whirring sound, a noise of many propellers. The whole convoy, in one of its zigzagging shifts, had passed over our heads.

"Blow the tanks!" I called the command into the speaking tube, and to the surface we rose.

We had failed with the torpedo; we would have it out with our guns. It was a risky thing, thus to rise so near the convoy and stage a fight with shell fire, but then our submarine cruiser was designed to put up a good skirmish on the surface, and if the going got too hot we could dive out of it.

We came up gingerly, guiding ourselves by the sound of propellers. We did not want to bump against the bottom of a ship. Now we broke the surface, and in a moment the gun crews were scrambling on deck and forward and aft to the guns. There were all those vessels only a short way off. Pandemonium broke loose. Our guns fired as fast as they could.

Every ship that had a gun and was in range popped shells at us. There were explosions all around the U-boat, but the shooting from the ships was confused and bad. We might have sunk several right there by direct gunfire if it hadn't been for one of the auxiliary cruisers. She was too near for comfort in the first place, and now she came at us, her guns blazing away. She was shooting carefully and well. Her shells were bursting in the water a few yards from us.

"Below for diving," I shouted to the men at our guns.

We were just in time. Just as the water was closing over the conning tower a shell burst up there. The water deadened its explosion, but the shell fragments clanged loudly against our steel plates. This time there was no lack of depth charges. They crashed out a few seconds apart above us, but we had plunged too deep for them.

Our second attack foiled. *"Donnerwetter,"* we said, "this has got to stop." Up to periscope depth and a look around. The convoy was steaming on in the distance. Very well, we have a fast boat—up and after them. We came to the surface and ran at our best speed until we had caught up with the convoy.

This time luck favoured us. The auxiliary cruisers were slow and gave us time to get the range. In good shooting distance, we had a few minutes of precious target practice. We sent our shells as fast as we could at the nearest steamer. She stopped, badly hit. Then we turned on the next one. A few shells, and she was disabled. By this time one of the cruisers was headed for us at full speed, firing and trying to ram us.

The ocean swallowed us, and in a minute depth bombs came looking for us with their ugly banging voices. When they had their say we returned to periscope depth to see what could be done. The first steamer we had hit was sinking. The cruiser that had attacked us was taking aboard the stricken vessel's crew. The second steamer we had hit was lying well afloat. Patrol boats were standing by, and one of the larger vessels was preparing to take it in tow.

It was mid-afternoon now, and we still had several hours in which to finish off the disabled ship. Patrol boats had been called to the scene from near-by ports and were swarming around. We had to proceed very carefully, running submerged. It was sundown and dusk was gathering before we had manœuvred into position for a torpedo shot. The damaged steamer was listing. The towline had broken, and the attempt to take the vessel in tow seemed to have been abandoned. The crew was being taken off by patrol boats.

By now it was so dark through the periscope that the ships above were nothing but shadows. We were about to loose a torpedo when one of the shadows loomed much too close.

"Dive!" I called in haste.

We rested for a little while at twenty metres, listening to the sound of propellers above. I stood in the conning tower. Beside me were my two officers. The helmsman stood behind. Down below the men not on duty were eating supper. The noise of propellers died away. Slowly the *U-139* edged up to periscope depth. As I looked in the glass I saw a looming shadow in the twilight, a ship broadside to us and right in line for a torpedo shot. I wasted no time for inspection.

"First bow torpedo—fire!"

The torpedo left the tube, and we dived instantly. After a short wait came the shattering roar of the torpedo explosion. Less than a minute later there was a terrible crash overhead and our boat shook from stem to stern as if it had been cracked open by the giant blow. The lights went out. Water rushed in from above. The boat listed to one side.

I guessed what had happened. We had been very near the ship we had torpedoed and had drifted under her. And now she had sunk on top of us. She was the vessel we had hit with shell fire and was water-logged when the torpedo ripped her open. That was why she had plunged so quickly.

The lights flashed on with that sudden strange startlement that always accompanies lights flashing on.

"Man the pumps!" I yelled.

The water was still pouring down over us from above. The helmsman was trying desperately to close the hatch of the compartment above, from which the drenching shower came. The hatch had been jammed by the shock and would not close. The depth gauge showed that we were sinking at a terrific speed. The sinking ship was carrying us down with her. The sea was three thousand feet deep here in this place. We would soon be crushed like an eggshell by the pressure of the water. Not a word was spoken in the conning tower. Not a sound was heard save the rushing of water and the heavy breathing of the men. Above us sounded the cracking of depth bombs. What a mockery they seemed. There was just one chance.

"Air pressure in all tanks." I could feel my voice go false and strained as I tried to conceal the tone of wild anxiety.

The boat trembled and lurched as the compressed air blew the water out of the tanks. Could we shake ourselves loose? I could feel the boat sliding. The depth gauge showed that our descent was checked. Then the pointer swung quickly around. The sudden upward drag of the boat had disengaged it from the sinking ship, which had slid off and gone on to the bottom.

The *U-139*, with blown tanks, was rising like a balloon. There was no chance of stopping our ascent until we came to the top, and there the surface craft were waiting. We could hear their depth bombs bursting. Water still poured into the conning tower, but the pumps were able to hold it down. Our upper works had been smashed, and in the conning tower we were blind. Our three periscopes had been carried away. The hand of the depth gauge moved around inexorably. I called to the men to be ready for an order to dive the moment we broke the surface.

A sound of swishing and splashing, and the shower from above ceased to pour down on us.

"Dive!" I shouted.

Another of those eternities. We were in the midst of the boats that were hunting for us. The sound of depth bombs came from here and there. But the sea was pitch dark and we were not detected. Now we were nosing down, I held the boat just below the surface, where the leakage through the conning tower would be least.

Expecting to be run down at any moment in that hornets' nest of boats, we limped away a few feet below the surface, and presently the sound of bombs, where they were still gunning for us, was lost in the distance. After an hour we came to the surface. Nothing was near us. Far off to the south we could see searchlights sweeping about the scene of our late adventure.

Our upper works were hopelessly ruined. The deck was ripped up. Our three periscopes hung by a wire. We were a rather crippled specimen of U-boat. The next day we picked up a small steamer. Our luck still held out. She had a cargo of port wine and cement—just what we needed. With the wine we refreshed our bedraggled spirits and with the cement repaired the conning tower, filling up the breaks so that it was watertight once more. We were still without periscopes, but could put up a surface fight and could navigate the depths again—a blind fish, to be sure, but still a fish.

The end of the Kaiser's dread under-sea fleet. At Harwich, England, after their surrender.

The effect of a mine on a submarine. In all, 178 raiders of the deep lie somewhere on the floor of the ocean.

We continued our cruise looking for ships to attacl
with our guns. The wireless told us that our line wa
being rolled back in France. Yes, Germany was de
feated. We were filled with despondency. Off th
Azores the *U-139* had its last fight, and a brisk affaii
it was. We sighted a big steamer escorted by a Portuguese gunboat. We gave chase, but the steamer was
too fast. The gunboat attacked us. It was a puny,
antiquated thing and had no guns to match ours and
had only half as many men aboard as we had. I have
never seen a braver fight than that old piece of junk
put up. Those Portuguese fought like devils, firing
shell after shell from their popguns while we raked
them from stem to stern. Fourteen of their forty
men lay dead on deck and most of the rest were
wounded before the boat surrendered. We took the
survivors aboard as prisoners and sank their vessel.
Later in the day we sighted a ship, stopped it, put our
prisoners aboard, and sent them home. They had
fought so gallantly that they deserved all considera-
tion, and, besides, we had scarcely room enough
aboard our U-boat to take a score or so of men on
board. We thought, of course, the episode was ended
there, but there was a sequel. After the war one of
the officers of the *U-139* met one of our former prisoners, one of the officers. They had a celebration and
became fast friends. The Portuguese said that the
steamer that escaped us had aboard several American
generals who were returning to America from the
Western Front.

We were less than half way across when the wireless brought news of the armistice negotiation. U-
boat warfare against the United States was suspended,
and we were ordered to return to Germany. We got
back to Kiel on November 14, 1918. As we steered
into the harbour we saw the red flags of the revolution
flying.

CHAPTER XXXVII

THE TRAGIC END—HOME AND MUTINY

He drew out a gold cigarette case, snapped it open, and handed it to me, showing me the inside of the cover. The shiny yellow surface was covered with scrawls, names scratched in the metal, hasty signatures.

"A remembrance of the end," he said.

It was Commander Gustav Siess speaking, the U-boat commander who had already told me of his early adventures in under-sea warfare.

"I was in the Mediterranean for a couple of years," he went on, "and then the end came. Germany was collapsing, Austria falling apart. Already the revolution in Austria had begun. There was a revolt at the port of Cattaro, which was our base. In the hands of the revolutionaries, it was a base for us no longer. The German U-boat fleet in the Mediterranean had lost its home. There was nothing to do but start back to Germany. The squadron started out on what was to be its last voyage. I, as the oldest commander at the Cattaro base, was in command of the flotilla.

"Some of the boats at the station were unfit for so long a trip. We destroyed them. The remainder numbered fourteen, and so we were fourteen when we started. I wanted a memento, and passed my cigarette case around. Each man scratched his name, and you can see them there. How many of the fourteen got safely back to Germany with their boats? Thirteen. One was lost. Another gained a fine victory,

Captain Kukat. He sank the British battleship *Britannia.*"

I had heard from other sources of that last voyage of the Mediterranean squadron back to Germany during those final days of the World War. The British knew the U-boats would have to clear out of Cattaro and try to make their way back to Germany, and of course pass through the narrow strait of Gibraltar. They came, just like a swarm of foxes being driven through a narrow bottle neck, and you can bet the hunters were there in force. One of those who made the memorable voyage was Commander Hartwig who at the time was in command of the big *U-63*. He told me a vivid story.

"The strait between Gibraltar and Africa, nine miles wide, was crowded with vessels, destroyers, patrol boats, gunboats, torpedo boats, submarine chasers, and I don't know what else, while overhead airplanes circled, ready to drop bombs. Everything was in readiness for our coming. Our fleet of fourteen U-boats had cruised along more or less together, but for a passage of the strait there was no thought of flotilla formation. Every man for himself.

"I had planned to go through on the surface at night. I could make better speed and trusted to dive out of the way of any enemy that spied me. The surface run was impossible, though. The weather was very clear, and the *U-63* was constantly being discovered by enemy craft even before we got through the strait. So were the other U-boats.

" 'Allo, allo!' the air was simply crammed with that word. It was the war warning—submarine sighted. 'Allo, position so and so.' The wireless kept the world informed where this boat was and that one.

"So under the surface we went. The craft were so thick above and searched the water so thoroughly with lights that it was impossible to show a periscope, even for a few seconds. We groped along blindly, heading in the direction that would take us through the narrow passage. We could hear the propellers of the vessels above, a steady hum, like a swarm of angry bees. The noise was our guide. When it had died away we would know that we were through the strait.

"We prayed for silence and after a while silence came. The buzz of propellers grew faint and died away. Then up we came. I intended, if the coast was clear, to make a dash out to sea on the surface. We broke water and then . . .

" 'Dive!' I yelled.

"Straight ahead, not five hundred feet away, was a big destroyer. She came streaking at us, and it seemed certain that we would be rammed. And if we were not rammed the depth bombs would surely get us. I have never seen another situation where I was so thoroughly sure that we were done for.

"She missed ramming us by an inch, and then the depth bombs came. Then a curious turn. The very closeness of our danger saved us. The depth bombs were exploding directly below us. They had been set for ninety feet, at which depth we would have normally taken refuge. But the enemy was on top of us so fast that we had not had time to get any deeper than thirty feet.

" 'Hold a level course,' I commanded.

"The depth charges ripped and tore the water below us, but we slid along safely above them. The destroyer was so sure she had nailed us that she flashed a wireless message reporting our destruction.

"We stayed under water after that and did not come up until we were well out in the Atlantic. Then we got wireless calls from the other boats. All drew together and ran along as a flotilla. One boat was missing, the *U-34* under Commander Johannes Klasing. The lucky thirteen kept on together around the north of Scotland and down through the North Sea. We put in at one of the Norwegian fjords, and there got our first news of the revolution in Germany. We could not believe our ears. But at least there was no revolution aboard our submarines.

"The red flag of revolution floated over Kiel. Mutiny reigned aboard the ships in the harbour there and the red flag flew from mast heads. But we, at least, kept to our duty till the last. The thirteen U-boats of the Cattaro base came into the harbour in war formation, with war flags fluttering in the breeze."

The only U-boat of that Cattaro flotilla, except those blown up, failing to get back to Germany was the one lost at Gibraltar. She was the last U-boat lost during the war. The *U-34*, under command of Commander Johannes Klasing, was accounted for by the British Q-ship *Privet*. The submarine was sighted by patrol boats and then by the *Privet*, which appeared to be only an innocent tramp. The U-boat gave fight to its seemingly feeble adversary, when at short range the *Privet's* disguise dropped away, and she sank the submarine with direct hits of eleven shells. That was the night of November 8 and 9, 1918, just two days before the Armistice.

On that same night the British battleship *Britannia* was sunk. Captain Kukat of the *UB-50* was stealing his way through the strait when he got a chance to launch a torpedo at the giant. He hit it squarely and then hit it again with another torpedo. The ship remained afloat for several hours. Two hours after the torpedoing, the crew, which was still aboard, sighted a periscope. It was Commander Kukat's or that of some other boat. *H.M.S. Britannia* opened fire with her guns for the last time. A rain of shells fell near the periscope, which disappeared. The *Britannia* then threw out a consignment of depth bombs. She could not remain afloat much longer, though, and her crew was taken off. Only forty men were lost. She was the last British warship sunk by submarine attack during the war—the last of the five mighty British men-o'-war that were successfully torpedoed. The others were the *Triumph*, the *Majestic*, the *Formidable*, and the *Cornwallis*.

The drama closes with a brief, grim epilogue— German U-boat against German battleship. And this final tale was told me by the under-sea skipper who tells likewise of the first great submarine exploit, Lieutenant Spiess, who was Weddigen's second officer that historic day when the *Hogue*, the *Cressy*, and the *Aboukir* were sunk.

People wonder why the great German High Sea Fleet surrendered so supinely. In England, navy men look blank when they mention it. They are strong in their statements that the Germans fought splendidly at sea. Yet they hauled up the white flag without a fight. The British wouldn't have done that. They would have struck a last blow. In answer to that the Germans say that the crews of the German warships, affected by Red propaganda, mutinied, and, save, for that, the German fleet would have sallied out for a last fight. There are rumours that the fleet was ordered to put out to sea and go down with colours flying. Indeed, it was the belief of an intended heroic self-immolation that provoked the mutinies among the sailors. They thought they were going to be sent out in their ships to deliberate glorious destruction.

Commander Spiess tells us that no such thing was comtemplated. Instead, a vigorous final stroke by the High Sea Fleet was the plan. Naturally, the sailors were not informed of the strategy of the High Command. Sailors never are. The German Army was making its last stand in Flanders. On land the Central Powers were crumbling. So the fleet wanted to try and offset this by taking a long chance. The great ships in massive array were to strike at the English Channel and the communications between England and France. They were to be within reach of their bases on the German coast, so as to be in a favourable strategic position for a battle or retirement. Meanwhile, the entire submarine fleet was to be thrown across the North Sea to lie in wait there. If the British Grand Fleet elected to hurry south to attack the German ships while they were attacking the Channel, then they would have to run the gauntlet of the submarines. Then a gauntlet of mines, which German small craft were to spread behind the line of submarines. Between the attack of the U-boats and the destruction wrought by mines Great Britain's naval squadrons might be seriously crippled before they closed with the German fleet.

The fleet was ordered to make ready for this project. The men of the submarines remained staunch, but the battleship crews mutinied. And then the menace of U-boats was turned against these traitorous men-of-war.

"In the Jade," said Commander Spiess, "the squadrons were being concentrated for sea. The submarines were anxiously awaiting orders to stand out. I had command of the *U-135,* a new boat, big and fast. Early on the morning of October 31st I was ordered to report immediately to the commander of the U-boat flotilla.

"The commander wore a grave face. I had already heard rumours of disaffection in the fleet, but the question he asked me seemed to put me in another world.

" 'Are you absolutely sure of your crew?'

" 'Yes, certainly, Commodore,' I answered mechanically. What a question, as if one should be otherwise than certain of one's crew. It seemed as if I were being transferred to a new realm of thought.

"The commander went on to inform me of what I already knew, that several battleships had mutinied, particularly the *Thuringen* and the *Ostfriesland*. He then sent me to the fleet commander, and again I heard that question, 'Are you sure of your crew?' Of course I was. He thereupon ordered me to take the *U-135* and accompany two harbour boats and a company of marines under Lieutenant Grimm and try to arrest the mutineers aboard the *Thuringen* and *Ostfriesland*. I asked for written orders. No, they could not be given me. I was to act on my own responsibility. That was how far the demoralization had gone.

"The two harbour boats and the *U-135* proceeded to the mutinous battle ships. We could have taken stern measures, but at the last moment we were placed under the orders of the squadron commander, and the measures taken were less stern. We acted under immediate orders. I placed the *U-135* between the two mutinous battleships, ready to torpedo one or the other with bow or stern torpedoes. Lieutenant Grimm and his marines boarded the *Thuringen* with fixed bayonets.

"The mutineers barricaded themselves in the bow of the battleships. Unfortunately, they were given five minutes to surrender. They should have been fired upon at once. They yelled and howled: 'Don't shoot, brothers.' The five minutes' grace had almost elapsed when I saw a torpedo boat coming toward the *Thuringen* at full speed with guns cleared for action and the signal flying: 'Am about to fire.' Then the torpedo boat swerved off and the signal flag came fluttering down. The mutineers had surrendered. If her guns had opened on the forward part of the battleship where the mutineers were huddled, my opinion is that the revolt in the fleet would have been checked.

"I was ordered to take the *U-135* and threaten the battleship *Heligoland,* on which there had also been disturbances. I held her under the menace of my forward torpedo tubes for a while. I had no orders to torpedo her, and there were no red flags flying. Finally I was called back to the *Thuringen.* The mutineers were being taken off under arrest. Then followed the arrest of the rebels aboard the *Ostfriesland.* The same procedure was employed as in the case of the *Thuringen.*

"These measures were feeble, and were not enough to check the revolutionary movement in the navy.

Our High Command had learned nothing from the history of the British. Whole British squadrons had mutinied during the Napoleonic wars. The English way was simple: Go alongside the mutinous ships, board and hang all the ringleaders. A Nelson would have had the German battleships that were first to mutiny anchored in the middle of the fleet and sunk by gunfire.

"After the leaders of the uprising had been taken off the mutinous battleships the vessels were sent to Kiel. This was a great mistake. The crews there were still disaffected, and these men instigated the revolt at Kiel."

Commander Spiess paints a melancholy picture of the last days of the German under-sea fleet. Revolution broke out in the ports. The crews of the U-boats remained staunch. The submarines left harbour and went from point to point, hoping to find a place that remained loyal. At every place, though, they found red revolt. They wanted to carry on and do their share in the last days of the war, but finally, with no loyal harbour to put into, they gave it up and returned to their bases, where the boats were taken

over by the revolutionaries. All did, save the *U-135*
and one or two others. These had acted against the
mutineers and the Reds had threatened vengeance.
So the flotilla commander gave them permission to
seek refuge in foreign ports. Whereupon they became submarines without a country.

They remained at sea for a few days. Then the
Armistice was signed. Better to face the Reds than
to end heaven knows where. So back to Wilhelmshaven. The faithful U-boat crews landed unmo-
lested by their revolutionary comrades.

Then followed the turning of the ships over to the
British. People wonder why the German officers did
not sink their vessels right there instead of facing the
humiliation of turning them over to the enemy. British officers asked me that question several times.
Commander Spiess states that the German naval officers were informed that the British would occupy
the Kiel Canal if the Germans did not surrender their
ships intact according to the terms of the Armistice.
They refused to sink them and handed them over
because of their desire not to cause an occupation of
German territory by the enemy.

And so the U-boats, together with the other ships
of the once powerful High Sea Fleet, went over to
England. The bigger ships of the erstwhile German
Navy went to the bottom at Scapa Flow, scuttled
by their own crews. The under-sea raiders were
divided among the Allies. Several sank when inex-
perienced crews ventured out to sea. Von Arnauld de
la Perière's big cruiser, for example, was given to the
French, and on a trip out with her French crew she
foundered with all on board.

The World War was over. The raiders of the
deep were back in harbour, such of them as had not
been given the iron coffin for a tomb. The campaign
of the under water was done. All that remained

was to reckon the score and to foot up the bill.

The Germans, from start to finish, laid down the keels of 811 submarines. But most of these were still unfinished on the ways when the war ended, and of course they never struck a blow. Less than four hundred were put into commission. And of these four hundred scarcely more than three hundred actually did any active campaigning. Such was the German under-sea fleet in magnitude.

Its losses in proportion were terrific. One hundred and ninety-nine boats were lost. Of these, one hundred and seventy-eight were sunk by the enemy! Seven were interned in neutral ports. Fourteen, which were disabled, were sunk by the Germans themselves. Of the one hundred and seventy-eight boats sunk by the enemy, about forty were blown to smithereens on the horns of mines, sixteen were torpedoed by British submarines, and one by a French submarine. About a dozen were sunk by the mystery Q-ships and six were swooped upon by airplanes and demolished by aerial bombs. Others fell victims to nets, destroyers, cruisers, patrol boats, chasers, armed fishing steamers, trawlers, and armed merchantmen. Some were rammed, some shelled, some destroyed by depth bombs. The fate of a score or so of U-boats was never explained. They simply left their bases and never came back, and the Allies have no record of destroying them. Most of these, no doubt, can be charged up to mines.

One outstanding fact is, not the numerical strength but the numerical weakness of the U-boat fleet. At the outbreak of the war the Germans had but twenty-nine submersibles and these were very primitive indeed. Two of them were out of service for repairs and three were not quite finished. In February of 1915, when the first unrestricted submarine campaign was declared, twelve more under-sea craft had been added to the fleet. From the total must be subtracted several boats that had been sunk. This was truly a feeble force with which to begin a blockade of the British Isles. Even at this point the building of under-sea raiders was not pressed fully. The Germans little dreamed that the war would last long enough for boats recently begun to be of any use. It was only after it was apparent that the titanic struggle was destined to be a long-drawn-out affair that the German dockyards began turning out submarines as fast as they could, and even then there was a lapse when, after the Battle of Jutland, naval construction forces were put to the task of repairing surface ships.

On the other side of the ledger, here is what the raiders of the deep accomplished. They sank ships of war, from mine sweepers and destroyers to huge battleships of the line. But it was not in attacks on naval craft that the U-boats found their most effective work. It was against trading vessels. In all, they sank 18,716,982 tons of shipping, of which ten millions were British. The total number of these ships destroyed was between five and six thousand. During 1917, in that one year, when the under-sea activity was at its height, seven and a half million tons went diving to the bottom—and the British Empire faced its doom. But how few of us realized it at the time!

Take the comparative weakness of the German under-sea fleet and the prodigious destruction it accomplished, buckle those two joints together, and you will have a bit of logic that tells of what a mighty part was taken by the raiders of the deep in those years when the world was mad.

THE END.

INDEX

INDEX

355

Fanning, U. S. S., the *U-58* of Kapitänleutnant Amberger is sunk by the, 222.
FELDKIRCHNER, Lieutenant, commander of the *U-17,* 34.
FELDT, Commander Richard, raids American coast in the *U-156,* 286.
FITZMAURICE, captain of the *Triumph,* 66.
FORD, Henry, 43.
Formidable, the British warship, 131.
FORSTMANN, commander of the *U-39,* 123.
FRANZ, Commander, takes the *U-152* into American waters, 286.
Freja, Moraht meets and takes the, 276.
FREMANTLE, Admiral, a passenger aboard the *Russell* when she sinks, 164.
FRIEDRICH, Prince Eitel, 46.
Fritzoe, it arrives without escort at the enemy's port, 122.

Gallia, Von Arnauld in the *U-35* sinks the, 151.
GANSSER, commander of the *U-33,* 123.
GEORG, Ritter Karl Siegfried von, captures fishing trawlers in the North Sea, 118.
GERLACH, Commander Helmuth, in command of the *U-93,* 192.
GLIMPF, Commander, his boat, the *UB-20,* is sunk by aërial attack, 235.
Glitra, is sunk by the *U-17,* 34, 51.
Gneisenau, the cruiser, 130.
Gratangen, the *U-64* sinks the, 274.
GRIMM, Lieutenant, 348.

Grosser Kurfürst, the, 107.
Güntzel, 131.

Hamburg, S. M. S., underwater manœuvre directed at the, 14.
HANSEN, Kapitänleutnant Claus, his notable career in the *U-41,* 109; the adventure with the *Pearl,* 111.
Harpathian, S. S., goes down to Von Nostitz, 317, 323.
HARTWIG, Commander Kurt, escapes from the sinking *Dresden,* 164; is assigned to a U-boat command in the Mediterranean, 165; he sinks the *Porto di Rodi,* 165; the *Cornwallis* is one of his prey, 165; tells of his return from the Mediterranean in the *U-63,* 343.
HASHAGEN, Lieutenant Commander Ernst, his story of the *Fritzoe* incident, 121; attacks the British *Prize,* 187; a cruise aboard the *U-22,* 208; he meets the *Luckenbach* and the destroyer *Nicholson* and adds the *Orama* to his victories, 220; he sends the *Dupetit-Thouars* on its final plunge, 222.
Hattie Dunn, the *U-151* sinks the, 296.
Hauppage, it goes down to the *U-151,* 296, 323.
HAUPT, 262.
Hawke, H. M. S., the *U-9* sinks the, 30.
HEIMBURG, Korvettenkapitän Heino von, his story of the engagements between submarines, 132 ff; the sinking of the *Medusa,* 134; the incidents of the *Amalfi* and the

ff; the *Gratangen* provides a surprise, 274; he sinks the *Moreni*, 275; the *Freja* falls into his hands, 276; his most stubborn fight with a merchant ship, the *Amiral de Kersaint*, 277; sinks the *Ausonia*, 277; the *Minnetonka* is taken, 279; his desperate battle with the *Lychnis* and the *Partridge II*, 279 ff.

Moreni, the spectacular sinking of the, 275.

Nicholson, the American destroyer, goes to the aid of the *Luckenbach*, 220; it takes revenge on the *U-58*, 222.

NOSTITZ UND JANCKENDORF, Commander von, raids American waters in the *U-151*, 286 ff; his boat encounters the *Port Said*, 289; an attack on the *Huntress*, 290; the *Hattie Dunn* and the *Hauppage* are his victims, 296; the *Edna* is sunk, 297; his boat takes the *Isabel B. Wiley* and the *S. S. Winneconne*, 308; the *Jacob M. Haskell* is his prize, 310; the *Edward H. Cole* goes down to him, 311; he sinks the *Texel* and the *Carolina*, 312; captures the *Samuel G. Mengel* and the *Edward R. Baird*, 315; sinks the S. S. *Eidsvold*, 316; the S. S. *Harpathian* goes down to him, 317; he takes the *Vinland* and the *Vindeggen*, 319; captures and sinks the *Pinar del Rio*, 320; the *Heinrich Lund* is taken by, 322; the *Samoa* and the *Kringsia* are captured on his return from America, 327;

the British *Dvinsk* is taken, 328; he is counter-attacked by the *Kronprinz Wilhelm*, 328.

Nürnberg, the cruiser, 130.

Oldenburg, the *U-151* converted from the, 287.

Orama, Commander Hashagen destroys the, 221.

Orduna, it encounters the *U-20*, 104.

Ostfriesland, is disciplined for mutiny, 348.

Parkgate, the *U-35* encounters the, 159.

Partridge, II, with the *Lychnis* sinks the *U-64*, 283.

PASHA, Enver, 73.

Patagonier, the *U-35* sinks the, 160.

Pathfinder, H. M. S., the sinking of the, 8, 16, 51.

Pearl, it surprises the *U-41*, 111.

Phaleron, Von Spiegel sinks the, 180.

Pinar del Rio, is taken and sunk by Von Nostitz, 320.

PIQUOT, Lieutenant, the commandant at Donnington Hall, 190, 203.

POHLE, Commander, 131.

Pommern, S. M. S., Lieutenant Spiess an officer aboard, 10, 130.

Porto di Rodi, Hartwig sinks it in the Ionian Sea, 165.

Port Said, encounters the *U-151*, 289.

Primo, the *U-21* sinks the, 52.

Primola, Von Arnauld, in the *U-35*, sinks the, 151.

Prinz Adalbert, is torpedoed by the English in the Baltic, 241.

ABOUT THE EDITOR

GARY E. WEIR received his doctorate in history from the University of Tennessee, Knoxville, in 1982. After a year on the faculty of the U.S. Naval Academy, Dr. Weir joined the contemporary history branch of the U.S. Naval Historical Center in Washington, D.C., where he wrote *Building American Submarines, 1914–1940* and *Forged in War: The Naval Industrial Complex and American Submarine Construction, 1940–1961,* winner of the 1993 Theodore and Franklin D. Roosevelt Naval History Prize. He is currently preparing an official history of naval oceanography. His other publications include *Building the Kaiser's Navy: The Imperial Naval Office and German Industry in the Tirpitz Era, 1890–1919* and articles for the *Naval War College Review, Mariners' Mirror, International History Review,* and *Naval Engineers Journal.*

He is an associate professor of history for the University of Maryland, University College, and the recipient of fellowships from the McClure Foundation, Office of Naval Research, and the German Academic Exchange Service (DAAD).

The Naval Institute Press is the book-publishing arm of the U.S. Naval Institute, a private, nonprofit, membership society for sea service professionals and others who share an interest in naval and maritime affairs. Established in 1873 at the U.S. Naval Academy in Annapolis, Maryland, where its offices remain today, the Naval Institute has members worldwide.

Members of the Naval Institute support the education programs of the society and receive the influential monthly magazine *Proceedings* and discounts on fine nautical prints and on ship and aircraft photos. They also have access to the transcripts of the Institute's Oral History Program and get discounted admission to any of the Institute-sponsored seminars offered around the country.

The Naval Institute also publishes *Naval History* magazine. This colorful bimonthly is filled with entertaining and thought-provoking articles, first-person reminiscences, and dramatic art and photography. Members receive a discount on *Naval History* subscriptions.

The Naval Institute's book-publishing program, begun in 1898 with basic guides to naval practices, has broadened its scope to include books of more general interest. Now the Naval Institute Press publishes about one hundred titles each year, ranging from how-to books on boating and navigation to battle histories, biographies, ship and aircraft guides, and novels. Institute members receive significant discounts on the Press's more than eight hundred books in print.

Full-time students are eligible for special half-price membership rates. Life memberships are also available.

For a free catalog describing Naval Institute Press books currently available, and for further information about subscribing to *Naval History* magazine or about joining the U.S. Naval Institute, please write to:

Membership Department
U.S. Naval Institute
291 Wood Road
Annapolis, MD 21402-5034
Telephone: (800) 233-8764
Fax: (410) 269-7940
Web address: www.navalinstitute.org